praise for Women of Destiny

Women of Destiny is one of the most anointed,
inspirational and informative books I have ever
read—period. Every pastor should read
this outstanding book.

CHE AHN
PRESIDENT, HARVEST INTERNATIONAL MINISTRIES
PASADENA, CALIFORNIA

Cindy Jacobs brings clarity and insight to
the controversy surrounding a woman's place
in ministry. Delicately, yet boldly, she presents
a fresh, historical and biblical interpretation
of God's Word on the issues facing today's
woman of destiny.

BETH ALVES
PRESIDENT, INTERCESSORS INTERNATIONAL, INC.
BELLEVUE, TEXAS

I can't think of anyone more qualified today to
write about the importance of women in ministry
than Cindy Jacobs. *Women of Destiny* lays a solid
theological basis for women in ministry
and will encourage thousands to
join in the harvest.

JOHN ARNOTT, SR.
PASTOR, TORONTO AIRPORT CHRISTIAN FELLOWSHIP
TORONTO, ONTARIO, CANADA

Cindy Jacobs has written a powerful book that will
impact the whole Church, particularly in its attitudes
toward women in ministry. I highly recommend
Women of Destiny to men as well as women,
especially to pastors who can strategically
encourage gifted women to become all that
God has destined them to be.

LUIS BUSH
INTERNATIONAL DIRECTOR, A.D.2000 & BEYOND MOVEMENT
COLORADO SPRINGS, COLORADO

In *Women of Destiny*, Cindy Jacobs handles sensitive
controversies with wisdom and love. She deals with
practical issues in a straightforward manner and
addresses spiritual issues with confidence and
authority. Her book lays another foundation stone
in the road for women who would find and
live out their biblical destiny.

FRANK DAMAZIO
SENIOR PASTOR, CITY BIBLE CHURCH
PORTLAND, OREGON

Every woman who is struggling with God's call on
her life should read *Women of Destiny*. Every man
who questions a woman's call need only read it with
an open heart and mind. A vital contribution to the
literature of gender reconciliation, this book is
biblically sound and long-awaited.

JOSEPH L. GARLINGTON, SR.
PRESIDENT, RECONCILIATION! MINISTRIES INTERNATIONAL
PITTSBURGH, PENNSYLVANIA

praise for Women of Destiny

Women of Destiny is destined to greatly bless the Body
of Christ. Of all that has been written or said on the subject, Cindy Jacobs comes closest to expressing God's true
thoughts concerning His own creation called "woman."
Thank you, Cindy, for lovingly and boldly co-laboring
with Christ in setting all of God's creation free.

BILL HAMON
FOUNDER AND PRESIDENT
CHRISTIAN INTERNATIONAL MINISTRIES NETWORK
SANTA ROSA BEACH, FLORIDA

As the Holy Spirit labors over the Church to bring
forth reconciliation among believers, our focus has
been on racial or denominational issues that separate
God's people. All the while, however, the greatest
single issue of unbiblical discrimination has been the
widespread posturing against women in ministry.
Cindy Jacobs's voice deserves to be heard—and taken
seriously. It just may be another gentle whisper
of the Spirit saying, "Open your hearts wider."

JACK W. HAYFORD
SENIOR PASTOR, THE CHURCH ON THE WAY
VAN NUYS, CALIFORNIA

Women of Destiny is bursting with passion for people
and for the advance of the kingdom of God. Women will
be affirmed and men will be challenged. I am grateful for
Cindy's contribution to the growing body of literature on
gender equality in Christian ministry and leadership.

DR. GARY D. KINNAMAN
SENIOR MINISTER, WORD OF GRACE CHURCH, MESA, ARIZONA

praise for Women of Destiny

Women of Destiny is an open door of opportunity
for the Church. Step through and relearn what
God's plan for every woman has always been.
Cindy Jacobs provides ample illustrations from
Scripture, history and her own personal life to
illuminate God's desire for His daughters.

DENNIS D. LINDSAY
PRESIDENT, CHRIST FOR THE NATIONS
DALLAS, TEXAS

In *Women of Destiny*, Cindy Jacobs bares
her soul and honestly shares her own struggles
in answering God's call on her life into ministry.
She speaks to women in the pews—those who
may not take the time or have the inclination
to study the theological questions regarding
the role of women in ministry—and encourages
them to accept God's call on their lives.

LORRY LUTZ
INTERNATIONAL COORDINATOR, A.D.2000 WOMEN'S TRACK
AUTHOR OF *WOMEN AS RISK TAKERS*
COLORADO SPRINGS, COLORADO

Cindy Jacobs has done it again! She has produced
what we're sure will become a classic—a book
that releases women to the higher destinies for
which God has created them.

JOHN & PAULA SANDFORD
FOUNDERS, ELIJAH HOUSE
POST FALLS, IDAHO

praise for Women of Destiny

With balance, sensitivity, wisdom and integrity, Cindy
Jacobs brings great insight to a very controversial
subject. Lay aside your paradigm for a time and allow
Women of Destiny to further enlighten you to God's
plan for all of us—both women and men.

DUTCH SHEETS
AUTHOR OF *THE RIVER OF GOD* AND *INTERCESSORY PRAYER*
SENIOR PASTOR, SPRINGS HARVEST FELLOWSHIP
COLORADO SPRINGS, COLORADO

In *Women of Destiny*, Cindy Jacobs has dared
to bring up the "woman" issue, which churches
have swept under the carpet for generations.
Fine-tuned through careful research, she has
written a classic that should be read by men as
well as women. It's liberating for both sexes.

QUIN SHERRER
AUTHOR OF *HOW TO PRAY FOR YOUR CHILDREN*
AND *A WOMAN'S GUIDE TO SPIRITUAL WARFARE*
COLORADO SPRINGS, COLORADO

We loved this book! *Women of Destiny* gives
scholarly answers to questions about the role of
women in ministry. This timely book is critical
to the Church as it moves into the 21st century.

EDDIE SMITH
NATIONAL FACILITATOR OF PRAYER MINISTRIES, MISSION AMERICA
ALICE SMITH
INTERNATIONAL PRAYER COORDINATOR, U.S. PRAYER TRACK
A.D.2000 & BEYOND MOVEMENT, HOUSTON, TEXAS

praise for Women of Destiny

In *Women of Destiny*, Cindy Jacobs writes with
passion about the biblical case for women in ministry.
This is an important book.

VINSON SYNAN
DEAN, SCHOOL OF DIVINITY, REGENT UNIVERSITY
VIRGINIA BEACH, VIRGINIA

Women of Destiny is an honest, insightful and scrip-
turally sound book that erases any need for women to
view themselves as second-class citizens in the Church.

IVERNA TOMPKINS
AUTHOR AND SPEAKER, COSPONSOR, WOMEN OF THE
WORD CONFERENCES, SCOTTSDALE, ARIZONA

God has a wonderful plan for every woman.
Cindy Jacobs helps women to throw off the shackles of
despair, discouragement, guilt and shame to walk in the
freedom that God has designed for them.

ELMER L. TOWNS
AUTHOR OF *RIVERS OF REVIVAL* AND
FASTING FOR SPIRITUAL BREAKTHROUGH
DEAN, SCHOOL OF RELIGION, LIBERTY UNIVERSITY
LYNCHBURG, VIRGINIA

In a day when there is considerable confusion over gender
issues in the church and in the home, Cindy Jacobs cuts
through the fog like a spiritual laser beam. No other book
I know on this subject matches the superb combination of
biblical and pastoral integrity of *Women of Destiny*.

C. PETER WAGNER
AUTHOR OF *PRAYING WITH POWER*
PROFESSOR, FULLER THEOLOGICAL SEMINARY
COLORADO SPRINGS, COLORADO

Women of Destiny

Cindy Jacobs

Regal

**A Division of Gospel Light
Ventura, California, U.S.A.**

Published by Regal Books
A Division of Gospel Light
Ventura, California, U.S.A.
Printed in U.S.A.

Regal Books is a ministry of Gospel Light, an evangelical Christian publisher dedicated to serving the local church. We believe God's vision for Gospel Light is to provide church leaders with biblical, user-friendly materials that will help them evangelize, disciple and minister to children, youth and families.

It is our prayer that this Regal book will help you discover biblical truth for your own life and help you meet the needs of others. May God richly bless you.

For a free catalog of resources from Regal Books/Gospel Light please contact your Christian supplier or call 1-800-4-GOSPEL.

Cover Design by Barbara Levan Fisher
Interior Design by Britt Rocchio
Edited by Karen Kaufman

Library of Congress Cataloging-in-Publication Data
Jacobs, Cindy
    Women of destiny / Cindy Jacobs.
        p. cm.
    ISBN 0-8307-1864-8 (trade pbk.)
    1. Women in church work. I Title.
    BV4415.J33 1998
    248.8'43—dc21   98-16372
                                                                          CIP

2 3 4 5 6 7 8 9 10 11 12 13 14 15 16 17 18 19 20 21 22 23 24 / 06 05 04 03 02 01 99 98

Rights for publishing this book in other languages are contracted by Gospel Literature International (GLINT). GLINT also provides technical help for the adaptation, translation and publishing of Bible study resources and books in scores of languages worldwide. For further information, contact GLINT, P.O. Box 4060, Ontario, CA 91761-1003, U.S.A., or the publisher.

This book is lovingly dedicated to my mom

Eleanor Lindsey

a great woman of faith and prayer, and my heroine.

Contents

Foreword

by Jane Hansen
International President of Aglow International

This is a day and hour when God is moving mightily in many unprecedented ways in and through women. Cindy Jacobs confirms this truth with her timely message, *Women of Destiny*

God, today, is restoring women to the place He has ordained for them to hold from the foundation of the world.

I was reminded as I read Cindy's manuscript that the "woman question" in our day is much like the "Gentile question" in Peter's day. Peter's theology did not allow for the inclusion of the Gentiles in the plans and purposes of God, and he thought he had a biblical basis for his stance. It was only when he saw the anointing of the Spirit fall upon Cornelius's household that he fully understood: The Gentiles were full heirs in the kingdom of God.

In that moment Peter could only say, "Can anyone keep these people from being baptized with water? They have received the Holy Spirit just as we have" (Acts 10:47, *NIV*). In other words, "Should not these be fully received into the Body of Christ? They have received the Holy Spirit just as we have." No doubt, Peter left that place with a new fervor to examine the Scriptures.

Could this amazing truth have been found in the written Word of God? It could. It had been there all along, but until that moment Peter did not have eyes to see it.

Such is the case concerning women Cindy does the Body of Christ a great service as she carefully sifts through the "difficult passages" of Scripture pertaining to women, to help us uncover what has been there "all along." Drawing upon many scholarly resources, Cindy courageously leads us through the morass of seemingly contradictory biblical statements. She shows us that there is no disharmony between Scripture and what has been demonstrated since the beginning of time: Women, without a doubt, are full heirs in the plans and purposes of God. This truth was forever sealed and became evident to all that long-ago day in Jerusalem when the Holy Spirit fell upon the waiting believers, male and female, equally equipping them to function as full members of the Body of Christ. Yet many still do not have eyes to see.

In this work, Cindy confronts the myriad issues that discourage women from taking up their God-ordained call. She describes her own wrestlings with the strongholds that threatened to prevent her from fulfilling her destiny in the call of God, knowing that women everywhere who love the Lord will identify with her struggles.

Through the examples of many "heroines of faith" throughout history, your own faith will be expanded to believe that God also has a distinct plan and purpose for your life, one that will not be diminished nor hindered by your womanhood, but rather specifically enlarged and strengthened by it. You will come away from this work with new encouragement and a greater biblical understanding of your destiny as a woman.

Foreword

by John Dawson
Founder, International Reconciliation Coalition

Jesus chose men as His disciples. This is not surprising given the fact that He was single and constantly traveling, but much has been made of it. Few subjects are more important than the role of women in spiritual leadership. What does the Bible teach? Does your tradition or mine contain the whole counsel of God? Do we really understand God's view of gender?

This book goes a long way in providing necessary encouragement for any woman with the call of God upon her life. Scholars will have to evaluate Cindy's interpretation of difficult texts, but I have listened to the debate about women in ministry long enough to be certain of this one thing: Our understanding of the Scripture is not a done deal and the points Cindy has raised are valid and worthy of consideration.

This is not a book written to men, but I recommend it to my brothers. The male reader may feel like an eavesdropper listening to an intimate conversation between sisters, but we have been invited to do so with good reason. Do not flippantly peruse this book seeking to discover and dismiss the central arguments; instead take a journey through the heart and mind of your sister in Christ, who has brought blessing to many and is pleading for a thoughtful hearing.

I read this book with some embarrassment. I am part of a patriarchal religious culture in which women who serve ministries are usually treated with great kindness but seldom taken seriously as leaders. This is less so in missions, but very evident in evangelical institutional life on the home front. We are snared by the sheer momentum of religious tradition.

The anointed partnership of Deborah and Barak is evident again in our generation and must not be hindered. Women of God, please find the encouragement you need in Cindy's teaching and testimony to press on into the full inheritance God has marked out for you. My sister, God intended that you be adored by a loving father who praised your accomplishments and cherished the beauty of your uniqueness. You were supposed to have felt unconditionally loved and completely safe in the company of male friends and relatives. You were supposed to have been released into your full potential in the family of God without any prejudice regarding your gender. I know you have wounds, but a new day is coming.

When I have publicly acknowledged the failures of men at reconciliation gatherings, I have seen such longing in the eyes of Christian men. I look around, collecting permission to speak from the eyes of my brothers. Sometimes they even shout, "Yes! Say it! That's right!" We are so sorry; please forgive us.

I believe that the recent movement of reconciliation between cultures is a prelude to the biggest healing of all. The wounds inflicted by men and women on each other constitute the fundamental fault line running beneath all other human conflicts. If gender difference is used as the justification for the devaluation of one part of humanity, then the door is open for the selective devaluation of all of humanity based on some difference from a perceived ideal. Gender conflict is the biggest reconciliation issue of all, outside of our need to be reconciled to God the Father.

One of the lessons we have learned in interracial reconciliation is that all parties need to begin at a point of open acknowledgment that we carry prejudice (fears and preferences) in our hearts. I had lived in the Black community in Los Angeles for two years before I began to understand that I was clueless. At the beginning of my experience I would have protested to anybody that I didn't have a prejudiced bone in my body, but I was only revealing my blindness.

For centuries, we White people have communicated a belief in our superiority and sometimes we do it most blatantly when we are trying to be kind. Subtle things betray our inner attitudes. Our tone of voice, posture and mannerisms all communicate a deep-seated conviction that we are superior. For this I had to repent and apologize before God and before non-Western peoples.

I believe we are at a similar point in our efforts at gender reconciliation. We men will get nowhere until we humble ourselves before God and admit that we are imperfect and desperately need revelation about the state of our own hearts. Are women to be involved in Christian leadership? I have begun to suspect that that question is a trick query from hell.

The question should be, Given the difference between male and female, in what aspects of leadership do we desperately need females to serve? Two obvious areas come to mind: (1) How to relate to God. Given the fact that we are corporately female, the bride of Christ, women have an advantage in understanding this, our most important relationship. And (2) How to bring to birth the purposes of God. Our male physiology is an intrinsic handicap in understanding the spiritual process by which things in God's kingdom are created: worship, conception, gestation, travail and birth. Most of the great intercessors of the Bible were men, but the metaphor they used to describe their experiences was often that of a woman in travail. Do these natural strengths exclude women from other types of leadership? I do not believe so. Just because females are observed to be nurturing does not mean they are not suitable for the rigors of governmental office in the Church.

This book is partly biographical. It tells the story of one of today's most controversial but deeply loved Christian leaders.

Cindy takes risks. She communicates her own struggles with complete vulnerability. She tells her personal story in ways that are sometimes painfully honest, and in so doing, has given us an inspiring read, not unlike Kathryn Kuhlman's *Daughter of Destiny*. This is an important book.

Acknowledgments

I can hardly believe I've finally finished writing this book! It's taken me years plus hours of prayer. There are so many people that I want to thank. First, of course, is the Lord Jesus Christ. Thank you, God, for never letting me stop, even though I wanted to quit a number of times.

Next, I want to thank my husband, Mike, who loves me and has been there for me throughout the ups and downs of writing *Women of Destiny*. I also want to thank my children, Madison (Mary) and Daniel, for putting up with a writing mom.

To all my good friends at Regal, thanks for believing in me and for wanting a book to be written that would release women into everything God has called them to be. Kyle Duncan, you lifted me up time and time again through our phone conversations when I would hit a slump in trusting God that I could, indeed, finish the course. Bill Greig III, you've been great to allow me to write what has been in my heart. Kim Bangs, you encouraged me greatly.

The two guys who spent the most blood, sweat and tears in the writing are Dr. Gary Greig and Bayard Taylor. Thanks for putting up with my lists of questions and inquiries about what the Greek and Hebrew really say concerning the woman question. You're going to have a special star in your crowns for this project!

Karen Kaufman, my editor, what a great woman of God you are to take on the editing of a book about women and the Church. I know the warfare has been severe, but you have been a true soldier of the Cross.

Polly Simchen, my secretary, you are the best there is. Thanks for all of your hard work as you cleaned up the manuscript for me.

To all those who have prayed for me, I could not have written this book without the prayer shield you put up for me. I pray God will pour back abundant blessing upon your heads. Please don't stop praying. We've just begun!

Last, but not least, I want to thank Dutch Sheets, my pastor, who is a brave man to agree to be my spiritual covering. You're the best! Thanks for standing with Mike and me throughout the years of our friendship and for believing in the call of God upon women.

Cindy Jacobs
Colorado Springs, Colorado
January 12, 1998

The Role of Women in the Church

Writing this book about the role of women in the Church has caused me to ponder the plight of women in my own generation throughout the world: brides being burned in India, Chinese women being forced into unwanted sterilizations and the impoverished women who represent the majority of civilization's poorest people. Pictures of hurting female faces flood my mind: Women with lovely almond-shaped eyes spilling over with tears, and some with dusky ebony complexions—all yearning for an answer to life. Again and again their questions resound in the corridors of my mind: *Cindy, what does God want from my life?*

As I've gazed into those eyes and listened to the brokenness in their voices, I see mirrored images of years past when I too struggled with those same issues as a young woman aching to find purpose and destiny. Certainly Christ is the answer, but the subject of women in ministry has caused great debate in most Christian circles. Earnest men in the pastorate are wanting to release the women in their churches, but they are seeking a balance and solid biblical basis to do so. Some, dealing with gender-to-gender issues which are potential fire bombs of destruction to marriages are feeling their way in the Spirit for a path of reconciliation.

According to Dr. David Barrett's encyclopedia *Our Globe and How to Reach It* (published in 1990), 84 million women have been genitally mutilated to date. Women make up 70 percent of the world's poor, and 75 percent of the world's sick and disabled. Two million are raped each year. There are 200 million battered women in the world; 23 percent of all married women are battered, and that number grows by 15 million women per year.[1]

Women work 62 percent of all the working hours and receive 10 percent of the world's income, while they only own 1 percent of the world's property and make up 35 percent of the paid labor force. There are 950,000 ordained clergy in the world and 50,000, or 5 percent of them, are women.

It is for these women that I have written this book. Their only hope is the gospel of Jesus Christ. For where the gospel is preached, its transforming power changes lives. I believe it is a new day for men and that, should the Lord tarry, in another 10 years these statistics will look amazingly different.

Frankly, I approach this book with quite a bit of personal trepidation. I remember specifically begging the Lord to prevent me from having to address some of the issues I will carefully pose and tenderly discuss in this book. I do not purport to be an expert, however, I will share practical thoughts with you, my precious friends, on this subject. To say that I have "the fear of the Lord" on my life as I tackle this volatile issue is an understatement. Some of it may be just plain fear...period.

Is there such a thing as being too vulnerable? Probably. Writing this book has stretched my ability to bare my soul and face the fear of human criticism. I have tried to give up the writing of this book at least 15 times. This is my third and most prayerfully written book to date. I summoned the strength to press on in writing it because deep in my heart is the feeling that I may be paving the way for a whole new generation of women—many just young babes. And I'm still optimistic enough to believe that when they grow up, many of the issues I've grappled with will be settled or at least answered to a large degree.

Some of the women who read this book will weep and laugh and say, "I've found myself!" It is with that hope tucked snugly in my heart and with much love to all of my gender, who are fervently desiring to be used of God, that I have written *Women of Destiny.*
Blessings!

Cindy Jacobs

Note
1. Dr. David Barrett and Todd M. Johnson, *Our Globe and How to Reach It* (Birmingham, Ala.: New Hope, 1990).

The Journey

The year was 1950 and a struggling seminary couple knelt in earnest prayer. They were presenting a very special request to God. It seemed strange for them to ask such a thing in light of their present circumstances. "Lord," they prayed, "please give us a baby girl." They had lost a child through miscarriage and already had a precious son. God answered their heartfelt petition in August of 1951, and that is how my journey began.

I've always been deeply touched by that story. It has given me a sense of destiny and purpose through many turbulent times as a woman minister. Perhaps the Lord knew I would need the extra confidence that such a blessed beginning gives so I would have the strength to finish the course God had set out for me.

People sometimes pose this question to me, "Cindy, did you ever dream you would be traveling around the world speaking to thousands of people when you were a little girl?" The answer is no. I had absolutely no inkling. However, I have always had the sense of God's hand on my life for something very special, even as a tiny child. Maybe there are those of you who have felt something similar.

Even people who have been in terrible rebellion, those who have a call of God on their lives, will later recount how God saved them from disaster or a potential life-threatening circumstance, time and time again. For you who are praying for lost loved ones or rebellious children, this should give you great comfort. God is faithful—always!

I have chosen to start this book with an intimate sharing of my life because most who will read it will be women, and women are born with a God-given need to know about each other in a detailed fashion that is somewhat foreign to male thinking.

For the men who are reading, please feel welcome in the following pages. You are extremely important in helping women find God's plan for their lives. Some of you men who delve into *Women of Destiny* are called of God to affirm and bless the work that God is doing through your wives and daughters, female friends or the feminine gender in your local congregations.

I Love You, Daddy

The man who influenced my life the most as a child was my daddy. I adored my daddy as I grew up. He was a Baptist church planter and had a passion for starting churches. During those days, we didn't have an understanding of the role of the apostle in the church, so Dad rather puzzled us. We would start a church one place and it would grow very rapidly. Then he would go into this building program, and within a period of only a few years he would have a thriving congregation. However, to our great consternation, he would then get this itch or need to move on and do it all over again! We now know that he was called as an apostolic leader to raise up new works.

As you can imagine, I moved quite a bit. I guess it could have really messed me up except for one factor—there was a lot of love in my family. I didn't doubt for one minute that I was loved. Dad, even though he had been a gang member in New York City, had been born in Georgia, and still had a bit of a soft drawl at times. Often I would reach for his big hand that wore a size 12 ring, look up into his face (he was almost six feet tall) and say, "I love you, Daddy."

And he would always reply with a grin, "I love you too, darlin'."
Food wasn't always easy to come by in those days. I remember times when we would receive big cardboard boxes full of food. The church called it "a pounding," which makes absolutely no sense, but it sure was fun to receive. We would get all kinds of exotic delicacies that people had been given for Christmas but hadn't sampled—pickled pigs' feet and things like that. I loved it!

Sweetheart, Your Father Is in Heaven—I'm Your Daddy

Prayer was important in our home. Each night (until we all became scattered asunder with jobs, school, etc.) we would kneel by one of our beds to pray. I was always small for my age, so my nose never reached the top of the bed in a kneeling position. We'd take turns praying, one at a time. For some reason the youngest always started, which was fine with me, because I'm the middle child and that put the pressure on my sister, Lucy. I'm convinced my life as an intercessor began on that bedroom floor—down on my knees, listening to the deep rumble of my daddy's voice and the sweet, soft Texan accent of my San Antonio-born mom.

My parents had an effective way of teaching, which went straight to the heart. I remember one day when I was in college. The Jesus People Movement was in full swing, so it was in vogue to pray, "Dear Jesus," instead of, "Dear God," or, "Our Father." That evening after I prayed for the meal, my daddy looked up, his gray eyes filled with sadness as he queried, "Honey, how did Jesus teach His disciples to pray?"

I replied, "Our Father, who art in heaven."

He softly instructed me, "Then pray that way."

Another time I decided I would call my daddy, "Father." I thought it sounded rather important. Dad was working on something in the backyard at the time. He stopped and simply said, "Sweetheart, your Father is in heaven—I'm your daddy." He wasn't being mean. I knew what he meant. The awareness of God in heaven was often brought to the forefront in our home.

Those of you who read my book *The Voice of God* (Regal Books) know that my daddy went to be with the Lord when he was 49 years old. I have thought from time to time, *Now I have a Father and a daddy in heaven.*

Born to Bear Fruit

Because Dad loved to start churches, circumstances were usually in a pioneer stage. This was great training for me as I learned to canvass neighborhoods. (For those of you not familiar with the term "canvass," it simply means going from house to house to either visit or leave a flyer about the new church.)

Early in life I begged Mom and Dad to let me take piano lessons, so I played hymns for the church from the time I was 10 years old. And because Sunday School teachers were often scarce—as we usually had quite a few new converts—I would sometimes teach the little kids younger than I with big, colorful, poster-sized Sunday School pictures that told the story on the back.

Life as a Baptist pastor's daughter wasn't always easy. I remember moving to a little Texas town during the third grade where everyone was either Catholic, Czech or somehow related. My life in that community was often full of rejection—subtle and otherwise. Years passed before I realized that there wasn't something terribly wrong with my personality and that my being overlooked and left out was simply a matter of prejudice. Thank God for the secondhand bike my dad fixed up for me. I loved to whiz down the country roads exploring God's world and sensing the weight of His presence. God and I talked—a lot.

When I was nine, I went to church camp in Prescott, Arizona. The Holy Spirit was so precious during the meetings and I loved to hear the missionaries' stories. I related in *The Voice of God* how the Lord called me during the camp session. One thing I didn't tell was my struggle over what I was to be. The night service was sweet as we sang the old hymns of faith, such as "Count

Your Many Blessings, Name Them One by One." I felt very close to God. That afternoon in my quiet time I had surrendered my life to the Lord, but now I knew I needed to "make it public," as we called it.

Finally, the moment came when the speaker gave the invitation. Wafting through the night air came the strains of the camp song I loved, "I Have Decided to Follow Jesus."..."No turning back, no turning back." I knew I couldn't turn back. I had to go. Feeling nervous and a little embarrassed, I moved out from the wooden bench where I had been sitting. Quietly, I knelt at the front. The song went on, "Though none go with me, still I will follow." Tears coursed down my cheeks. My heart was bursting with love for the Lord. I sang over and over with the melody, "I will go Lord—anywhere. Just tell me what You want me to do."

At the end of the invitation time, one of the workers handed me a commitment form to fill out. I sat down and studied the boxes: pastor, evangelist and missionary. I wasn't sure about missionary, but I never dreamed I could be a pastor or evangelist, so I signed up with the Lord to go to the mission field.

It's interesting how choices we make even in our earliest years affect our lives. My interests as I grew up were in interior design and music. No one in my family played the piano, but as I said earlier, I had an intense desire to learn. Unfortunately, there was no money, so my mom wrote to my grandmother who sent us the money for my lessons. My first piano had been stored in an old firehouse so the keys were warped and looked rather wavy. I didn't care. One piano teacher told my mother that I was too little to reach the pedals and that my hands were too tiny to stretch wide enough to play, but that didn't daunt my mom. She believed in me and found another teacher.

Years later, the piano lessons placed me in good standing—I was granted a music scholarship to what was then Grand Canyon Baptist College. I honestly believed I had discovered my niche in life. This must be what God wanted of me.

I once heard the parable of a beautiful tree which, as it matured, grew beautiful flowers. The tree, seeing the flowers, came to the conclusion that it was a flower tree and that it would always be a flower tree. But as spring progressed, the flowers dropped off and little hard balls began to form where the flowers had once given the tree its sense of splendor. This was most confusing to the tree, which no longer knew what it was. Time passed and the little hard balls eventually matured into luscious ripe apples. Eventually the tree realized it was meant to bear fruit and not flowers.

The apple tree's story is much like the passages of God for those who are called. Many times young leaders will assume their eventual destinies by the beginning flowers of their callings. That's exactly what happened to me with music. I loved to play Bach, Beethoven and so forth—so much, in fact, that I thought this would be my call.

Years later I was offered a job teaching voice at a Bible school and my desire to take the job was so strong that I had a hard time hearing God's will for me. Even though my schedule was full of speaking engagements that I would not be able to fulfill if I took the job, I still struggled for a yes from the Lord. Finally, in the wee hours of the morning, the Lord gently instructed me to finish the course by preaching the gospel, not by teaching music. I heard Him say in a still, small voice, "Cindy, the call to music is the call of your soul (or emotions), but the call of your spirit is to preach the gospel."

When Man Closes a Door, God Opens a Window

Emotions can color the decisions we are to make that will eventually affect our destinies. We must be cautious when feelings begin to dictate our actions. Let me explain.

When I first started ministering in Argentina during 1990, I fell so in love with that nation that I wanted our whole family to move there. I even dialogued about the move with some Argentine leaders. One day when I was riding in a taxi to a meeting in Buenos Aires, the voice of the Lord said in my heart, *Daughter, I will allow* *you to give **your heart** to this nation, but not **your life**. I have called you to the nations of the earth and you must not move—you would get so focused on this one place that you would not fulfill your calling.* I knew I had to obey His voice rather than the voice of my emotions.

I completed my bachelor's degree in music and went on to study a fifth year for my master's in teaching music. The fact that I studied music and desired to use my gift for the Lord will help you understand one of the challenges or tests that came before me as a young married woman in my church.

God Will Make a Way

Mike and I lived in California and went to a little fellowship with only about 50 members. Mike worked all night for an airline and would sleep during the day, so I often attended church alone on Sunday mornings. One Sunday the pastor approached the back of the church where I was sitting to talk to the man on the other side of me. He leaned across me and in a quiet voice asked, "Homer, would you stand and lead a song this morning? We don't have anyone who can do it."

Homer, obviously very uncomfortable with the thought, shot back, "Pastor, you know that I can hardly carry a tune!" The pastor walked away and led the song himself.

Now Mike and I were personal friends of the pastor, and he was well aware that I was working on my master's degree in music. In fact, the week before I had been observing my professor as he directed the Burbank Symphony for my orchestral conducting class. Part of my training was in conducting symphonies, but now *because I was a woman*, I could not even stand in front of my church to lead a hymn! As a 23-year-old who wanted to use her gift for God, that was a heartbreaking moment.

What did I do? Well, I knew I had several options: One, I could go away bitter and never return to the church. Two, I could stir up trouble against the pastor. Three, I could make a godly choice and seek the Lord for how I could use my musical training in a church that didn't believe women could do anything from the pulpit. I chose to pray and forgive the pastor; then I started a youth choir.

What transpired was glorious! That little choir became the best sound around and many of the youth made commitments for the Lord Jesus. I really grew through that experience.

God will always make a way for you if you are obedient to Him.

Young leaders, men or women, please read this carefully: God will always make a way for you if you are obedient to Him. Nothing will stop you from using your God-given gifts. If a door closes, look for the window. Be creative. When life is full of frustrations and tests, don't give up.

Many people ask me, "Cindy, why has God used you all around the world for His kingdom?" Well, it's not because I'm more gifted than most or a better speaker. I earnestly believe it is because when there were obstacles in the way of what God called me to do, I trusted Him to make a way where there was no way. Has it been easy? No. Has it been worth it? Yes!

Ladies, you may at times have unique challenges in pursuing your destiny, but your attitude along the way will make or break you. If you choose bitterness or anger, or get eaten up inside with how unjust the system is or how prejudiced some men are against women, then you will never survive in the ministry or be successful in your life either. And remember ladies, being prejudiced against men is just as ungodly as the other way around.

It takes a lot of courage to follow the call of God—many times, more courage than you can personally muster. This is why you need to have an intimate walk with the Lord.

Obstacles are inevitable. There will be storms. And friends, sometimes God doesn't take the storm away—He just tucks us in the eye of the storm where we will be protected from its raging.

My War, His Will

At other times, however, the storms we experience come from our own struggles to follow His will. God touched me when I was 31 years old and told me to pick up my cross and follow Him in taking the gospel to the nations. Well, I had a terrible struggle accepting the call. In fact, during that time I had a brilliant idea! I would offer my husband, Mike, in my place! You see, I never dreamed I would be the one preaching. For some time I had prayed and believed God that Mike would preach and I would be his loyal intercessor. That nice neat package wouldn't have offended anyone.

The wrestling with God began in earnest when I realized God was not negotiating. He wanted *me* to preach, not Mike. Now, this was about as foreign to my thinking as my signing up for the "astronaut program." Anyone who knows me would double over laughing at the thought of me doing anything that requires athletic ability. When we played volleyball in school, I ducked when the ball came my way!

The war was on! I gave the Lord plenty of reasons why I couldn't possibly preach. "God," I pled, "didn't You notice that I am the *wrong gender*? Besides, Lord," I whined further, "I don't like women ministers. They have those high, squeaky, unpleasant voices. So God, don't ever ask me to preach, especially over radio!" (I have lost track of the number of times I have preached or been interviewed on radio throughout the world since then.)

The next horrible thought that zinged through my brain was, *Oh, God! What about my children?* I winced at that. You see, I lived in a little Texas town where some of the men didn't have a very high regard for women ministers! I didn't want anyone to hurt my kids. I'm afraid my next statement wasn't very religious: "God, I'm not laying my children on the altar of any ministry." I was unwilling to see my children mocked, made fun of or isolated as I had been.

For nearly a two-year period, I paced the floor after everyone was asleep at night, fighting the call. Again and again the voice in my head screamed, *No, no, I won't do it!* Rebellion was running deep. *Why me, God? Please God, no!*

Struggling Veterans Who Preceded Me

I began to read autobiographies of others who had also struggled with their sense of destiny.

Aimee Semple McPherson

One day I came across a book about the life of Aimee Semple McPherson, who founded the Foursquare denomination. The story related her struggle with the Creator. She had been a missionary's wife whose husband died while they were newlyweds on the mission field in China. Aimee was widowed with a small baby to care for. In desperation, she came back to America to raise her little daughter.

About that time, Harold McPherson, just six months older than Aimee, asked for her hand in marriage, declaring his love for her and her little girl. Aimee agreed to wed with one stipulation: that all her heart and soul were really in the work of the Lord, and that, "If at any time in my life He should call me back into active ministry, no matter where or when, I must obey God first of all." They married on February 28, 1912, under those conditions.[1]

For a while, Aimee attempted to stay at home and forget the call of God upon her life. She and Harold were living at her mother-in-law's lovely home in Rhode Island. She had also given birth to a baby boy during that time, and took up collections for the Salvation Army in order to augment their income. Finally, however, as Aimee tells in her own words:

All through these strenuous days and that of the comparative quiet of our Providence home, a Voice kept hammering at the doorway of my heart. It shouted, "Preach the Word! Do the work of an evangelist!"

"Impossible, Lord!" I would protest. "Impossible!"

"I have called thee a prophet unto the nations," echoed the Voice.

"No, Lord, I cannot go!" I would reiterate. Then would come a paralyzing silence which ensues when a telephone is disconnected. Returning to the privacy of my own room, I weepingly sobbed, "Oh Jesus! Jesus! Jesus!"[2]

Aimee's health broke under the strain. She suffered a major operation and steadily grew worse. All the time the Voice inside her kept bidding her to keep her pledge to preach the Word. To continue in her words:

Finally, my condition became critical, and I was taken into a separate room to die. A nurse sat by me in the early hours of the morning, watching my flickering pulse. Through the death silence which was broken by my own painful breathing, came the Voice of the Lord in trumpet tones, "NOW WILL YOU GO?"

Lying there face-to-face with the Grim Reaper, I realized that I was either going into the grave or out into the field with the gospel. I made my decision and gasped out the words, "Yes—Lord—I'll—go!"

Instantly new life and warmth surged through my being.[3]

It helped to know that I wasn't the only one who had ever kicked against the pricks to answer the call of God (see Acts 9:5; 26:14, *KJV*). Not only that, but the consequences for saying no suddenly loomed large before me. Maybe it wouldn't be too healthy to tell God no—I didn't want to take that chance.

Sister Gwen Shaw

Other women have also wrestled with accepting the fact that God had a call on their lives. One of them was Sister Gwen Shaw, who is the head of the End-Time Handmaidens. The Handmaidens consists of a large network of intercessors who must fast 21 days before they can become an official part of the organization. Sister Gwen tells the story of her call to China during a revival in her Canadian Bible school days in her book *Unconditional Surrender*:

> It was around 11:00 P.M. when I entered the building and found my way to the classroom downstairs, where students were praying. As soon as I knelt, I felt a great burden for intercessory prayer come upon me. I put my head down under the chair and the Holy Spirit began to travail inside of me. Hour after hour I wept and wept. Today as I look back, I know it was that God would give me another chance to do His will and fulfill His calling on my life.
>
> After this experience, I looked at my watch. It was now 3:00 A.M. In the other room there was still a lot of praying going on, so I got up and went in there.
>
> As soon as I went in, I saw something I had never seen in my life before. One of the students was travailing for China. The Holy Spirit was weeping and calling through the student, "I'm calling you to China. I need you in China. Won't you go to China? China. China."
>
> I looked around at those in the room and I wondered, "Who could God be calling to China?" The fact that it might be me never dawned upon me. After all, God couldn't call me—I was married now, and anyway, I didn't like the Chinese people. I was even afraid of them.[4]

The call of the Spirit persisted until one teacher asked Gwen, "Why don't you pray about it?" She consented and in her own words:

> Immediately, I began to feel a strange new burden grab hold of me for a nation I had never thought about. "I must be imagining this," I thought. God surely wouldn't call me. What would Dave [her husband] say?[5]

Gwen's heart was so full of questions that she said at last in desperation, "Lord, if it is me You are calling, then You will have to put me on the floor. I'm staying in this chair." Suddenly the power of God hit me like a stroke of lightning and threw me on my back on the floor. I thought God was killing me! "Lord, I'll go! I'll go!" I cried in desperation.[6]

Upon arriving home, Dave was not at all happy about the decision his wife had made. He sarcastically announced that she might go to China, but he was "going to Hawaii." Gwen's heart was broken, so she cried out to God. The Lord faithfully intervened. The same Holy Spirit who had dealt with Gwen later prophesied through a visiting prophet over Dave that he was called to North China. This should be encouraging to those of you who feel a call of God even though your spouse doesn't.

As a matter of fact, I came close to calling off my wedding because Mike insisted that he didn't have a call of God on his life. I broke up with the poor guy about 10 times because of it. The last time we broke up, Mike moved from Phoenix to Los Angeles, where we had met at a Baptist church.

After Mike left I was terribly sad. I didn't eat and was totally miserable. Finally, he called and quoted Matthew 18:19,20: "Again I say to you that if two of you agree on earth concerning any thing that they ask, it will be done for them by My Father in heaven. For where two or three are gathered together in My name, I am there in the midst of them."

"Honey," he said, "somehow I feel that if we will let God be in the midst of our marriage, everything else will turn out OK."

Later on, Mike did receive a call and we started Generals of Intercession together in 1985. We've had many challenges, but God has truly been with us all the way.

Can Any Good Thing Come Out of Weatherford?

People often ask, "Cindy, what happened after you said yes to God and accepted His call?" The truth is that I had no idea what to expect after I surrendered my life to full-time ministry. There certainly didn't appear to be much danger of anything too drastic happening to me because, after all, I lived in Weatherford, Texas—population 12,000. How could anyone find me there? In fact, some of us used to jokingly say, "Can any good thing come out of Weatherford?" We hadn't even started Generals of Intercession yet. What a good place to hide. Right? Wrong! God can find you anywhere. (See Psalm 139.)

When I agreed with God to preach the gospel, I taught Children's Church and was also leading worship. Sundays were busy because I had to arrive early to work with the praise team, lead the worship for our little church, slip out and teach 40 to 50 children from 5 to 12 years old and then slip back in to finish the service at the piano. It may sound overwhelming, but I actually thrived on it. God was at work! The children were praying for each other and God was causing short legs to grow, mosquito bites to disappear and warts to fall off. We had a great time! Nearly 100 children were born again in a year's time.

When God Calls Us, He Equips Us

God actually started things off in a big way when I visited my in-laws in Phoenix, Arizona. We went to lunch with Faye Darnell, the women's pastor of a large charismatic church with nearly 5,000 members and between 200 and 300 women meeting in the weekly women's meetings. I had a nice time and we agreed to meet the following day for the Bible study.

Had I known what God had in store for me that day, I would have been scared out of my wits! The Lord, however, had faithfully prepared me by waking me at 6:00 A.M., impressing me to fast for the day.

At the meeting, I was puzzled by the strong sense of God's presence upon me until Faye asked me to minister prophetically to 12 ladies. I agreed and as I prayed, the Spirit of God moved powerfully. Not only did the 12 ladies fall under the power of God, but others in the room were also touched. Faye urged me to continue. The strong sense of God's Spirit rolled in like a thick cloud filled with His glory. I ministered for three more hours.

When I returned to Weatherford, I received a call from Faye asking me to prayerfully consider ministering at her church's next ladies' retreat. She told me about the well-known person who had ministered the previous year and then said, "Cindy, we could get some big-name speaker, but we are hungry for the anointing and we want you to come." Frankly, I was astounded.

God wants to minister through you and
me in His power and not our power.

Mike and I prayed and sensed this appointment was of the Lord so I said yes. Then the struggle began!...What had I done? To say that I was fighting intimidation would have been the understatement of a lifetime! It's moments like this that the devil sits on your shoulder and whispers in an intimidating voice *Who do you think you are? You know you can't do that! What will you say that will have any meaning to those people?* Actually, it really wasn't very difficult for him to practically demolish me with those cutting words, because they exactly mirrored my own! Fortunately, when you and I feel totally inadequate, we are actually ready! God wants to minister through you and me in *His* power and not *our* power.

My one "plus" was that I earnestly wanted to obey God. I had more fear of the Lord on me than fear of man. (Believe me, I had tons of fear of man in me in those days!)

Next, I was overcome with a deep sense of emotional insecurity. I rehearsed a list of numerous other women who could do a much better job than I and tried to get God to change His mind.

(Some of you are grinning right now because you've had a similar experience, or else you're going through one right now!) Perhaps I should have given up on convincing God to change His mind by now, but then you've probably also noticed that I can be very stubborn and hardheaded at times.

Throughout these emotional roller coaster rides, I was also earnestly beseeching God for the subject matter I was to teach during the retreat. Faye had asked me to teach three times. *Three times!* I thought with sheer terror. *God, I haven't taught more than one time anywhere in my life!* Major panic set in as I sought the Lord for something to say during *all that time!* Thank God for praying friends who helped me through that big step.

Leaping into the Dark

When I was a little girl my daddy used to preach about faith. I remember hearing him explain that it was like a little girl looking down into a dark basement and her daddy saying to the small child, "Jump, honey. I'll catch you!" The little girl couldn't see her daddy, but she could hear his voice. That leap into the dark for her daddy's arms was faith. Friends, I was leaping into the dark and hoping God was going to catch me.

The day the retreat began I felt assured about the message God had given me, but I had no idea how long it would take to teach the series, "Releasing Bitterness and Judgments." I'll never forget the first session. Faye introduced me and I walked to the front. Fortunately we had one of those old wooden pulpits instead of the new Plexiglas kind. Those Plexiglas ones are merciless: they show all of you—even your shaking knees. You can't even take your shoes off if your feet hurt without the whole world knowing!

My knees were shaking and inside I was fervently praying, *Oh God, please don't let them know how scared I am! Oh God, help me!* But then, all of a sudden, I sensed the same presence of the Holy Spirit as I had at the weekly Bible study! It enveloped me like a garment and the words simply flowed out of my mouth.

Boy, was I ever relieved! In the end, not only did I have enough material—I had too much!

God did all kinds of things that weekend. We laughed and cried. People were able to forgive the unforgivable. The miracle anointing flowed. I'll never forget when I gave the Word of Knowledge for healing (a supernatural insight that a certain type of healing was taking place) that someone had a corn on her foot and that God was healing the problem. Now, this was kind of corny (pun intended!), because we were at a retreat center in Cornville, Arizona!

A lady named Juana laughingly said, "It's me, it's me!"

"Well, take off your shoe and look," I urged. She did and the corn fell right off her foot onto the floor! Wow! It was great!

People were set free, especially from bitterness. One lady who began manifesting a demon fell on the floor. I started casting the evil spirits out of her. And when I called out "rejection," the spirit manifested. It caused her to pound the floor as it left with a whiny voice saying, "I'm the last one, I'm the last one." What a glorious deliverance!

What did I learn? I hardly know where to begin. I learned that if I stepped out in obedience, God would show Himself strong on my behalf. I learned that He is greater than my fears, insecurities and those thoughts that rise up to intimidate me. I learned that if He's working through me, I don't have to worry about what I lack because He will speak through me—and He isn't at all insecure or lacking in any good thing! Good lesson, huh? I'll share more about this and other lessons I learned while ministering in chapter 11, "Anointed to Serve."

When God Opens the Door, No One Can Shut It!

There was a real shifting of gears in my life that weekend. Other people quickly heard word about what had happened and sent me invitations to speak. It has always been my philosophy to let the Lord make the way. I've never sent out resumes asking to speak or tapes to solicit engagements. The Lord has opened all the doors. In fact, He has opened so many doors that I've had to run to keep up with Him.

I do want to balance my experience by saying that I know some people generate their entire incomes from speaking engagements. In those early days, Mike worked for American Airlines so we didn't have to use love offerings for living expenses. But people who live entirely by faith may have to initiate finding contacts and being selective about where they can afford to speak. Either way, if it isn't the Lord's will, the doors will usually shut rather than open (see Rev. 3:7). I thought we had quite a big measure of faith before 1991, but now I realize my faith was in Mike's paycheck. Today, God is the one who guides and provides every detail of our lives.

This was the beginning of my being thrust into ministry, which began in 1981. So much more has transpired and will be woven throughout the pages of this book. The next chapter, "Secret Pain," is critical as you discover God's plan and purpose for your life. No matter what God calls you to do in life, striving to be a whole person in Christ is essential to finishing the race well. Let's take the journey together...

Notes
1. Aimee Semple McPherson, *The Story of My Life* (Dallas: Word Inc., 1973), p. 72.
2. Ibid., p. 72.
3. Ibid., p. 75.
4. Gwen Shaw, *Unconditional Surrender* (Jasper, Ark.: End-Time Handmaidens, Inc., 1986), p. 62.
5. Ibid., p. 64.
6. Ibid., p. 64.

Secret Pain

Rapid thoughts ran through the woman's head. She knew she could be in grave danger if caught. Her body was weak and she was totally destitute. *What have I got to lose?* she pondered. A sense of her isolation, along with loneliness and shame, shot through her emotions. Familiar despair felt like myriad knife wounds in her soul.

Slowly, she dropped to her knees and began crawling through the crowd. Every once in a while she would stand to take her bearings to see how far she had come in executing her plan. It seemed fail proof. The crowd was so large and many were jostling and pushing each other just for a look at this incredible rabbi. Surely He would not notice just one more person tugging on the hem of His garment.

Carefully, she inched her way toward Him and, at last, reached out. *Just one touch...I know I will be healed of this issue of blood,* she told herself. At last she was almost close enough to touch the border of the fringe trailing from His side. For one split second she faltered. *What if I am discovered and stoned because I have made the rabbi unclean? How could I possibly get away in this throng? Too late now,* she decided, and made the plunge.

What could be happening to me? Her thoughts were in a

turmoil. A warmth emanated from her womb. The terrible pain subsided and a peace such as she had never known seeped into her troubled mind.

Quickly, she came to herself and looked around in a panic to see how she might hide herself and make her escape. Then she heard a voice crying out in the crowd that filled her full of wonder and fear at the same time. "Who touched Me? I felt virtue leave My body." And then she knew. It was the Rabbi, the one they called Jesus. He was calling her name.

Her first thought was to run—flee away! But then, she remembered the sound of His voice, and was aware in a keener way of the strength and wholeness now coursing through her once diseased body. Gingerly, she stepped out of the crowd and fell down at His feet and said, "Rabbi, it was I. I'm the one who touched the hem of Your garment."

She was aware of His eyes as she shyly lifted her face upward to His tall, strong frame. *Those eyes,* she marveled, *who could be afraid of anyone who has eyes such as His?* They were tender and loving, yet strong and full of power.

Somehow she knew she could trust Him. There was a sense of being fully protected from all those who would seek to harm her because she had come out into the crowd when she was unclean. With a trembling voice she told her story:

"Master, I've gone to the best physicians in the land for the last 12 years. I used to have quite a bit of money and many friends. Now, I have spent all and no one has helped me but You. You were my last hope. I'm not quite sure exactly what has happened to me, but I know I am well. Oh, thank You, Master, thank You!" she exclaimed.

Lovingly, the Master looked down into her mist filled brown eyes and pronounced, "Daughter, it was your faith that made you well! From this day you are whole and free of your disease!"

The crowd just melted back as she cautiously climbed to her feet. She *was* well! The weakness was gone and joy burst from her soul! With one last look at Jesus she practically floated away into her new life. (See Matt. 9:20-22.)

Private Pain in Public Pews

Have you ever asked yourself the question, *Why did Jesus call her out of the crowd?* It is unthinkable that a loving God would have a desire to humiliate the already broken woman. Did He have to ask, "Who touched Me?" Wouldn't He have already known?

Perhaps He called her out of the crowd because her disease had not only affected her on the *outside*, but it had also greatly damaged her on the *inside*. The woman had suffered for 12 years and was weary of life. She had, in all probability, been separated from those she loved—at least from any kind of a human touch—and most likely suffered deep physical and emotional poverty. I believe the Lord called her out of the crowd to bring healing to her inner person and lift the shame and disgrace off of her. Jesus, the Rabbi, pronounced her "clean."

Many who enter our churches today come with secret pain that they don't want to talk about. Maybe you are one of them. It deeply saddens me to know that people sometimes slip into church to find comfort only to leave again without being made whole.[1]

Why do people hide their pain? One of the many reasons might be that people often have a big problem trusting other brothers and sisters in the Lord. There is also the issue of shame and rejection.

Let's take a look at the culture of the Church. In many cases we come together and say to each other, "How are you today?"

"Fine, thank you," we might reply.

No matter how terrible we may be feeling, the polite reply is, "God has been good to me." Well, I'm not negating that God has been good to us, but many of us are not honest! We are *not* fine! In fact, we might have just told a big lie! There are situations in our lives causing us deep distress and we need help.

Our *how are yous* are often only perfunctory and we seldom listen for a response. Eye contact is rare and heart-to-heart sharing is rarer still.

We need to listen not only to what people say with their words, but also with their faces, noticing whether their eyes are happy or sad and checking out their expressions. Jesus, who was

Undealt—with pain is like an infection that when left untreated can destroy our destinies.

pressed on every side, took notice of someone who simply touched His garment for a moment. He is our example. I want to be like Him in everything I do and say. Unfortunately, I fall very short.

In Touch with the Out of Touch

Some people are in touch with others and out of touch with themselves. They stuff their pain, they deny their pain and they project their pain by blaming others. But God did not create us to carry our hurts. Undealt-with pain is like an infection that when left untreated can destroy our destinies. If we are to become all God intends for us to be, we must allow the Holy Spirit to ferret out all the hurt places within us and heal our broken hearts.

Healing begins with truth. We must be willing to look at what my mother calls, "our beasts in the basement." However, the basement may be the floor of reality, and instead of kicking all our junk downstairs, we need to have a spring cleaning. Of course, it's much easier to hide from the truth. Counselors call this *denial.*

I once saw a funny, but true, *Peanuts* cartoon. Lucy was trying to tell Snoopy (who was dancing around and around in glee) just how terrible the world is.

"Snoopy," rebuked Lucy, "with all the terrible things happening in the world today, how can you be so happy? You must be in denial."

Snoopy replied with a big grin on his face, "I'm the king of denial."

For some, denial is survival, but that's not God's highest and best. There's a lot of pain and cause to be offended that comes from daily life. The Bible says in Matthew 18:7, "Woe to the world because of offenses! For offenses must come." Whether we like it or not, we will all be challenged by offenses in our lives and the pain they cause.

In the early days of my ministry, every little word of criticism would wound my heart to the core. Rejection is one thing that women ministers usually receive quite a bit of (as does anyone in Christian leadership, for that matter).

A friend called me one day and asked me what I was doing. "I'm in bed," I told her, "and I've stapled the covers over my head and I'm not coming out!" Everyone has days like that. Maybe you're having one today.

One of the most memorable prophecies I have received was, "Daughter, I'm going to give you the hide of a rhinoceros and the heart of a dove." I have to admit that I am still very much in process on both counts. In the introduction, I confessed my reluctance to writing this book. I had to count the cost because I know that not everyone will embrace the message it brings to women. I hope I have rhinoceros hide!

Secret Sins Cause Leaky Lives

Many people have so much secret pain stored up inside that it spills out, hurting those around them. One day I asked a counselor friend why a person we know acts the way she does. Her response was, "Cindy, that person is so full of anger that she's like a big sponge that is totally saturated and it just leaks out all over people who get close."

What's important is that *you* aren't the one who is leaky! One of my favorite prayers is, "Lord, keep me from secret and hidden sins" (see Ps. 19:12).

A pastor friend was terribly hurt by a breach he had with a great and respected leader who had mentored him. He had given up all hope of reconciliation, but as we talked he realized that a stronghold of offense had been built up in his mind because he had been rejected. We made a covenant to pray and ask God to restore not only that broken relationship, but also others in his life. One by one we saw God answer our prayers with other people. Then finally the one breach that had caused him the most pain was mended in a supernatural way.

As you read this pastor's story, you may be thinking of those with whom you have had a breach. It might be your mother, a child or a friend. This causes a deep pain in your life. Believe God to heal the situation. Don't give up on believing, because *nothing* is impossible with God.

If I am speaking to you, would you be willing to stop reading right now and make a list of those with whom you need to reconcile? You might even want to pray the following prayer:

> Lord, I guess that I have believed that there is something You cannot do. I have given up on trying to reconcile this situation so I am going to believe there is nothing impossible or too difficult for You. Please heal this breach with _____ and restore our relationship.

I thought about waiting until the end of the chapter for that, but I didn't want you to suffer one moment longer. I pray you feel a lot better right now.

How Can a God of Love Have So Many Rotten Kids?

Years ago I began to come to grips with my own secret pain. Most of it resulted from being a pastor's daughter. In fact, by the time I was 18, I couldn't stand some church people. I had watched them behave ungratefully toward my parents, and sometimes, downright mean. One day I concluded that I loved God, but I couldn't stand His kids!

I remember standing by my mother when this lady approached her and started criticizing my dad. I was a 16-year-old fireball who didn't take this too kindly. My mom kept me a little behind her, probably so I wouldn't tell her off. Actually, I was thinking, *Mom, if you will move a little more to the right, I'll let her taste my fist!*

My mom patiently listened to everything Mrs. Big Mouth said and then with a look of peace on her face murmured, "I am so sorry that you feel that way, because *we love you so much.*" All the strength went out of my anger as I listened in wonder to my mother show the love of Christ to this totally unlovable person!

By coming from the opposite spirit, the situation was reversed. Mom was a victor rather than a victim. Her victory came through her own choice and maturity in Christ.

We can make similar decisions in our lives. Scripture tells us to bless those who curse us and do good to those who hate us (see Matt. 5:44). If we do this, we will receive a blessing from above: "Blessed are you when [people] revile and persecute you, and say all kinds of evil against you falsely" (Matt. 5:11). Notice the scripture doesn't say *if*, but *when.*

Once when I was sad because of false accusations being spoken against me, my husband, Mike, wisely said, "Cindy, Jesus was perfect and they falsely accused Him." This brings us to an important principle:

You will never be so perfect that you will escape being misunderstood.

At times when I hear what my accusers are saying about me I chuckle and say, "I can't understand why they'd say those things about me because I'm such a nice person!" (Well, mostly I am.) Honestly, many misunderstandings are cleared up when you meet the person you are having a problem with and sit down and dialogue.

Forgiveness:
The Antidote for False Accusations

Let me take a few moments to deal with the subject of false accusations: an area of secret pain that is often pulled into the public arena. Accusations often get mixed up with gossip and grow and multiply alarmingly. For example, once I had a little mole removed and people phoned my office to verify if I had cancer! Why are we so apt to believe the worst about each other?

Could it be that we've been listening to the accuser of the brethren? The devil works day and night trying to kill our faith, rob our joy and destroy our reputations. We would be wise not to listen to him. Pastors are accused of manipulation and control because they try to correct sinful situations in their churches. Many women who are strong leaders are accused of being Jezebels (i.e., controlling and manipulative women who act like Jezebel did in 1 Kings 16—2 Kings 9 in the Bible. Would it make you feel any better to know that I've been accused of being one myself?) However, accusations are not gender specific. At one time or another, all believers will have to learn how to deal with them.

So what should you do when you are accused? First, you will have to deal with the sting of it in your emotions. (The magnitude of the pain will depend on how much rhinoceros hide you've developed.) My friend Peter Wagner, a forerunner in the area of church growth and prayer and spiritual warfare, gets shot at often. When he hears of a new criticism written against him, Peter just grins and says, "Did they spell my name right?" I really admire him. I don't always fare so well. Sometimes my first reaction is to want to beat 'em up (a real joke for someone five foot two and three-quarter inches like me), or demand an immediate apology!

But forgiveness is what Jesus modeled and so must we. After we work through the angry or hurt stage (or a mix of both) and forgive, we need to pray for wisdom.

Although our first inclination might be to confront, that

might not always be the best plan. John Maxwell, of Injoy Ministries, is a foremost expert on leadership who said at a Breaking The 200 Barrier seminar at Fuller Seminary:

You can either add water or gasoline to a fire.

If you're not careful, you will make the situation much worse. (This is hard to believe at the moment it happens!)

If the Lord tells you to confront the situation, follow the biblical pattern set forth in Matthew 18:15-17:

1. Tell the person his or her fault. Make sure it is between you and the offender alone. If the person hears you, you have gained your brother or sister (see v. 15).
2. If he or she will not hear you, take one or two more to confront (see v. 16).
3. If he or she refuses, tell it to the Church (see v. 17).

The gravity of some situations is so intense that if you are married, it is better to go as a couple—such as in a case when the accusation has been made before a congregation. You may also want to ask someone in spiritual leadership to go with you.

Remember, Jesus acted like a lamb led to the slaughter before His accusers. Even though I have been written against and slandered on the radio, very few times have I answered my accusers. One day my teenage daughter queried, "Mom, who is (so-and-so) and why doesn't he like you?" This was a perfect opportunity to model Christ's forgiveness before my daughter. It hurt me more that my daughter had heard the accusation and suffered than the fact that I had been spoken against over the airwaves.

I might add that none of these people came to me to dialogue before they publicly bashed my name—a clear violation of the Matthew 18 passage. But I was still able to show my daughter how things should have been handled and explain that suffering accusations can be a growing experience. Through the suffering we learn more compassion and tenderness toward others. How we handle the situation can either work a weight of glory (see 2 Cor. 4:17) or destroy us. I have a favorite saying about times such as this:

Satan has meant to break me through this, but I choose to allow it to make me more broken before the Lord.

Purify My Heart, Lord

If you want to be a pure and broken vessel for the Master's use, then your intimate prayer sessions with the Lord should include a time of asking God to uncover secret sins, anger, hurts and offenses. Allow the prayer of David in Psalm 51 to be your example. (At times I deceive myself that something didn't really hurt, but later I make some kind of caustic statement about it and discover I've not fully dealt with it to the depth that is needed.) Warning: Don't pray this way if you don't really mean it, because He will do it! Sometimes in the most public places.

For instance, during the 1980s I was speaking at a large church for the Sunday night service. I had spoken for its women's retreat just prior to the service and God had revealed a deep wound in my heart concerning the city where that church was located. You see, my dad had pioneered a church there and it had been hard—very, very hard. Remember the story about Mrs. Big Mouth? This was the same city. I had amazingly shoved my deepest pain into a big mental closet. I guess if Snoopy was the king of denial, I was the queen.

Immediately after I was introduced, the Lord spoke to me in my heart, *Cindy, you can't get up and preach to these people. Your heart is not right. You hate this city and the denomination your father was a part of here.*

Now "hate" is a strong word, but it was true. I was angry about the mistreatment my dad and our family had suffered. Of course, a good Christian girl wouldn't consciously harbor hatred and anger, so I was not in touch with those feelings at all.

Why was I so angry? The Lord gently whispered into my spirit, *Cindy, you believe they are responsible for your dad's death.* Wow! That insight hit me like a ton of bricks! It was true though.

A little family history is needed to understand the depth of my emotions. My dad had been a pastor who planted churches. For some time he had longed to become a missionary and wanted to be supported by the missions board. The board had helped us with $25 a week years before, and now he was applying for regular support.

When Dad approached those in charge of missions at the denominational headquarters, he was offered a proposal: "Albert, how about cleaning the buildings for us while we process your application? We need a janitor and you need to provide for your family."

My dad was a very humble man. Although he was a highly educated seminary graduate, he felt it wasn't beneath him to become a janitor. So night after night, he would clean the headquarters building. Sometimes I would go with him and help. Never did I hear him complain that the job was too menial.

After a substantial period of time, Dad approached the missions board to find out what had happened to his missionary application. Although numerous churches had given him commendable references, his request had been denied because one church had submitted a negative reply.

To put this in perspective, that church had run off every pastor they'd ever had prior to my father. In fact, the previous pastor had left in the middle of the night, leaving only a letter of resignation on the pulpit. Even though it was a tough place, Dad had stuck it out. The church grew and even added a parsonage. And now the church he had strived so hard to build and preserve would lay its final blow to my daddy's pastoral career.

From that day forward, my dad was not the same man. He never pastored again. Even though God used him mightily with young handicapped high school students, he never quite recovered from that disappointment. Finally, he died at age 49—one month short of his fiftieth birthday. He was too young to die. I believed his death was the result of a broken heart.

When I finally got in touch with those feelings, a volcano of emotion began to erupt within me. Shaking, I explained to the congregation what was happening. I told them the story, and asked the elders of the church to come forward to pray for me. Thank God for covenantal friends who can be trusted with sensitive issues of the heart. As I knelt, they came quickly and laid hands on me.

A confession flowed out of my mouth. James 5:16 says, "Confess your sins to each other and pray for each other so that you may be healed" (*NIV*). I needed to be healed because I was full of private pain. The reason Scripture instructs us to confess sin is that confession is part of the healing process. I said some ugly things such as, "I have hated that denomination, God, and I have hated its denominational leaders. They couldn't have killed my dad in a more painful way if they had used a gun to shoot him in the head!"

I couldn't believe what I was hearing myself say. The confession went on with, "And God, I hate this city for what it did to my family. It was such a hard place to start a church. We suffered so deeply, God. The church either wouldn't or couldn't pay us enough to even provide the basic necessities of life, and we were hurt."

I had flashbacks of going to the store with my mom and asking her to buy some cookies. Mom cried because she only had $10 to buy a week's worth of groceries—she couldn't afford to buy cookies. I grieved as I recalled images of Mom and Dad wearing old clothes that should have been discarded years before. (Pastors and their families often suffer deeply as they sacrifice to start churches.)

After I had vented for a while, I felt like a clock that had been too tightly wound and the spring had let go. During those moments I could also see how my brother and sister were hurt by what happened. Thank God that He restores: Today (as of this writing) my brother is teaching English in China and my sister has her degree in counseling. God is a redeeming God!

At last, a glorious sense of peace and joy filled my heart as my friends prayed for me to be healed. I was just beginning in ministry at that time, but I believe as a result of my willingness to be open and honest, God honored what happened that day. God has opened doors all across the world for me since then. My dad may not have become a missionary on this earth, but I did! And I am believing for a double portion of anointing to shake the nations of the earth.

You might be a pastor or child of a minister and relate to this story. Many times, as I have shared, leaders' children have come and fallen into my arms, weeping. A pastor in Mexico told me how he has gone with holes in his shoes because there is not enough money to fix his soles.

Even if you are not in full-time ministry, you may have been hurt by someone so deeply that you have never been the same. You are why I have written this chapter. I don't want you to hurt, but most of all, your heavenly Father doesn't want you to keep carrying secret pain in your heart. My friend, Ed Silvoso, says that people get shipwrecked in certain areas and times of their lives and they are never the same. It stunts their spiritual growth. First Timothy 1:19 puts it this way:

> Having faith and a good conscience, which some having rejected, concerning the faith have suffered shipwreck.

Rebuilding from the Wreckage

I have seen shipwrecks happen to people other than myself in myriad ways. I've seen those with the gift of giving hurt when large sums of money they gave to a ministry were later misused and those in charge were proven unworthy of their trust. They then became wounded and crippled in the area of their greatest strength. Thus, their strength became their stronghold. I've seen pastors who have been so hurt that they've left the ministry and never used their pastoral gifts again. They are now soured toward the ministry, and unless they are healed, their pastoral destinies will erode in the sea of bitterness where they were shipwrecked. Perhaps I'm talking to you right now. If so, the following are some suggestions to help you receive healing:

1. Pray, asking the Holy Spirit to reveal any areas where you are carrying secret pain.

2. Make a list of the people and situations in which you have been hurt, abused or offended.
3. Ask God to give you a person(s) who can pray with you as you confess your faults. (Of course, you can pray privately and forgive and ask God's forgiveness, but James 5:16 speaks directly about confessing our faults one to another.)
4. The more vulnerable and truthful you are willing to be about the situation and your pain level, the deeper the healing you will receive. (Helpful tip: Bring a big box of tissues because you will probably need it.)

Years ago I was diagnosed with a grapefruit-size tumor behind my ovary. After the doctor read the sonogram, he advised me to have it surgically removed. I asked him if we could wait 10 days so my husband and I could pray for my healing. He was a bit skeptical, but said it wouldn't hurt to wait for that time period.

I earnestly began to seek the Lord for healing. Then, one day I received a call from an intercessor in California who gave me a word: "Find the root and pull it out, then you will be healed." I began to ponder this. At first I had no revelation about what had hurt me enough to cause this large mass to grow within my body.

Suddenly, in a flash of inspiration, I knew what it was! I had been deeply hurt by a male pastor who didn't believe women should be in the ministry. The rejection had affected me in my femaleness! (I have found this to be the case for lumps in the breasts also. In fact, medical science is now making similar discoveries. Women who have lived with a critical father or husband often have problems with fibroid tumors or other female-related illnesses.)

I began to search the Scriptures regarding healing. When I read James 3:16—"For where envy and self-seeking exist, confusion and every evil thing are there"—I knew I had found the key to my healing. We had already prayed and anointed with oil, but this one thing I had not done: I had not confessed my hurt, anger and unforgiveness against this pastor to anyone else.

Mike and I invited a couple over with whom we felt close. I knelt down and confessed my pain in detail. As I confessed that I had not truly been able to forgive this pastor, even though I had tried, I started to weep until tears were wetting the carpet in front of me. Then, when I finished, they anointed me with oil and asked God to heal me.

I still had the pain in my body (from the tumor pressing against my spine) after the prayer, but something was different inside of me. I knew I was healed. When I went back to the doctor he was totally stunned and amazed! It was absolutely gone! Not only that, but I had the blessing of witnessing to my Hindu doctor as a result of the miracle.

There are serious consequences when we don't forgive others and receive a release from the pain and bitterness of the situation. I like the illustration that Ed Silvoso, forerunner on prayer evangelism, gives about forgiveness:

Suppose a visiting evangelist comes to your church and borrows your car. The man is a former drug addict who seemingly is being used of God in a wonderful way. Later you find out that the man has driven to the airport, sold your car, and gone to South America.

You would probably be furious, feeling betrayed by the evangelist. "He used me!" you would probably fume. "He was a minister of the gospel!"

Who must take the initiative to forgive? The thief? No, the one in the right! There is a deep vulnerability towards bitterness that he has to overcome. Does the thief have to overcome bitterness? No. He is in South America, oblivious to the pain you are feeling!

This reminds me of the story told in Matthew 18:31-35:

So when his fellow servants saw what had been done, they were very grieved, and came and told their master all that had been done.

Then his master, after he had called him, said to him, "You wicked servant! I forgave you all that debt because you begged me. Should you not also have had compassion on your fellow servant, just as I had pity on you?"

And his master was angry, and delivered him to the torturers until he should pay all that was due to him.

So My heavenly Father also will do to you if each of you, from his heart, does not forgive his brother [or sister] his [or her] trespasses.

Quin Sherrer and Ruthanne Garlock (two of my prayer partners for years) have some good insight on the need to forgive:

Forgiveness through Christ is the cornerstone of our reconciliation and relationship with God. Knowing this, Satan attacks our capacity to give and receive forgiveness. He provokes us to indulge our grievances and hold on to our bitterness by telling us over and over, "The person who did this to you doesn't deserve to be forgiven!"

Only Christ's sacrifice has the power to free us from sin and its bondage. Yet Jesus fixed a condition for that freedom in His parable of the unmerciful servant. In this story the king represents God and the servants represent us, His children.[2]

We put forgiveness in its proper perspective when we realize that any injustice we have suffered from another person is small compared to our own sin against God.[3]

Some secret pain can only be forgiven through the grace of Calvary. One of the most powerful stories I have ever heard about forgiveness comes from the life of the great Dutch leader, Corrie ten Boom. For those of you not familiar with her story, Miss ten Boom and her family harbored Jews during World War II, for which they paid a high price. Almost all of her family died in concentration camps, including her favorite sister, Betsie. The following story is her personal recount of a time when years later

Corrie came face-to-face with a jailer from the concentration camp where her sister had died:

> It was a church service in Munich where I saw him, the former S.S. man who had stood guard at the shower room in the processing center at Ravensbruck. He was the first of our actual jailers that I had seen since that time. And suddenly it was all there—the room full of mocking men, the heaps of clothing, Betsie's pain-blanched face.
>
> He came up to me as the church was emptying, beaming and bowing. "How grateful I am for your message, *Fraulein,*" he said. "To think that, as you say, He has washed my sins away!"
>
> His hand was thrust out to shake mine. And I, who had preached so often to the people in Bloemendaal the need to forgive, kept my hand at my side.
>
> Even as the angry, vengeful thoughts boiled through me, I saw the sin of them. Jesus had died for this man; was I going to ask for more? "Lord Jesus," I prayed, "forgive me and help me to forgive him."
>
> I tried to smile. I struggled to raise my hand. I could not. I felt nothing, not the slightest spark of warmth or charity. And so, again I breathed a silent prayer, "Jesus, I cannot forgive him. Give me Your forgiveness."
>
> As I took his hand, the most incredible thing happened. From my shoulder along my arm and through my hand a current seemed to pass from me to him, while into my heart sprang a love for this stranger that almost overwhelmed me.
>
> And so I discovered that it is not on our forgiveness any more than on our goodness that the world's healing hinges; but on His. When He tells us to love our enemies, He gives, along with the command, the love itself.[4]

Perhaps it's your own family that has hurt you. Many people have to forgive their parents, or even their own children.

I recall when I had unforgiveness against my still small babies. Mary (Madison as she prefers to be called today) hardly ever slept through the night and I was bone weary most of the time. Then later, when Daniel was born, the doctors thought Daniel would probably never walk because he didn't have muscle tone in his left leg. I spent hours soaking off his little cast while he cried and cried. Even though I knew in my rational mind that it wasn't Madison and Daniel's fault, and that it was, in fact, the situation that frustrated me, little things the children did started grating on my nerves until I was a wreck!

The Lord showed me that I needed to forgive my children. At first it seemed crazy that I should forgive a little baby and a small child for things that weren't their fault, but I did what He asked me to do. One by one I asked God to bring to my mind situations from their infancy to toddlerhood where I had resented what they did. One by one I forgave. When I finished, I somehow felt clean inside—released from past frustrations, and able to be a much more loving, patient mom.

One of the hardest things to do is to love a rebellious or, perhaps, strong-willed child or teenager. My daughter has always been a young, emerging leader and thus tested my leadership to the max! I remember how we went to a Bible study at a very large church one time when Mary (Madison) was only three. I only turned my eyes away from her for a few short moments when all of a sudden I heard a strident voice coming from the direction of the church's bookstore screeching, "Whose child is this?"

To my absolute horror my sweet child had spun a rack of little mini-books around so fast that they had gone flying all across the store! I was absolutely humiliated! I was tempted to look the other way and say, "Child? What child? Did I come in here with a three-year-old, blonde-haired child looking just like that one?"

Sherrer and Garlock tell the story of how Audrey forgave the pain caused her by Vic, her prodigal son, in their book, *How to Forgive Your Children*:

A few days before 18-year-old Victor was to graduate from

high school, he learned he'd failed his Advanced English course and would not be allowed to walk down the aisle with his classmates for commencement. Three days later, Audrey found a note on the windshield of her small yellow station wagon which read: *Mother, Dad...I have to get away. Don't worry, Vic.*

Audrey was shocked. "Vic had never given me any problem," she told me. "I had such high expectations that he would serve the Lord with all his heart in whatever career he chose. I had another child who was retarded, a husband who was terribly mixed up and not serving God, and now I had a lost son. I had to call on the Lord for help."

Audrey searched frantically for Victor, and finally located one of his close friends. "If you hear from Vic, please have him call home," she begged.

That night the telephone rang. A weak voice on the other end of the line breathed a terse message: "Mom, I'm all right!" Vic cut the connection, leaving her no clue as to his whereabouts.

"I had one choice, and I knew it," Audrey shared as she recalled the experience. "If I were to survive emotionally, I had to forgive Vic for the disappointment I felt because he was not graduating and for his leaving home without so much as a good-bye. I also had to lay down my pride, my hurt, and finally my anger. I'd be tormented over what he had done to me and worrying about where he was if I didn't. So, I made the choice: I forgave Vic, releasing all my pent-up feelings as I committed him once again into God's care."[5]

Although Audrey changed her outlook, the prodigal didn't immediately come home. In fact, it was three long months before he would come home. God led her to a friend of Vic's because she felt in her heart that he might be in the area. When she finally saw him again, he was thin, living in a bad section of town and wearing threadbare clothes.

Her first words were simply, "Hello, Vic."

He replied, "Hello, Mom. I missed you"—music indeed to a mom's ears.

Sometimes restoration is a process and not the microwave kind of fix we would like it to be. For those in the midst of the process, I recommend Marcia Mitchell's excellent book, *Surviving the Prodigal Years* (Emerald Books).

It may also help you as you forgive and receive healing from the subsequent hurt to study some of the books written by Quin Sherrer and Ruthanne Garlock. They are excellent and go into depth in the area of forgiving in many different areas. (See the "Recommended Reading" at the back of this book.)

This chapter has been extremely critical because a woman will never reach her highest potential, either in the home or the church, without being a whole person in every way.

You're going to love reading the next chapter. Part of our restoration as individuals comes through the friendships God brings into our lives on an everyday basis.

Notes
1. Note: I am grateful to Rich Wilkerson for his book *Private Pain* for the concept I used to begin this chapter. I highly recommend his book, published by Harvest House Publishers in 1987.
2. Quin Sherrer and Ruthanne Garlock, *A Woman's Guide to Breaking Bondages* (Ann Arbor, Mich.: Vine Books-Servant Publications, 1994), p. 181.
3. Quin Sherrer and Ruthanne Garlock, *A Woman's Guide to Spiritual Warfare* (Ann Arbor, Mich.: Vine Books-Servant Publication, 1991), p. 125.
4. Corrie ten Boom, *The Hiding Place* (Grand Rapids: Fleming H. Revel, 1996), p. 238.
5. Quin Sherrer with Ruthanne Garlock, *How to Forgive Your Children* (Lynnwood, Wa.: Aglow Publications, 1989), pp. 66-67.

Dear God,
I Need a Friend

My husband, Mike, used to play basketball on Sunday afternoons at the little park near our home in Weatherford. He teased that he would hang around under the basket until the younger guys would throw the ball to him. (The truth is that Mike is actually a good athlete. But he enjoys luring an innocent partner who is quite rusty and out of shape onto the basketball court: rather like, "Come right in," says the spider to the fly!)

Mike had played with basically the same group of guys for nearly six weeks and I had even gone down once to be his best cheerleader. So one day when my sweaty, stinky, but happy husband arrived home from an action-packed day on the basketball court, I queried, "Honey, what are the guys' names that you play ball with?"

A totally blank expression came across his face. "Names... well...," he stammered, "well, I don't know any of their names."

Now, to my feminine mind-set this was a shock! He didn't know anything about these people he had played ball with for six weeks? Unthinkable! It simply did not compute!

Surely I must have misunderstood that he *knew nothing*

about them. So I probed deeper, "Well then, are they married? Do they have children?"

Searching his face, I saw to my dismay, the same blank look. The realization that he knew absolutely no details of their lives finally dawned upon me.

The Gender Gap

Have you ever watched men play basketball? They are really physical. After a good shot, they pat each other on the rear end and otherwise express glee in ways a woman would *never* think of! (Okay, some women who are on a college team might do this, but they would probably know a lot about each other first.) I was incredulous! I would have to know someone really, really well to physically act like that, and then I still probably wouldn't do it.

On the other hand, have you ever watched women get together for the first time? Their goal is to bond with each other and they do so by gathering information. When two women have become friends, they know practically everything about each other—everything except maybe their social security numbers! I'll go into more detail about the differences between men and women in the chapter entitled "Gender to Gender." But for now, it is sufficient to say that the way most men and women cultivate friendships is quite different.

The Friend You Can Depend Upon

You may find that the title of this chapter, "Dear God, I Need a Friend" resonates in your heart. For most of us it does. And that's why I'm going to talk to you about letting God be your very best friend. God, through His Son, Jesus, wants to be first in our lives in order of priority. He is a friend who will never fail you. In fact, He is a "Friend who sticks closer than a brother" (Prov. 18:24).

The attributes of God are far beyond what even your best friend could attain. Let's consider a few of them together. He is...

1. Always available. (His line is never busy or out of order.)
2. Never a gossip or willing to treat us unjustly.
3. Unconditional in the way He loves.
4. Generous in every way.
5. The most attentive listener.
6. The best counselor, always giving unbiased advice.
7. Never selfish or self-seeking.

Pretty outstanding attributes, huh? In looking over the list, I feel I have a long way to go at being a good friend.

But the Bible tells us that Moses was a friend of God and that "the Lord spoke to Moses face to face as a man speaks to his friend" (Exod. 33:11). Imagine having that kind of closeness with Him!

Perhaps Moses could talk face-to-face with God because he didn't have anything to be ashamed of. Moses must have walked before God with what the Scriptures refer to as "the fear of the Lord" upon His life.

So what is the fear of the Lord and how does one develop it? I say, "develop," because it certainly isn't instinctive to our carnal nature. Joy Dawson, an international Bible teacher, author and intercessor is one of the people who influenced my life most in learning about the fear of the Lord.

The Wise Friend Hates Evil

Joy Dawson taught me that one product of walking in the fear of the Lord is "wisdom." I want to be wise to help my family and friends and "the fear of the Lord is the beginning of wisdom" (Prov. 9:10). We begin to develop wisdom when we realize how casual our attitudes have been toward sin and how much our culture has polluted our thinking about right and wrong. We cannot be a friend of God when we have lost our understanding of what pleases and displeases Him in His holiness because sin is what separates us from God.

Joy Dawson gives four distinct levels of attitudes toward sin in her book, *Intimate Friendship with God:*

Level One: The person who does not sin because the consequences are too great. This person lusts after someone else in his or her heart but does not commit the sin of adultery or fornication with his or her body because of the consequences being too great. Or he may hate someone else and wish that person were dead, but does not murder him because of the consequences. Obviously, there is no hatred of evil and, therefore, no fear of the Lord.

Level Two: The person who lives by the Golden Rule. He wants peace at any price and cannot understand anyone who is so radical that he would try to change the status quo of his life or anyone else's. This person can be full of the sins of selfishness and self-righteousness without being aware of it. He may go to church regularly every Sunday and give his tithes, pay his bills, grow six cabbages and give one over the fence to his neighbor. He often does good deeds. If you came up to him and said, "Do you fear the Lord?" he would be most indignant that you would even ask such a question of him. "Of course," he would reply. In fact, the "of course" could mean, "How could you have been so unobservant? How insensitive to the obvious!"

If you asked him, "How long has it been since you spent more than an hour in prevailing prayer for the lost souls of men? What is the depth of your commitment to the Lord Jesus Christ for the lost souls of men to be reached by your witnessing to them on a personal basis? What is your prayer life in relation to the millions of Muslims, Hindus, Shintoists, animists, Buddhists, Communists, atheists, humanists, and nothingists who have no knowledge of God's plan of salvation or assurance of eternal life? What concern have you for the unreached millions of the world?" In all honesty he would have to answer, "Very little, or none at all."

There is no fear of the Lord manifest in these sins of selfishness, prayerlessness, self-centeredness, complacency, and self-righteousness. There is no acknowledgment, let alone any hatred, of these sins in the person who lives on this level.

Level Three: The sincere Christian who earnestly desires to please the Lord Jesus Christ. He does not want to sin and is deeply concerned when besetting sins are in his life. He wishes he could find an answer as to why he is always having to confess over and over again the same sins. Perhaps he commits the sins of criticism and of judging others; the sins of pride, always drawing attention to himself in conversation; the sins of unbelief in being unable to trust God, as manifested in fear, doubt, and disobedience. Or maybe it is the sins of lust, covetousness, jealousy, or resentment—to God or man. He is deeply concerned and longs for freedom.

Level Four: The person who has the fear of God upon him. He hates sin; therefore, he seldom sins. If he does, there is a quick awareness of sin, immediate repentance, and a willingness to humble himself before others if directed by the Holy Spirit to do so.

Joy Dawson goes on to say that "we have sinned because we have chosen to sin, because we love sin. 'Through the fear of the Lord, a man avoids evil'" (Prov. 16:6).[1]

As her son and my friend, John Dawson, would say, "That will clean your plow." I have *the fear of the Lord* on me just typing the four levels!

Humility: The Quick Fix for Human Messes

I often think of how little puppies are sometimes trained with a very short leash. If they run out too far ahead, their owners pull back on the leash and they find themselves splayed out on all fours. This is how the Lord is with me at times. Once I plant the fear of the Lord as my boundaries, if I simply think of running in the wrong direction, my heavenly Father, in His mercy, pulls back on that leash and I find myself falling on my face in an extremely humbling position.

I am thankful to know that God loves me enough to keep me from straying outside of His love (see Heb. 12:10). I want to clean up my messes quickly and run to fellowship with Him. I want Cindy Jacobs to be a person He can trust to do whatever He needs done with integrity and compassion. I know that it will take all of my life to be the kind of friend that Moses was with God, but then God is no respecter of persons, so I believe it is attainable.

I have learned that one way God manifests Himself to us is through the friends He sends our way. Although our primary need is friendship with God, we can also ask Him for a friend "with skin on," so to speak. The unconditional love of a covenantal friendship is healing and a great source of strength and comfort (see Eccles. 4:12). A real friend is one who sees us at our worst moments and still thinks that we are special.

Ruth: A Model for Friendship

Both men and women need friends, but their friendship needs are very different. For now I will primarily focus on the kind of friends women need. (Men, you might want to stick around and not tune out at this point, because the following insight will be helpful in your relationships with those mysterious beings called "women.")

One of the most beautiful stories of friendship in the Bible comes from the book of Ruth. This book flourishes with lessons we can apply to our daily lives. As you read about Ruth, notice the qualities she brought to her friendships and ask yourself which of these qualities you need to cultivate.

Let's begin by contrasting this book's main characters—two women brought together during distressing times in a covenantal relationship: Ruth, a young gentile daughter-in-law, and

Naomi, a bitter, disillusioned, older Jewish mother-in-law. Their diversities can conjure up all kinds of mental pictures for us. Ruth was probably quite beautiful and most likely could have had her pick of handsome young men. She didn't need Naomi.

Obviously, Ruth would have known about the notoriously strict religious laws of the Jewish people because she had married into a Jewish family. So why would she choose to go with Naomi to Bethlehem?

Undoubtedly, she knew that if she traveled with Naomi, she would be forfeiting the protection of her own people and choosing instead the hard, cold ground and hostile surroundings in order to make the journey. This was a serious choice weighted with possible dire consequences. And yet Ruth made that choice.

Ruth Was Covenantal
The dialogue between these two women is often sung at weddings, representing the love between husband and wife; but, as we know, it was actually a healthy, covenantal love between two women:

> Entreat me not to leave you,
> Or to turn back from following after you;
> For wherever you go, I will go;
> And wherever you lodge, I will lodge;
> Your people shall be my people,
> And your God, my God.
> Where you die, I will die,
> And there will I be buried.
> —Ruth 1:16,17

Naomi had not only won Ruth's personal affection, but her life had also caused her daughter-in-law to have a conversion experience for which she abandoned her pagan gods for the one, true and living God. What an impact a friendship can make!

As we read through the book of Ruth, we notice that Naomi had another daughter-in-law, Orpah. But these two women were quite different in the ways they demonstrated friendship. Let's compare them:

Ruth	Orpah
An intelligent love of choice.	An emotional love of feeling.
Quiet fidelity.	Passionate affection.
Love that bore testing.	Love that failed in adversity.
Genuine spiritual basis for conduct and decisions.	Selfish biases for decision making.
A resolute exercise of the will.	An easy change of emotions.[2]

Ruth Was Patient

Bitter people, such as Naomi, are usually difficult to be around. And Naomi might have been short with Ruth from time to time as she processed the grief of her husband's death. But Ruth's love was so healing that even Naomi was softened by it.

I am convinced that the love of God can penetrate any soul, no matter how hurt or angry. I would encourage you not to abandon your friends when they are going through bitter times such as the loss of a child, husband or parent. That is the time when they need you most. And that is also the time when they are least able to reciprocate your love. But the Scriptures tell us to love even when we don't receive it in return (see Matt. 5:44,46).

Ruth Was Diligent

I personally admire Ruth as much as any woman in the Bible because of her excellent character qualities. She didn't have a lazy bone in her body. Rather than going out to glean the fields, she could have said to Naomi, "Look, old woman, get up and go help me find some food. I have lost as much as you have. Not only that, but I'm in this crummy foreign land and I don't understand the customs!"

Ruth Was Long-suffering

Instead, however, Ruth was tender to Naomi—who must have been in deep shock, and steeped in shame and embarrassment for having to return to Bethlehem empty-handed. Most likely her old neighbors who had tried to dissuade her and her husband from leaving were wagging their tongues and saying to each other, "Didn't we tell them not to go to that godforsaken place? Well, she got what she deserved!" Ruth was sensitive to the pain and shame of her mother-in-law. She had met the living God and her actions showed it.

Because Ruth was now God's child, He directed her right to the field of one who would become her husband and kinsman redeemer (i.e., a type of Christ. The kinsman redeemer was a relative who could "redeem" the inheritance of a dead relative. Isn't this a romantic story?) The Bible says Ruth *happened* upon the field of Boaz (see Ruth 2:3).

Ruth Was Grateful
Ruth worked tirelessly all day and when she met Boaz, she fell at his feet in gratitude. (Probably lifted those beautiful brown eyes up at him through her long dark lashes and he just melted!) What man could resist such a humble, grateful woman?

Ruth Was Committed
When Ruth ate the lunch Boaz provided, she saved some for Naomi, knowing she was hungry at home. She could have reasoned that she, after all, was the one doing the hard physical labor!

By chapter 3, we see that Naomi was getting healed of her despair and wanted to see that Ruth had security. She advised Ruth to appeal to Boaz as her kinsman redeemer. This strategy was based upon knowledge of Levite marriage (see Deut. 25:5-10). By this practice a widow became the wife of her husband's brother or another close relative in order to produce a child who would inherit her first husband's estate and preserve his name. Ruth's loyalty to the tradition of her husband's people and her desire to care for Naomi by marrying someone within the family was a tribute to her commitment to the family of her deceased husband.[3] Of course, we know that Boaz was a symbolic picture of Jesus, who is our Kinsman Redeemer—the Lord who redeems us from our sins and provides rest and relationship for all who lay their lives at His feet in submission to His lordship.

Ruth Was Teachable

Ruth did exactly as she was told by Naomi, which shows that she had a teachable spirit and a willingness to listen and learn from her elders. When Naomi tried to instruct Ruth about how to approach Boaz, she could have said, "Now listen, Naomi, I recognize that you know a lot about Israel, but I know much more about men than you do. You're from the wrong generation and obviously out of touch with how to get a man to notice you."

Ruth Was Obedient

There are great blessings to be gained from obedience—not blind obedience, but loving, godly obedience. The Bible says that obedience is better than sacrifice (see 1 Sam. 15:22).

I love to read from *The Woman's Study Bible* (Thomas Nelson Publishers) because of the richness found in the margin notes regarding the interrelations of women. One of the boxed-in points discusses mutual commitment between the women (Ruth and Naomi):

Gratitude on the part of one awakens loyalty in the heart of the other.

Selflessness on the part of one demands unselfishness from the other.

Bitterness in one gives opportunity for creativity in the other.

Interest from one is rewarded by responsive communication in the other.

Counsel from one bears fruit as accepted and honored by the other.[4]

One of the great themes of the book of Ruth is that of restoration. Dr. Fuchsia Pickett says:

The book of Ruth ranks among the greatest books of the Bible for teaching true, spiritual restoration, foreshadowed in the redemptive love of Boaz for Ruth. [5]

Godly Friendships Bless Both People

Naomi instructed Ruth to go to the threshing floor and lie down at Boaz' feet and say to him, "I am Ruth thine handmaid: spread therefore thy skirt over thine handmaid; for thou art a near kinsman" (Ruth 3:9, *KJV*).

In Eastern culture, "to spread a skirt," or covering, over someone was a symbolic act offering that person protection. More than that, it involved entering into covenant with a person for

New friends may have been brought into our lives just for the moment, or the meeting could be some God-ordained, lifelong connection that will change the course of our destinies.

the sake of redemption. Even today, in many Eastern countries, to say that a man puts his skirt over a women means that he married her.[6] (What a bold woman Ruth was! She was in all practicality proposing to Boaz!)

In asking for Boaz to cover her, Ruth was declaring, "I need a redeemer. I am a widow, disgraced, with no inheritance. You can take my shame, my poverty, the bleakness of my future and give me an inheritance. You can totally redeem me, if you will."[7]

This beautiful friendship brought redemption and restoration to *both* women. Ruth got a new husband, and had a young son. She became the mistress of the house where she had gleaned. Naomi received inheritance and her son's lineage was passed on. Not only were both women totally restored, but the generations also show that both King David and *the* Messiah, Jesus Christ, who redeemed the sins of the world, came from their heritage.

This story touches me deeply because my friends are among the greatest treasures God has given me. I have one friend whom I have known since the second grade. Even though we rarely see each other, I am always amazed and delighted by the way we pick right up in our relationship as if we had never been apart. This is a covenantal love.

Some friendships, like that of Ruth and Naomi, go beyond simply being a satisfying relationship for a brief period of time—they are God ordained. Joy Dawson has taught that God appoints the seasons of our friendships. New friends may have been brought into our lives just for the moment, or the meeting could be some God-ordained, lifelong connection that will change the course of our destinies.

The following are a few examples of friendships in the Bible:

- Esther and Mordecai: "niece" and "uncle";
- David and Jonathan: shepherd boy and prince;
- Mary and Elizabeth: mother of Jesus and mother of John.

These kinds of covenantal friendships are supernatural in their purpose. Have you ever met someone with whom you felt an immediate bond in friendship? This is an indicator that God will be doing something significant through the meeting. Of course, this goes way beyond the feminine gender. Mike and I are extremely close to a number of other ministers and their families who have had a tremendous impact on our lives: Chuck and Pam Pierce, Peter and Doris Wagner, John and Julie Dawson, Ed and Ruth Silvoso, Dutch and Ceci Sheets and others.

I don't hesitate to say that we are family to one another in many ways. We have laughed, prayed, cried and mourned together. Many of us have been on the front lines of the battlefield and been shot at so many times that we have had to pray each other out of intensive care. We know that we can call each other any time of the day or night, but we don't abuse the privilege.

Cultivating Closeness

One of my close female friends of many years is Beth Alves of Intercessors International. We've had numerous Holy Spirit adventures together. For example, several years ago I went through a deep valley of despair. Finally, in my intense discouragement, I decided to quit the ministry. I'll never forget calling Beth on the phone and leaving a sobbing message. I was crying so hard that my voice was indistinguishable. Beth shared with me later:

"I got home and Floyd [Beth's husband] was playing back the calls on the answer machine."

A voice came over the machine and Floyd said, "Beth, who in the world is that woman?"

Even though my voice was almost unrecognizable, Beth knew. Beth is my friend and it's not the first time she has heard me cry.

"Floyd, that's Cindy, and something is terribly wrong!" she exclaimed. Beth called and called until she reached me. When I explained the situation and my decision, she said, "Cindy, don't do anything rash. You go rest and let me carry your prayer burden for the next three days." Beth not only prayed, but she also *fasted*. Within three days I was able to press on in the ministry.

Maybe you're thinking right now, *I sure wish I had a friend like that*. Well, friendships like Beth's and mine are forged in the trenches of life. We have walked through so much together that we have built a foundation of trust. I've stayed up nights praying for her and her children and vice versa. Friendships such as ours require a substantial investment of time and energy. They don't just happen—they are cultivated!

Many people are waiting for someone to knock on their doors with a cake and an announcement, "Hi, I'm your new best friend and I've come to lift you out of your doldrums!" Even though this is not out of the realm of possibility, friendships usually don't happen that way. The Scriptures tell us that, "A man [or woman] who has friends must himself [or herself] be friendly" (Prov. 18:24).

Sowing Seeds of Friendship, Reaping a Harvest of Friends

Because we moved so often when I was a young girl, I remember being unbearably lonely. Then finally one day in the fifth grade, I made a decision that if I was going to have friends, it was up to me to start the relationships. I didn't know that I was actually tapping into a scriptural principle. It just worked! When I met someone I hit it off with, I would invite that person to my house after school. I also began thinking of kind things to do for people, and before long, they were responding. I wasn't interested in joining the most popular crowd—I just sought out people with similar interests who liked to read and discuss books or ride bikes with me.

When we would move, I corresponded with friends from that area as long as they wrote back so I wouldn't be entirely disconnected from relationship. I introduced my new friends to my old friends through their letters and the cycle of friendship expanded.

I also learned to develop friendships with people of all ages. I talked to neighbors when they were outside—especially the senior citizens. I had many hours of great fun while I raked their yards, walked their dogs or sat and ate cookies with them. A neighbor of my grandmother's whose name was Mrs. Lippy—I always called her "Mrs. Mississippi"—left me a 100-year-old plate that today hangs on my dining room wall. What a treasure!

Now I'm learning from Generation Xers and feel a great call to them. Many have told me about their fears and challenges, and although we relate on a different level—some call me "Mom"—they enrich my life. I once came home from a trip to find eight of them in the house while my own child had run an errand. "Hi, Mom," they chorused. Bewildered, I searched each face to see if I recognized any of them. I didn't. But they let me know that my kids had told them they would love me and that they could call me "Mom."

Letting God Be Lord of Our Friendships

Friendships have ebbs and flows, and these transitions shouldn't be threatening. If only young girls could realize this when they feel that their lives are over because Dottie has a new best friend. There are times when I am extremely close to a particular person, but then the Lord seems to start taking us in different directions for a season of our lives. It doesn't mean that we don't still have deep affection for one another, but we are going different ways. One or two years later we might just take up at the same place again. Of one thing you can be certain: If God is giving you a friend who is part of your future destiny in Him, He will see to it that you find each other again.

My friendship with Janna is a perfect illustration of how this happens. In 1990 Communism had not yet fallen in Russia, so I went with a team from Aglow International to pray that the doors would open for the ministry there. One of our Russian contacts was a young woman in her 20s named Janna. I fell in love with this young woman, and it broke my heart to have to leave her in Russia. We had some special times of prayer together and pondered on what God might have for us in the future.

When I left Russia, I lost track of Janna, even though I often prayed for her and asked God to help her move to America. She had deeply touched my heart as a friend and I felt she had a big destiny and calling in God. Sometimes I would pray, "Lord, please help me to find Janna again."

Several years later I was in Seattle, Washington, for an international board meeting for Aglow when I received a message asking me to call a young man we had met in Moscow. I was delighted to make contact with him again. Little did I know that I was about to receive the surprise of my life. Steve said, "Hello, Cindy. There's someone here who wants to talk with you." A moment later I heard a familiar voice with a Russian accent. It was Janna! I started jumping up and down, hollering and crying over the phone. It was a miracle!

Through many divine interventions, Janna and her husband

finally moved to the United States and she now works for Gospel Light, the publisher of this book. Janna translates Sunday School material into the Russian language. God works in mysterious ways, His wonders to perform!

Friendship Through Evangelism

One powerful way God uses friendship is through evangelism. There are many, many lonely people behind the closed doors in your neighborhood. Oftentimes they will see Jesus through reading your life and caring attitude towards them. My friend JoAnna Cinnani has a ministry to the lost through friendship and prayer evangelism.

JoAnna's guiding principle is to "Preach Jesus, but if at all possible, don't use words." Although this may sound unusual, I assure you that at the right moment she knows how to lead people into a saving relationship with the Lord.

In an interview in the *Navigator's Community Newsletter*, JoAnna shared that the way Jesus related to people was through a natural progression of friendship. His winsomeness made Him attractive and approachable, but He never let it interfere with challenging people to make hard choices.

She went on to illustrate how Jesus didn't condemn or judge the lost—He loved them and won their love. For example, His exposure of the woman at the well gave her hope rather than making her feel shame. JoAnna attempts to model her life and relationships after Jesus' example so others see how He:

1. Touched hearts by caring for people and fostering a sense of family.
2. Was a remarkably open man, listening as well as advising, and sharing stress and sorrows.
3. Was a deeply compassionate man, reaching out to those scorned and shunned by others.
4. Was obedient to God, performing in a quiet, unpretentious manner.

5. Was a first-class servant who voluntarily laid down His life for our sakes.
6. Was confrontational and exasperating when necessary, compelling people to make difficult choices as with the rich young ruler and in dealing with the Pharisees.
7. Addressed root problems in people's lives through an abiding love, something we have trouble doing unless we have the dynamic, transforming life of Jesus in our hearts.

While following the example of Christ, JoAnna also does her behind-the-scenes homework in prayer and spiritual warfare. She goes on to challenge the readers:

When we approach our neighbors, friends, and coworkers, have we truly laid a foundation of prayer? Have we asked the Holy Spirit to guide us with His agenda each day? Are we asking God to impose His sovereign right in our interactions? Is prayer a common occurrence in our daily activities? Are we calling on God's way rather than man's way in dealing with the world we encounter?[8]

JoAnna has been a special friend to me in many ways. When we moved to Colorado from Weatherford, Texas, I left behind two good friends who would help me clean house, or do whatever I needed. These friends ran errands for me when I was overwhelmed or went shopping with me on the spur of the moment. One day, I realized I was lonely for that kind of a friend so I prayed, "Lord, I'm lonely and I need friends like Laurie and Margarita." Soon I met JoAnna, who is Italian like my friend Laurie, and full of "salsa" like Margarita.

Before I went on our prayer journey to Vietnam in 1996, I became very, very sick. The day before I was supposed to leave, I was so sick that I couldn't even get out of bed to pack! JoAnna came to my house, looked in my closet and packed everything for my trip. It was an adventure just discovering what was in my suitcase on that trip! Thank God for the gift of friendship!

What keeps people from developing close friendships? Sometimes it is fear. We may have been deeply, deeply hurt through what might be called "friendly fire."

Maybe you have been "wounded in the house of [your] friends" (Zech. 13:6). This is a very deep pain. However, you will be the loser if you don't allow your heart to be open and receive the healing of the Lord that comes through friendships. It is a risk worth taking.

Some married women expect their husbands to give them the kind of friendship they need to receive from women. This expectation can actually put a strain on the marriage. While I consider my husband my best friend, I know He doesn't like to hash, rehash and go over the details of situations to the degree I need to. When a woman gets hurt, she needs to talk about it—sometimes more than once! This can actually lessen the pain for her, but it can also drive men crazy, as they usually discuss an issue once, conquer it and want to put it to rest.

Friendship Qualities
That Enrich Our Lives

Women in countries other than America sometimes express friendship in different ways than we Americans do. In Argentina, I would think nothing of holding hands and walking down the street with my good friend, Marfa Cabrerra. In America, however, I would be reluctant to do so because people here think holding hands is only for lesbians. I think Americans often rob themselves of the sweetness of pure relationships in which they can hug or even kiss on the cheek without feeling strange. Sometimes I love to hold my mother's hand. Often when we are at church and someone prays, she will reach out and take my hand. What a precious, precious gift that is!

Have I convinced you to enrich your life with deeper friendship? I hope so. Here are some tips for growing and finding new friends:

1. Pray, and be honest before the Lord. Tell Him, "God, I need a friend." You might even be specific just as I was about my need for a friend who could help me at home in my personal life.
2. Be open to looking back at past friendships and allow the Lord to heal you of any bitterness, pain or abandonment that would cause you to build walls and not receive the good gifts God wants to send your way.
3. Look around you for people in your neighborhood or church who are alone. Many singles need community in their lives and might enjoy spending holidays and other special times with you.
4. Pray for your neighborhood or perhaps your coworkers, asking how you can express Christ to them through friendship.

One of the greatest women of prayer that I know is Mary Lance Sisk. Mary Lance teaches on neighborhood praying. She told me the story of how a young mother moved into a developing subdivision where only a few houses had been built. This mom would bundle her little ones up and put them in a stroller to walk and pray over every lot on her street. She would ask the Lord for the salvation of each person He wanted to move onto those lots. Now years later, Mary Lance reports that almost every person on her whole block is a Christian.

I pray that God will give you a strategy for your neighborhood. Maybe you'll have a ministry of baking bread for new people who move in, or block parties where you open your home. You can make a difference through loving, interactive friendships.

With this theme of allowing God to use you to make a difference in the world you live in, I invite you to turn to the next chapter entitled, "Women of Destiny."

Notes

1. Joy Dawson *Intimate Friendship with God* (Grand Rapids, Mich.: Chosen Books, 1986), pp. 51-53.
2. *The Women's Study Bible* (United States: Thomas Nelson, Inc., 1995), p. 437.
3. Ibid., p. 437.
4. Ibid., p. 440.
5. Dr. Fuchsia Pickett, *The Prophetic Romance* (Orlando, Fla.: Creation House, 1996), p. 29
6. *The Women's Study Bible*, p. 108.
7. Ibid., p. 108.
8. Carrie Wagner, *Community* (Colorado Springs: Jan./Feb. 1997), pp. 1-2.

Women of Destiny

Have you ever asked yourself, *Why was I born?* Do you struggle with a sense of purpose and belonging? Each person has been uniquely formed and destined to accomplish specific tasks and goals. And yet, I have talked to many women who have said they wish they had been born a man! They tell me, "Life would be so much easier...," or "Men have it so good and women have it so much tougher."

The point is that if you are born a female, God wanted you to be one! You were given life by God to be a woman of destiny and to impact the lives around you. But in order to do that, you must discover God's purpose for your life and fulfill it to the very best of your ability. Perhaps you could make an impact like Susanna Wesley whose children, John and Charles, grew to be mighty reformers for God's kingdom. Remember, the Lord has called you for "such a time as this," just as He called Queen Esther (see Esther 4:14)!

It's true that some of you will have bigger mountains to climb and greater challenges to overcome than others. Some will have been raised in abusive homes, the drug culture or other difficult places. Others will have had the advantage of more money or greater educational opportunities. Fortunately, it's not what you have, but Whom you know that makes the difference!

Little Becomes Much
in God's Hands

History is full of women who believed God would turn their dire circumstances around and, therefore, saw amazing miracles. Consider the woman from 2 Kings 4:1-7. Talk about a bleak situation!...Her husband had died, and the creditors were threatening to make slaves of her two sons if she didn't pay the debt her husband left behind. (You may be in a similar circumstance, although you are more likely to be in danger of eviction than the enslavement of your children.) This woman needed a miracle! What did she do? She went to the prophet of God who asked, "What do you have in your house?"

This probably seemed like a strange question to the widow, but she graciously replied, "Nothing at all, except a jar of olive oil."

Often we think we are in a barren place without hope, but I assure you, there is something in the house—either a talent, ability or tangible item, such as a jar of oil, that can be multiplied to bless us. God will not leave us comfortless.

This widow was in a seemingly deep-end situation, but God had a plan for her. The prophet told her to borrow as many empty pots and pans from her neighbors as she could find. Then he instructed her to lock herself in the house and pour oil into the borrowed vessels from the one full container she already had. When she obeyed the prophet, she stepped into the realm of the miraculous.

Imagine the scene...her boys running back and forth, eyes wide with amazement as the oil kept pouring and pouring. Finally, perhaps a little out of breath, the boys said, "Mom, that is the last pot." Surely she must have looked around in wonder at the full vessels of oil and marveled!

She must have gathered up her skirt and gone running to find Elisha. I'm certain he would have been grinning when he instructed her to go pay her debt and then live off the money she made from selling the rest of the oil.

God Knows Your Address

Several years ago I was ministering in Argentina at a large church. The meeting was packed and the balconies were overflowing with people. Right in the middle of the meeting I stopped and the Lord spoke quietly into my heart, *Cindy, someone here is planning to commit suicide. Tell the person not to do it.*

Feeling the urgency of the situation, I interrupted the message and gave the Word from the Lord. When I finished the sermon, the pastor gave an appeal for the suicidal person to come forward. Slowly, a lady about 30 years old dressed in a white blouse and dark skirt made her way to the front. Softly, in a rather muffled voice, the young woman whispered that she was being evicted from her house and had planned to shoot herself and her three children when she arrived home from church. At that point, she drew a gun out of her purse and put it in the pastor's hand. "Pastor," she said, "when I heard God speak to me through Cindy, I knew He would make a way, and my children and I would not be out on the street."

No doubt the woman had prayed and God had intervened. I sure was glad that I had been faithful to the Holy Spirit's nudging and stopped in the middle of the message to tell her that God had a better way!

Anchored in the Purposes of God

You may feel stuck and controlled by the circumstances around you, when in reality, God has a plan to lift you out of the midst of your problems or despair. Romans 8:28 says, "And we know that all things work together for good to those who love God, to those who are the called according to His purpose."

If we study this verse carefully, we see that things work together for good to those who have "the anchor of purpose." All things may not be working together for good because we are aimless and don't know our purpose. We could interchange the word "purpose" for "destiny."

Down through the ages God has used women in powerful ways to influence their families, churches and nations. Many women have told me, "I know that God has called me to be a mother." And yet other women such as Elizabeth Dole, head of the American Red Cross, feel their place is to be serving and leading in business or government. The issue is not what you are doing, but whether you are doing what God has ordained for your life at this time. Romans 8 promises that nothing will be able to separate us from the love of God, but sometimes we are unsuccessful and miserable because we are not in our place of purpose or destiny.

Women of Courage and Valor

History reveals that no matter what their beginnings, women have been able to rise to the forefront when God was involved. For example, Catherine Booth was a sickly woman who often stayed in bed for days at a time, yet she never let her poor health stop her from doing the Lord's work. She sacrificed to "reclaim" women from lives of prostitution, and persevered until 1890 when she finally died of cancer at age 61. By the time God called her home, Catherine Booth had impacted the whole world through the Salvation Army.

Another woman who greatly changed the face of our nation was Frances Willard. When I went on a prayer tour of the Capitol building in Washington, D.C., I was impressed by the marble statue of her standing beside a pulpit engraved with the words "For God and Country." This inspired me to scurry to the history books. There I learned that this great woman of God lived from 1839 to 1898 and was one of the best-known female temperance leaders of the nineteenth century. She was active in founding and directing the Women's Christian Temperance Union (WCTU), the largest nineteenth-century women's organization.

Frances Willard's life and ministry illustrates how closely the temperance movement was aligned to religious activities. In spite of intense opposition, temperance work offered the only viable public ministry for many women of the nineteenth century.

Frequently, the religious activity associated with the WCTU involved evangelistic outreach to men.

The WCTU department of evangelistic work sponsored Bible readings and gospel work in prisons and police stations, as well as among railroad employees, soldiers, sailors and lumbermen. Willard's work was not limited to the United States. Indeed, the WCTU was probably the first large-scale women's organization to spread worldwide. By the 1880s, the White Ribbon Missionaries were organizing chapters in Asia, Africa, South America and else where throughout the world.

Closely connected with her work for temperance was her support of women's suffrage, for she believed that laws supporting prohibition would be enacted only if women had the ballot. As with her temperance work, Frances Willard claimed the direct leading of God:

> While alone on my knees one Sabbath, in the capitol of the Crusade state, as I lifted my heart to God, crying, "What wouldst Thou have me to do?," there was borne in upon my mind, as I believe from loftier regions, this declaration, *"You are to speak for women's ballot as a weapon for protection for her home."*[1]

Frances worked with Dwight L. Moody during his Boston campaign, and Moody even invited her to preach at a Sunday afternoon meeting. Although she eventually felt it was not God's will for her life, she later said, "I deem it one of the choicest seals of my calling that Dwight L. Moody should have invited me to cast in my little lot with his great one as an evangelist."[2]

"Career Woman" Is Not a New Term

Some women of destiny are called to business, such as the woman who bought a field and planted a vineyard in Proverbs 31:16. In this biblical family, it seems that both the mother and father did some work outside of the home. Women today (especially Christian women) often feel guilty for having careers, and yet this Proverbs 31 woman was clearly praised for her contribution.

I believe God is raising up an army of women in ministry as well as women who own businesses. Recently, our ministry, Generals of Intercession, has been working with business leaders to help them develop prayer strategies for their companies. This, in part, led me to the study of an Asian woman named Lydia, one of the most fascinating and least talked about women in the Bible. Her story is told in Acts 16:13-15.

The events that led to Lydia's conversion are significant. Paul had received a vision from the Lord of a man who said, "Come over to Macedonia and help us" (v. 9). Prior to this vision, Paul had intended to go to Asia. Although he was restrained by the Lord from going, the Lord had a plan to begin to touch Asia through this little woman.

Lydia was named after a province in Asia Minor in which her city of Thyatira was located. Lydian women were famous for the manufacture of beautiful purple dye made from the murex, a shellfish.[3] But I've often wondered how Lydia came to live in the city of Philippi in Macedonia, because the two cities appear to be more than 300 miles apart. Did she come by a caravan, riding on the back of a camel? How did she, a single woman, manage to overcome the obstacles that might have come her way? Evidently God had a plan for her life that included being in the city of Philippi, on a river bank seeking to know more about Him—at the same moment Paul came into town.

The very fact that she was worshiping by a river is important historically. The place was probably a *proseucha*, a place of prayer and worship when there was not a synagogue. It was usually a spacious, uncovered amphitheater.[4] A regular synagogue could only be established when a core group of 10 adult men was present. For some reason, only women were in attendance when Paul arrived on the scene.

Lydia was hungry for truth. Notice God's strategy. Paul did not go into Asia, but his first convert in Europe was Asian. The Lord knows when the heart is ready to receive the truth. Not only was

Lydia born again, but her whole household received Christ and was baptized with her.

I believe Lydia had a gift of giving that influenced the church in Philippi, which was started in her home. Do you remember Paul's letter to the church at Philippi?

> As you well know, when I first brought the Gospel to you and then went on my way, leaving Macedonia, only you Philippians became my partners in giving and receiving. No other church did this. Even when I was over in Thessalonica you sent help twice....At the moment I have all I need— more than I need! I am generously supplied with the gifts you sent me when Epaphroditus came. They are a sweet-smelling sacrifice that pleases God well. And it is he who will supply all your needs from his riches in glory (Phil. 4:15,16,18,19, *TLB*).

It might even be possible that Lydia in some way helped to start the church in Thyatira found in Revelations. The letter to the leader there says:

> I am aware of all your good deeds—your kindness to the poor, your gifts and service to them (Rev. 2:19, *TLB*).

It is also interesting to note that the church in Thyatira had allowed the false prophetess Jezebel to bring heresy into the church. This is certainly a sobering note. We women must be very careful to stay godly and not manipulate or try to control.

When God Called, She Picked Up Her Hatchet and Went

One of the most colorful woman leaders in American history was a lady named Carry Nation. Her fame was based largely on her "smashing" of saloons with a hatchet. This activity was a result of what she described as a "divine call":

One day...I opened the Bible with a prayer for light, and saw these words: "Arise, shine for thy light is come and the glory of the Lord is risen upon thee."[5]

At the time, Carry worked with the WCTU in Medicine Lodge, Kansas. Her smashing was often accompanied by the preaching of an evangelistic message. What did it mean to "smash" a saloon? In her own words:

I threw as hard and as fast as I could, smashing mirrors and bottles and glasses and it was astonishing how quickly this was done. These men seemed terrified, threw up their hands and backed up in the corner. My strength was that of a giant. I felt invincible. God was certainly standing by me.[6]

Remember, this occurred around the turn of the century in the days of the wild, wild West. I wouldn't recommend that you take this exact approach today! However, what if God called you to pray earnestly every day for the pornography stores to close in your area? Would you be willing to answer that call?

Many women are being called of God to stand up for righteousness in their countries. If you were to see some of them, they might not appear that impressive at first glance. Many are silver-haired praying grandmothers. Others are teenagers taking a stand for abstinence in their schools. I like what Aglow says: "Ordinary women—extraordinary God!"

United We Stand, Divided We Fall

In 1985 I was in a time of prayer and fasting for the United States of America. On the third day of the fast, I asked the Lord, "How has Satan made such inroads into the United States? He isn't omnipotent, nor omniscient!"

The Lord answered, "He has a strategy and My people do not. Call together the generals (prayer leaders), and when each comes with a piece of the strategy, I'll reveal Myself in their midst."

My first book, *Possessing the Gates of the Enemy* (Chosen Books) tells the specific instructions I received. What I want to emphasize here is that the Lord told me we would be like John the Baptist, preparing the way for a move of unity. He said, "If the intercessors come together in the '80s, the pastors will come together in the '90s." Of course, that is just what is happening!

With help from many friends such as Sally Horton, B. J. Willhite and others, we Generals had a great first meeting. I'll never forget looking around the room of great prayer leaders that night thinking, *Lord, this is going to take a big miracle!* You see, some people had tried to discourage us from even attempting to get people from such diverse backgrounds together for prayer. They thought it would never work!

It was a challenge. As I scanned those in attendance, I reflected on what I knew about the organizations and churches they represented. One thought that everything was the result of demons, and the other thought Christians couldn't be oppressed by demons at all. Another believed we were perfected through suffering and the next one didn't think we should ever suffer anything as Christians. Interesting...very interesting!

God met us in a powerful way and the next morning I was still basking in the goodness of God. We had all felt that we needed to get together again for prayer and strategizing. However, right in the middle of the afterglow of success, the phone rang. Have you ever noticed how the devil follows you around on the heels of a great blessing! A distant relative of one of Job's friends was on the phone: "Cindy, my pastor said that if God was going to bring together the prayer leaders, He certainly would not use a woman!"

I couldn't believe what I was hearing! Truthfully, I was deeply shaken by the phone call. That night I didn't mention the call to Mike because he was really tired when he came home from his job at American Airlines. I thought to myself, *You can handle this. Don't make a big problem out of it.*

The next day, while I was minding my own business, the phone rang again. It was a lady. (I've generally found ladies to be much meaner to me about being in the ministry than men.) The voice on the phone said, "Cindy, *my pastor said that* (Oh no! I could hear it coming and I knew it wasn't good!) even if God wanted to use a woman to gather the generals, He wouldn't use a woman your age."

At the time I was 33 years old. (The year for both crucifixion and resurrection. At that moment we were in the crucifixion part!) Immediately, in my mind's eye, I had a picture of myself with a big bun on the back of my head, hair shot through with gray, rolled down hose and varicose veins.

I felt like shattered glass inside. One of my biggest fears was that I would get into presumption and move out of the will of God in my life. *What have I done?* I wildly thought. *How could I have been so stupid and ignorant?*

Any time God calls you to something new it seems that old sluefoot sits on your shoulder and asks, "Who do you think you are?" When I wrote *Possessing the Gates of the Enemy*, the devil tried to tell me again and again that nobody would read that book. As of this writing, it is being translated into 10 languages. Then, when I wrote my second book, *The Voice of God*, another "friend" said sagely, "Well, Cindy, you know some people only have one good book in them." Panic struck! I had signed a contract without being enlightened to that particular bit of info!

I called my mentor and spiritual dad, Peter Wagner, and poured my heart out to him. "Do you think I only had one good book in me?" I fearfully asked. "Have I overextended myself?" Thank the Lord that Peter was home to walk me through that valley of doubt. Peter explained that many people experience those same feelings when they write their second books. To say that I was relieved was a big understatement! When we finished talking, the peace of God had settled deep into my heart.

The Taunting Goliath Takes a Tumble

By the time I received the second phone call after the first Generals meeting, I was struggling intensely. I remember thinking, *Oh, God, I've been in terrible presumption! How could I do such a thing?* Mentally, I started making a list of both men and women older than I who could finish the vision.

When Mike arrived home that night, I was in a deeply spiritual state, but it wasn't the right spirit! I was depressed, discouraged and sitting on our bed crying my eyes out. (Believe me, I wasn't a pretty sight! Mascara was running down my face, my eyes were swollen and my nose was running!) Mike took one look at me and said, "What is the matter with you?" Then he grabbed a fist full of tissues, put them in my hand and instructed me to blow my nose.

"Oh Mike," I sobbed with that high squeaky voice women get when they've been crying, "I've made a horrible mistake. I thought that God spoke to me to gather the Generals of Intercession to pray for the nation." I then proceeded to tell him about the two phone calls.

Poor Mike. He has put up with a lot from me throughout the years. There's going to be a special star in his crown just for being married to me! When I had cleaned myself up a bit, he said, "I'm going to pray and get the Word of the Lord for this situation and I'll let you know what God says to me in a couple of days."

Good to his word, several days later Mike shared what he had received. "Honey, this is what the Lord spoke to me. When little David went to the camp of the Israelites, all the men were in battle array. Goliath came day after day and taunted them and mocked the God of Israel. Only David rose up to face the giant with the words, 'Who are you, you uncircumcised Philistine—to dare defy the armies of the Most High God!'"

He went on to say, "Cindy, you weren't God's first choice. He tried to call a man. You weren't God's second choice. He tried to use someone older than you. (This was getting more encouraging all the time!) You were God's third choice, but He knew that if He asked you, you would do it because of your obedience. He knew that you would do anything that He asked you to do."

From that time on Mike and I were partners in a new way. We cofounded Generals of Intercession together in 1985, and even though Mike worked with American Airlines until 1991, we conducted many meetings gathering leaders together to intercede and bring healing to their nations.

The Lord also sent some encouraging prophecies my way from people I hardly knew. One of them admonished me not to give the vision God had given me to another. The warfare in the early

Faith is "always in the red." When you are comfortable believing Him for one thing, God shakes you out of your comfort zone and says, "Now do this."

days was so strong (What am I saying? There still is a lot of warfare!) that every time we had a meeting, Mike and I would decide on the way there that it was the last one we would ever do. Then some prophet would show up at the place and start prophesying, "And the Lord says, I want you to take this vision around the world!" Have you ever felt really nonspiritual like you wanted to kick the prophet? We didn't want to go around the world! Just getting to that one little meeting had been so difficult that we wanted to quit!

Building Faith Muscles by Focusing on the Upward Call

I have to say that faith does grow with the vision. While we almost had our faith fail a number of times, we can believe for much more now than in the early days. I remember when we got an office outside of our home in 1991. We wondered how we would ever make the $200-a-month payment! Now we believe for tens of thousands of dollars for projects on a regular basis! As of this writing, the newsletter we started in 1992 is sent to at least 42 nations. We also learned that faith is "always in the red." When you are comfortable believing Him for one thing, God shakes you out of your comfort zone and says, "Now do this."

In this hour God is calling women, not as militant feminists who insist upon their rights and demand a place of service, but as those who will find their place in His kingdom. If God doesn't open the door for you, then it isn't one that you should go through (see Rev. 3:7).

Beverly LaHaye describes the call for women in her book *The Desires of a Woman's Heart*:

> Each woman's call is unique. For some obedience to God means being "thrown to the lions," so to speak, or cast into a hostile climate in which Christians and the Bible are scorned out of date and puritanical. For others, obedience to God may lead to a more quiet, private existence. The important thing, however, is to be obedient to God and "Stand firm. Let nothing move you. Always give yourselves fully to the work of the Lord, because you know that your labor in the Lord is not in vain" (1 Cor. 15:58).[7]

LaHaye goes on to say:

> Hundreds of thousands of women today are involved in organizations such as Concerned Women for America, Christian Action Council, Eagle Forum, American Life League, Enough is Enough and Mothers Against Drunk Driving, to name just a few. These women know who they are. They are confident of their worth; they see the decline in American society, and they are actively involved in trying to stop it.
>
> The committed women of Concerned Women for America, [the organization LaHaye has founded], for instance, are working in churches and neighborhoods to build a network of prayer and action. They are actively

working at the local, state and national levels to derail legislation and education that will harm their families. They
are concerned about protecting the rights of families
rather than their own personal rights. They are not primarily concerned about self-fulfillment, and they are not
chasing some nebulous ideal of happiness. They are seeking to fill a concrete need: preserving the nuclear family
and society from destruction.[8]

Remember the story in chapter 1 of the apple tree that thought
it was a flower tree? This story is symbolic of the many passages
or stages that both men and women go through in life. We all
experience changes in focus, occupations or even roles throughout the years. Few of us know what we will eventually do; however, the prophetic word will sometimes give us an inkling.

Believe His Prophets and Prosper
(2 Chron. 20:20)

When Dick Mills prophesied in 1984 that I would have a worldwide ministry, I could hardly comprehend what he was talking
about! At the time I was speaking for local women's meetings
with many invitations and had only ministered in Canada outside
of the United States. I had to grow into the prophecy Dick Mills
gave, which didn't say in detail, "Next year I'm going to speak to
you about a prayer army you'll eventually call Generals of
Intercession, then you will speak to national congresses for pastors and leaders all around the world."

But I'm so glad I didn't know! I wasn't ready yet. Frankly, it
would have scared me to know. To give you a frame of reference
for how far I've come in speaking before large audiences, I need
to explain about the days when we would have Wednesday night
"seasons of prayer" at my church. I was only in my 20s and fought
a measure of shyness. Each Wednesday the congregation would
pray aloud in what amounted to sentence-type prayers. Week
after week, I would say to myself, *The next time we have that*

time of intercession, I'm going to pray aloud. Somehow, when the time came, my tongue felt glued to the roof of my mouth! I just couldn't get the words out.

If someone had told me then that I would speak to 20,000 people at a time, I would have gone into a catatonic state! Thank God He has given me just what I could bear at the moment.

Later, after I had children, I was often frustrated that I didn't have more time to pray and intercede. The Lord would often assure me, "Cindy, the day is coming, when your children are in school, that you'll be able to spend hours in prayer." I learned to have small prayer breaks while I was washing dishes or rocking a baby. I would usually pray late at night or get up early to have my devotions.

Maybe you're a frustrated young mom feeling terribly guilty because you want to do more for the kingdom of God. Let me assure you that if you are feeling called of God and you are willing to remain obedient, a day will come when you will be able to do all that's in your heart.

Trusting Through the Seasons of Life

Life is a series of seasons, and we all experience winters, springs, summers and falls. As you read about these four seasons, ask God to show you where you are and what He is wanting to teach you during this season of your life.

Winter "Wonder Why It's Not Happening" Land

If you are in a winter season, you may feel rather dead or unproductive. It could be that God wants you to take a rest and allow the ground of your life to replenish itself. This is one of the hardest seasons for type A people (such as myself).

After I finally struggled to accept the call of God on my life, He then asked me to give it back to Him and take a hidden role of intercession. I felt like a spiritual Ping-Pong ball. Now that I had said yes, I had all this fire and wanted to go take on the world for Jesus Christ! Instead, He said, "Cindy, be still and know that I am God. I don't waste the anointing. Be assured that I know where you live and will use you in the proper time."

Some days I would cry out to Him, "God, I'm afraid that You're going to come back again before I get to preach one time!" Oh, it was so hard to wait! You feel as though God moved and lost your address. The heavens are as brass and you can even struggle with feelings of abandonment. But these preparatory times are necessary because they develop character and cause your roots to go deep, deep down into the soil of the Word.

Once the plan of God unfolds, it's as if you are on fast forward. That is when you will need all the Word you have deposited in yourself to survive the blessings of the other seasons.

Spring Is Bursting Out All Over

Life seems to be the most exciting during spring. This season is usually accompanied by a sense of great anticipation—you often feel as though you are about to burst inside with new life. You get this sense that something wonderful is about to happen, but you don't quite know what it is. That's how I felt in 1989 when Mike and I went to a prayer summit in Washington, D.C., sponsored by Ray Bringham.

One night during the summit, I tried to sleep but wasn't able to for all the excitement I felt. (I guess the only experience I can relate it to is how I felt on Christmas Eve as a little girl. We opened our presents on Christmas morning and I could hardly wait to pounce on my parents and drag their tired bodies out of bed!) The next morning we drove over to an executive council meeting for the National Prayer Embassy with Dr. C. Peter Wagner, his wife, Doris, and Len LeSourd—whom we had just met. Peter and Doris watched as we modeled prayer between England and the United States in something we now call "identificational repentance." They were fascinated and plied us with questions about how to heal nations.

I had started writing a book about prayer and had prayed some rather radical prayers such as, "God, if you want me to write a book, You'll have to help me. I need a mentor and I don't have a clue how to find a publisher." Right in the middle of our conversation Len, who was then the vice president of Chosen Books, leaned over and asked me, "Have you ever written a book?" Then he handed me his card.

Peter chimed in, "Cindy, I'm meeting with Jane Campbell, the editor for Chosen at 4:30 today because they want a book about prayer. They don't need my book, they need your book. Meet us in the cafeteria at 4:30 and I'll introduce you."

Since then my life has been a whirlwind. Peter Wagner has become my mentor, and he gave me guidance on my first book. In fact (to my absolute horror), he threw the first three chapters I had written in the trash! The point is that spring is a time for birthing new things into our lives.

At times during the spring of your life, you may be on the verge of a new thing and feel like a pregnant woman in her ninth month: you know, you're sort of grouchy and touchy; you know God is about to do something; you can feel it move inside of you, but you don't know what it looks like. Every day you live with the hope that God will reveal it to you so you can get on with your life.

Summer's Fruit Is Sweet, but Some Days Can Be Hot!
Summer is mostly a fruitful time. Although it may be rather hot in the amount of spiritual warfare that you experience, this season is generally quite productive. This is also the hour when you sense God's refreshing and blessing. It is during this time that you experience the richness of seasoned friendships.

Autumn Leaves Me Feeling Frazzled!
Autumn is harvest time, when the seeds you've planted have ripened in the summer sun and are ready to be picked. The vastness of responsibilities during this season, whether personal or in the Body of Christ at large, can feel overwhelming. Be cautious of great presumptions! If you move too quickly on the plans of God for the harvest, you can be premature and cause great destruction to the harvest. And if you don't watch for signs of storms in relationships, you can actually see most of your life's

work destroyed! This is a critical time to gather others around you who can speak into your life.

I do this on a number of different levels, both ministerially and as a woman. I have friends who have a special love for our family with whom I can share heart-to-heart when I am struggling. Others know more about what I am going through as a minister.

But this was not always the case. In the early days of ministry, I didn't know any other women in leadership. Even later on, those I knew either didn't have children or were much older than I, so they had different time factors to consider. Since I have usually been the youngest of my peer group, I have felt a little "out of sync," so to speak, with the rest of my group. I have had unique responsibilities and always felt like I was doing some kind of juggling act: trying to be supermom, the best wife in the world and yet spend enough time with God. Yes, autumn can be busy!

In addition to harvest, autumn is also a time of dying to self. Just as nature reflects transitions in its seasons, God likewise usually calls for the greatest changes in your life during autumn. Often He will reposition you for greater effectiveness. Sometimes He will have you leave one ministry to work in another, or ask you to quit your job to stay home more. It seems to me that God is currently repositioning a large part of the Body of Christ to prepare His Church for the end-time thrust of the gospel. Many people are physically moving to new cities and this kind of change requires great flexibility and patience. But the result will be greater effectiveness for His people and greater glory for His kingdom.

Breaking the Mold to Recast the System

Women of destiny have great challenges before them. At times God doesn't choose the most likely or even the most talented for high places. There are some women who have been in the winter season, in a seemingly hidden time, whom God is getting ready to release as a great blessing to the Body of Christ.

Young Esther was a woman such as that. The Bible tells us that she was an orphan. In addition, she had suffered the trauma of exile, not to mention the fact that she was the wrong race. She had at least three strikes against her. Obviously, Esther was too dysfunctional for God to use for anything important. Right? Wrong. He created her as a woman with great physical beauty and her Uncle Mordecai must have worked hard at developing her inner beauty. I wonder if she dreamed of being a queen when she was a little girl. Maybe, but probably not.

Esther was a woman who broke the mold for what a good Jewish girl should be. It must have required great courage and flexibility on her part to answer the King's summons. And yet God is calling women today who are willing to respond to anything He asks with a simple, "Here am I, Lord, send me."

This response may mean breaking the mold for society's stereotypes. The feminists cry, "You'll never be fulfilled unless you have an occupation outside the home." Other voices say, "You are a bad person if you feel God has anything for you other than keeping house."

Kari Torjesen Malcolm discusses some of the issues that prevent women from reaching the place and calling God has for them in her book *Women at the Crossroads*. I like her perspective when she says:

We forget so easily that Jesus promised that if we seek first His kingdom and His righteousness, all the rest shall be added to us (Matt. 6:33). If our love relationship with Him takes first priority, then all other relationships will find their rightful place in our hearts and schedules. The woman who focuses on Christ will therefore become a better wife and mother than the one who stays home all day out of a sense of duty, as a reaction or as a cop-out. To a woman who loves the Lord, the Word of God will burn as a fire in her bones, so that she must speak up for her Lord, whether the crowd be small or large, or whether the people be her own kin or those from a different culture.[9]

Breaking the Strongholds
That Strangle Destiny

In looking back over my life, I have been able to identify at least five major strongholds that I personally had to deal with in order to be released into my destiny. I think many women will relate to a number of these on differing levels.[10]

1. Strongholds of the Mind

I like the way Ed Silvoso describes this kind of stronghold:

> A mind-set impregnated with hopelessness that causes the believer to accept as unchangeable, situations that we know are contrary to the will of God.[11]

In other words, some of the ways we think and feel about ourselves and situations are contrary to God's will. Basically, there are ways we think and feel about ourselves that can actually stop us from reaching our destinies in God. These can be things such as childhood traumas, insecurities and/or inferiorities.

One of the major endeavors I believe all women should participate in is prayer. The enemy wants to make you feel like your situation is hopeless, your husband will never be born again, your child will always stay in rebellion, etc. These strongholds must be cast down as vain imaginations so we can run the race with diligence in intercession.

2. The Stronghold of Fear

One of the biggest strongholds we women struggle with is fear. Fear comes in many packages and hides behind lies. We sometimes self-righteously dress up our fears as, "It's simply not *me* to stand in public and pray."

We often fear others' opinions. Remember, at the end of our days, the Lord will ask each of us what we did with our talents. I hope that none of you have a backyard full of talents you've buried, such as gifts of music, writing, organization, serving, etc.

Fear will not be an acceptable excuse when we stand before the King of the universe, because He has given us all the ability to be overcomers through the blood of the Lamb. If we are feeling overtaken with fear, it hasn't come from God! He gives us "power, love and a sound mind" (see 2 Tim. 1:7).

Some of you need to dust off your talents and dreams and give them to the Lord. The difference between women who find their place in God's kingdom and those who never find it may simply be a willingness to be used of God. Everyone can do something. You can join a group of Moms In Touch who intercede for their children's schools or some other form of service that will get you out of yourself.

3. Strongholds of Intimidation

Intimidation often binds women. It occurs when we look at our shortfalls rather than at the greatness of God. Whether we are called to sing or testify, the enemy might say something such as, "People will think that you are full of pride if you do that!" He often points out the weaknesses in our personal lives and family situations, or tries to compare our abilities with those of others in order to produce an oppressive feeling that will restrain us from reaching our full potential in God.

4. Generational Strongholds

Some strongholds start long before we are born. We inherit them. You might say, "Wait a minute, Cindy, that's not fair!" Exodus 20:5 says God visits the iniquities of the fathers upon the children to the third and fourth generations. While we have been redeemed from these iniquities, we need to appropriate our freedom through the Name of Jesus Christ. I give a lengthy teaching on this subject in my book *The Voice of God.* These strongholds can produce curses such as sickness, poverty, insanity and so forth.

5. Strongholds of Tradition

Coming from the South in the United States, tradition was another of my big strongholds. Good Southern Christian women simply did not travel around the world and preach the gospel! As you can tell from reading this book, I struggled intensely with accepting the call of God upon my life as a minister of the gospel. It took me two full years before I even admitted to anyone that I was a minister—even after I was licensed! I just couldn't seem to get that "m" word out of my mouth. I guess I was afraid of people's reactions. Now, I am proud (in a righteous way) of sharing what I do in God's kingdom. I tell people, "I have a great boss and the retirement plan is out of this world!"

I've often wondered if Queen Vashti, in the book of Esther, refused to come when summoned by the King because it wasn't traditional for her to do so. When the King summons us, we must be sure that we are not being held back by tradition.

Lord, Send Me into My Call

You may have a genuine desire to become a woman of destiny and fulfill the high calling of Christ Jesus for your life. Be assured that the Lord is raising up a vast army of handmaidens all around the world. Don't be bound by the opinion of man (or woman). Simply follow God's leading. If God calls you to stay home full-time even after your children are grown, then do it! Maybe you are single and God is calling you to the mission field; step out! (We'll have a lot to say about this in the next few chapters.)

Please pray the following prayer with me right now:

Lord, I want to be a woman of destiny. I give You all of my life, my children, my family and other people's opinions of me. Here am I, Lord. Send me into my call. Help me to break down any strongholds that stop me from completely serving You. I will go anywhere You ask me to go and do anything You ask me to do as long as I know it is Your will for my life. In Jesus' Name I pray. Amen.

One way to strengthen your resolve to be a woman of destiny is by studying other heroines of the faith. You might consider the next chapter as a great "Hall of Faith" for those who have pioneered and paved the way for future generations. Maybe you'll find someone about whom you can say, "Lord, I want to be like her. She's my heroine. If she did it and finished the course, I can too!"

Notes

1. Ruth A. Tucker and Walter Liefeld, *Daughters of the Church* (Grand Rapids: Zondervan Publication, 1987), pp. 272-273.
2. Ibid., p. 273.
3. Finis Jennings Dake *Dake's Annotated Reference Bible* (Lawrenceville, Ga.: Dake Bible Sales, 1963), p. 142.
4. Ibid., p. 142.
5. Ruth A. Tucker and Walter Liefeld, *Daughters of the Church*, p. 274.
6. Ibid., p. 275.
7. Beverly LaHaye, *The Desires of a Woman's Heart* (Wheaton, Ill.: Tyndale House Publishers, 1993), p. 87.
8. Ibid., pp. 86-87.
9. Kari Torjesen Malcolm, *Women at the Crossroads* (Downers Grove, Ill.: InterVarsity Press, 1982), pp. 30-31.
10. Note: I first wrote about these five strongholds for a chapter entitled "Dethroning Strongholds" in Aglow International's book *Women of Prayer*. For a more complete study, please refer to pages 89-105 in that book.
11. Ed Silvoso, *That None Should Perish* (Ventura, Calif.: Regal Books, 1994), p. 155. I actually memorized this quote from Ed long before he wrote it in his book.

c h a p t e r   5

Heroines
of the Faith

Isn't it amazing how God chooses the foolish things to confound
the wise? Some of the greatest works for the Lord have been done
by women who by their physical form, background and other circumstances seemed the least likely to be used for God's kingdom
purposes.

During the Reconstruction Era in the United States after the
Civil War, a young, attractive, four-foot-three woman received a
call from God to spend her life in far-away North China. This lovely young lady came from a wealthy, aristocratic family during a time
when women were considered beautiful ornaments. If you have
seen the movie *Gone With the Wind,* you might have a perspective
of the culture during this time period. Young women from planta-
tion homes turned flirting into an art form, which they used in
attempting to twist the hearts of unsuspecting young men around
their little fingers. But this was not the case with Lottie Moon.

The Heritage of the Righteous

Lottie was a descendent of the Quaker theologian and preacher,
Robert Barclay, a Scottish man of God who pioneered with such

Quakers as George Fox and William Penn. Lottie's father was Edward Harris Moon, whose home, "Viewmont" in Albermarle County, Virginia, was not far from the homes of three American presidents: "Monticello" of Thomas Jefferson, "Montpelier" of James Madison and "Ashlawn" of James Monroe.

Her mother, a staunch Southern Baptist, was a positive force for good within her community. Because there was no church near their home, Mrs. Moon held services each Sunday morning in her parlor for neighbors, servants and her children. When there was no minister, she led the services herself.[1]

Not only did Lottie have a righteous heritage, but she was also highly educated. She was one of the first Southern women to obtain a master's degree, which she received in 1861.

For a short season Lottie was content with tutoring and working to change the South. But when her sister, Edmonia, left for China in 1872, Lottie's heart turned toward the mission field as well. She devoured her sister's letters and finally received her own call to China in the spring of 1873 after hearing a sermon preached on the text, "Lift up your eyes, and look on the fields; for they are white already to harvest." She was 33 years old.

Lottie had been in love with a young professor, but when he embraced Darwinism, she broke the engagement and never married. At times she would be racked with deep pangs of loneliness on the mission field.

On her journey to China (by boat, of course—no airplanes in those days) she wrote home during a bad storm:

As I watched the mad waste of waters, howling as if eager to engulf us, I think I should scarcely have been surprised to see a Divine Form walking upon them, as sweetly I heard in my inmost soul the consoling words, "It is I, be not afraid."[2]

Born in America, Changed in China

Lottie set up housekeeping with her sister in a 300-year-old house they called "The Home of the Crossroads." Homesick for

Virginia, Lottie planted Virginia Crape myrtle and, in front of her window, pomegranate trees like those at home.

Imagine, if you will, this pretty young woman with lovely soft features and dark, upswept hair, now living in China. She quickly adopted Chinese dress and ways and eventually looked quite Chinese. She would wear a plain Chinese coat and gown and embroidered satin shoes with soles made from fragmented soft garments too worn to be patched. Later, she estimated that her shoes for three-fourths of the year cost less than 80 cents, and her winter boots a little more than a dollar. She slept on a brick bed and ate food bought in the village market and cooked in Chinese kettles.[3]

Lottie often wrote extremely challenging letters home to the Southern Baptists:

> It is odd that the million Baptists in the South can furnish only three men for all China. Odd that five hundred Baptist preachers in the state of Virginia alone must rely on a Presbyterian minister to fill a Baptist pulpit. I wonder how these things look in Heaven. They certainly look very queer in China.[4]

Lottie Moon also stirred up the ire of some of her own people when she wrote of the position of women on the mission field:

> "What women want who come to China," she wrote, "is free opportunity to do the largest possible work....What women have a right to demand is perfect equality." Again she wrote, "Simple justice demands that women should have equal rights with men in mission meetings and in the conduct of their work."[5]

She received a barrage of criticism from other missionaries, such as Mrs. Arthur Smith, wife of a Congregationalist missionary who suggested that Lottie Moon was mentally unbalanced for craving such "Lawless prancing all over the mission lot."[6]

This should be comforting to readers whom people have thought were crazy because of the call of Christ. I have often (more in the early days of ministry) felt totally misunderstood and sometimes wondered if I *was* off the wall in my ministry of intercession.

Controversial Today, Commonplace Tomorrow

Because it is so appropriate, I want to interject something of my own personal life here. One day I had received even more than usual criticism about being a woman minister and I was weary of it. (You see, not only am I a woman minister, but one who teaches about healing nations and how to do spiritual warfare, etc.) Truthfully, I was murmuring to God about my situation.

The controversial things of today are the commonplace of tomorrow. Controversial people do great things for [God].

"God," I said, "it's not bad enough that I am a woman minister, but one who teaches on spiritual warfare! If I have to be a woman minister, couldn't I teach about color typing or something less controversial? Lord," I went on, "I'm tired of being controversial."

Even though I deserved to be zapped with fire from heaven right on the spot, God had mercy on me and gently replied, "Cindy, the controversial things of today are the commonplace of tomorrow. Controversial people do great things for Me. Just do My work." He went on to remind me of the barrage of criticism John Wesley received for using bar tunes as hymns. For his time, that was simply outrageous!

Fearless, Firm and Faithful unto Death

Speaking of those who have been outrageous and courageous for God, Lottie Moon traveled from village to village in a *shentza*or mule litter and commonly slept in vermin-infested inns. Often, the area she would travel through would be so dangerous that her carriers would take the precaution of muffling the mule's bells with straw. Lottie was as fearless and firm as a man, yet gentle and womanly.

In 1888 she challenged the women of the Southern Baptist Church with the plea, "Will you not, in appreciation of what Christmas means to you, share in the work of this area?"[7] That year $3,000 was given in response to her call. The Southern Baptists continued this yearly offering even after her death, and by 1992 had raised nearly a billion dollars for world missions in Lottie Moon's name.

She suffered many hardships including the Boxer Uprising during which she left China and went to Japan to teach. Many Chinese Christians were martyred during that time, not loving their lives unto death. When she returned to China, life became harder and harder financially until revolution broke out in 1911. The American Consul and many of Lottie's friends urged her to leave, but she stayed at Tengchow. The more her Chinese friends suffered under war, epidemics and poverty, the more money Lottie Moon gave to feed the poor. Finally, now in her 70s, Lottie simply stopped eating.

In December of 1912, Lottie bowed to the pressure to leave for the United States. She was frail and already dying of starvation when she boarded the ship. Four days later, as the ship sailed into the harbor at Kobe, Japan, this faithful warrior of the Cross slipped away into glory.

Those who loved her later received and buried her ashes in Crowe, Virginia. Lottie's gravesite bore a simple inscription: "Faithful unto death."

Ten years earlier Lottie Moon had said, "I would that I had a

thousand lives that I might give them to the women of China."
She gave her one life and its influence was multiplied a thou-
sandfold.[8]

As I finish writing this story, tears are coursing down my
cheeks. Inside me there is an answering cry that says, "Oh, God,
I want to be a heroine of the faith like Lottie Moon! I want to be
faithful unto death." It's not that I would desire to be a martyr,
but if the time came when a choice was given me between denying Christ or living, well, I settled that question a long time ago.
In fact, I did so when I was only 12 years old at church camp....

I'll never forget the night when my counselor chose me to be
in a skit where this question of martyrdom was being portrayed.
The skit was acted out in the outdoor amphitheater on the camp-
grounds at night. Spotlights illuminated different situations in
nations all around the world where Christians were given choices of dying or denying Christ.

My part was set in a Communist country where we were told
to kneel with guns pointed at our heads and given the test:
"Denounce Christ or die on the spot!" While getting ready for
the skit that night, those words played repeatedly in my head,
"Denounce or die....Denounce or die!" What would I do if the
situation were real? Would I choose Christ, or be a coward and
make the decision to denounce Him?

Later that night, the play seemed to come to life before me,
and when I knelt on the hard, rocky ground, I suddenly had no
doubt what my answer would be. I would never, never, never
deny Him! From that night forward, I became a "living martyr."
In a way, I died that night when I made my choice.

She Who Finds Her Life Must Lose It

History is full of women who gave their lives for the cause of
Christ. One of the earliest of those was Vibia Perpetua (181?-203).
Perpetua lived in Carthage, North Africa. This story especially
fascinates me because North Africa as of this writing is a stronghold for Muslim fundamentalists. (We are earnestly praying and

believing for this situation to change!) Roman Christians had brought the gospel to this part of the world during the reign of Emperor Septimius Severus.

Because Severus was fearful of the rise of Christianity, he issued an edict prohibiting any teaching or making of converts. New believers came to Christ realizing that the chances of living very long were minimal to nil unless God had a reason for them to escape persecution.

It's inspiring to study the writings of these early Christians, knowing that martyrdom was just a fact of life. In fact, it was considered a privilege to be a martyr! Early writings tell of Paul's conversion after the martyred death of Stephen. Most of us would not consider martyrdom synonymous with evangelism, but the Early Church thought very much in that manner.

Confident that their martyrdom would cause many to follow Christ in the pagan city of Carthage, believers knew that it might very well be their own blood that would be the seed of the Church. Perpetua was keenly aware of this at the time of her own baptism. She said as she came out of the water, "The Holy Spirit has inspired me to pray for nothing but patience under bodily pains."[9]

Can you imagine yourself in the place of this young woman in her early 20s? How would you react if you were arrested? To add to the intensity of the situation, she was nursing her baby!

Perpetua was arrested with five companions. While she was in prison, her father visited her time and time again, begging her to recant for his sake and the sake of her child. He would rage at her and leave, only to return again, beseeching her in a different way.

Later, two deacons succeeded in getting Perpetua and her maidservant, Felicitas, into a better part of the prison. Felicitas was eight months pregnant and concerned that she would not be allowed to go into the arena with her friends of the faith. She feared she would die with strangers rather than with her companions.

We have Perpetua's own words from the journals she maintained right up to the time of her death. As I read the following portion she wrote about her infant child, my heart was gripped as I thought of my own two children:

> I suckled my child, who was already weak from want of nourishment. In my anxiety for him I spoke to my mother, and comforted my brother and commended to their care my son. And I pined excessively because I saw them pining away because of me. These anxieties I suffered for many days; and I then obtained leave that my child should remain with me in the prison. Immediately I gained strength and being relieved from my anxiety about the child, my prison suddenly became to me a palace, so that I preferred to be there rather than anywhere else.[10]

Later, as her child was brought to her for the last time she confessed, "God so ordered it that it was no longer required to suck, nor did my milk inconvenience me." [11]

As I have studied the life of Perpetua, the following passage of Scripture has come to me again and again:

> "Do not think that I came to bring peace on earth. I did not come to bring peace but a sword. For I have come to 'set a man against his father, a daughter against her mother, and a daughter-in-law against her mother-in-law';...He who loves *father* or mother more than Me is not worthy of Me. And He who loves *son or daughter* more than Me is not worthy of Me. And he who does not take his cross and follow after Me is not worthy of Me. He who finds his life will lose it, and he who loses his life for My sake will find it" (Matt. 10:34,35,37-39, italics added).

Truly, the world was not worthy of you, young Perpetua! Oh God, I pray that I will follow You with such ardent love as my sister from Carthage!

The Dragon Slayer Who Triumphed over Death

Perpetua had some rather remarkable supernatural visitations from the Lord while she waited to be taken to her death. One was in the form of a vision in answer to her prayer that God would reveal to her the fate of her companions and herself:

> Last night in a vision, I saw a golden ladder of wondrous size reaching up to heaven; so narrow that only one could go up at once. On its sides were every kind of iron instrument, swords, lances, hooks, daggers. If one went up carelessly, one's flesh would be torn, and pieces would be left on the iron implements. Under the ladder was a dragon of wondrous size, which laid snares for those climbing it, and frightened them from the ascent.
>
> Now Saturus [her teacher] went up first. He had given himself up voluntarily after our arrest on our account, because he had taught us the faith, and he had not been present on the occasion of our trial. When he had reached the top of the ladder, he turned and said to me, "Perpetua, I am waiting for you; but take care that the dragon does not bite you." And I said, "In the Name of Jesus Christ, he shall not hurt me." The dragon, as if afraid of me, slowly thrust his head underneath the ladder and I trod upon his head, as if I were treading on the first step.[12]

Felicitas, whose concern was not that she would die, but *with whom* she would die, gave birth to a little daughter one month early. A warden mocked her birth pangs, saying, "If you cry out now, what will you do when you are thrown to beasts in the arena?"

Her reply was, "I myself suffer not, but then another shall be in me who shall suffer for me, because I am to suffer for Him."

The daughter who was born to her in prison was brought up by her sister.[13]

At last, the day of the martyrs' honor and glory came. They were to be taken to the arena. The conclusion of Perpetua's story is worth quoting in full:

> The day of their victory dawned, and with joyful countenances they marched from the prison to the arena as though on their way to heaven. If there was any trembling it was from joy, not fear. Perpetua followed with a quick step as a true spouse of Christ, the darling of God, her brightly flashing eyes quelling the gaze of the crowd. Felicitas too, joyful because she had safely survived childbirth and was now able to participate in the contest with the wild animals, passed from one shedding of blood to another; from midwife to gladiator, about to be purified after childbirth by a second baptism....
>
> For the young women the devil had readied a mad cow, an animal not usually used at these games, but selected so that the women's sex would be matched with that of the animals. After being stripped and enmeshed in nets, the women were led into the arena. How horrified the people were as they saw that one was a young girl and the other, her breast dripped with milk, had just recently given birth to a child. Consequently, both were recalled and dressed in loosely fitting gowns.
>
> Perpetua was tossed first and fell on her back. She sat up, and being more concerned with her sense of modesty than with her pain, covered her thighs with her gown which had been torn down one side. Then finding her hairclip, which had fallen out, she pinned back her loose hair, thinking it not proper for a martyr to suffer with disheveled hair; it might seem that she was mourning in her hour of triumph. Then she stood up. Noticing that Felicitas was badly bruised, she went to her, reaching out her hands and helping her to her feet....
>
> And when the crowd demanded that the prisoners be brought out into the open so that they might feast their

eyes on death by the sword, they voluntarily arose and moved where the crowd wanted them.

Before doing so they kissed each other so that their martyrdom would be completely perfected by the rite of the kiss of peace. The others, without making any movement or sounds, were killed by the sword; but Perpetua, in order to feel some of the pain, groaning as she was struck between the ribs, took the gladiator's trembling hand and guided it to her throat.

Perhaps it was that so great a woman, feared as she was by the unclean spirit, could not have been slain had she herself not willed it.[14]

The church father Tertullian added this postscript to Perpetua's life: "O most brave and blessed martyrs, you have gone out of prison rather than into one. Your dungeon is full of darkness, but you yourselves are light. Your dungeon has bonds, but God has made you free."[15]

Avenging the Blood of the Martyrs

Recently, the Lord has given me a word that He is getting ready to avenge the blood of the martyrs. This will be done by many receiving Christ where the blood of Christians is crying out to God from the ground. (See Gen. 4:10.)

The first time I gave this word publicly was at an Aglow conference. A lady from Rwanda, where hundreds of thousands have been killed, spoke the morning after the prophecy was given. When she stood to share, she started by saying, "I am so encouraged because I know God has heard my prayers." She went on to say that God had miraculously spared her life during the massacres. "However," she quietly said, "others of my Christian friends did not make it." She continued, "As I looked at their dead bodies, I looked up to heaven and cried, 'God, avenge the blood of the martyrs.'"

I know that it will be so. God is getting ready to avenge the blood of the martyrs throughout the world. Many thousands of people will turn to Christ in a great revival in Rwanda, as they will in Italy and Spain and other places where so much shedding of Christians' blood has occurred.

Why is this chapter on heroines so important? One reason is that throughout the years many books have been written about heroes, but very little emphasis has been placed on the exploits of great women. I believe mothers should read stories to their daughters about the women of God who have gone before them to prepare the way. In doing so, young women can learn from both the weaknesses and the strengths of these heroines to be more equipped for the unique questions a life of service to God will bring. For instance:

- Should I marry if I have a call of God on my life?
- What about having children?
- What kind of husband should I marry?
- How did other women settle these issues?

I have certainly made mistakes along the way that I believe could have been avoided if I had received a book such as this one to help guide me.

Joan of Arc, the Deborah of France

One heroine of the faith who was guided by God through visions and used to change the fate of a nation was Joan of Arc. She is often called the *Deborah of France.*

Joan of Arc lived from 1412 to 1431. She had a short life indeed— only 19 years. Apparently her visions began when she was about 12 years old and continued until she started her mission in France at age 16.

Young Joan was a shepherdess who lived in a small village and was the youngest of four children. Although some of the visions and voices she heard seemed to be from strange sources, such as martyred saints, I believe the Holy Spirit was speaking to her. Perhaps, in her ignorance, she did not have a complete understanding of the Voice of God, but the fruit of what she heard was good.

She called the Lord *"Messire"* ("my Master") and what she heard from Him was sweet and direct:

> Whenever I am sad because what I say is a command of Messire is not readily believed, I go apart and to Messire I make known my complaint, saying that those to whom I speak are not willing to believe me. And when I have finished my prayer, straightway I hear a voice saying unto me, "Daughter of God, go, I will be thy helper." And this voice fills me with so great a joy, that in this condition I will forever stay.[16]

(A parenthetical note: Some of you reading this book may be teenagers. God is going to use your generation in a powerful way! The Lord wants to find Deborahs in your generation to serve Him to change their nations—maybe not in exactly the same way, but in the way He would choose for your life.)

To understand a little of the political situation during Joan of Arc's time, France was in a war with England and their allies in France, the Burgundians, who were from the north of the Loire. Circumstances looked dire for the French heir to the throne, the Dauphin Charles, who had been disinherited by Henry VI and the queen mother, Isabella of France, who favored Henry VI.

When Joan was only 16, she started receiving more and more supernatural instruction and was called as God's emissary to her country's cry of distress. An older relative traveled with her in May 1428 from Domremy to Vaucouleurs (about 15 miles) to see the military governor who sent her back to her parents.

Joan was a mystic accustomed to waiting for spiritual guidance, so she simply went home and waited. This time she received more specific instructions, which she sent to the military governor. He in turn sent her with a letter to the Dauphin. But before she went, Joan proceeded to boldly cut her hair to a page-boy length and exchanged her red dress for the uniform of a soldier. She was highly criticized for this, and yet because she believed she had received divine guidance to do so, the criticism did not faze her. Dressed as a man, she was able to easily ride a horse and mingle with the soldiers.

God's favor to fulfill her mission was remarkably evident as this little teenager admonished tough, hard-drinking, foul-mouthed soldiers, warning them that God would not give them victory unless they became moral people. Astonished by her words, many soldiers made dramatic changes in their lives.

History doesn't portray the Dauphin as a particularly pleasant person. Rather he was described as incompetent, bored and ugly. Her statement to him as he talked to her in private was, "I am God's messenger, sent to tell you that you are the King's son and the true heir to France. And France is to be a Holy Kingdom."[17]

After being questioned for three weeks by clergymen at Poitiers, Joan was allowed to proceed with the divine guidance she had received earlier from the Lord to lead an army into battle at Orléans. She must have been an incredible sight, because the Dauphin put her in a glistening coat of armor to lead the troops. For a weapon, Joan chose a sword that had five crosses, given to her by a church, and she carried a banner sprinkled with holy water to represent her company.

I would love to have been a witness to this young Deborah of God as she told her company to repent and renounce their sins and take the sacrament together. After this exhortation, a noticeable change came over the men and they rose to the standard put before them. At the front of her company marched priests chanting psalms and hymns. (Reminds me of Jehoshaphat—send Judah first!)

The Army Won the Battle, the Nation Lost a Saint

Joan received specific instruction for the battle, and even though the wind had been blowing the wrong direction, it changed when the troops needed to cross the Loire River in small boats near Orléans. The Voice of the Lord then told her, "In God's Name go down against them, for they shall fall and not stay and shall be utterly discomfited; and you shall lose scarce any men. Arise and pursue them."[18]

The troops of the Lord took Orléans that day and Joan went on to lead four other battles. She then instructed the Dauphin to enter the city where the kings of France were traditionally crowned and saw that he was anointed with oil. (He was now King Charles VII of France.)

Finally, the day after his crowning, Joan was captured and tried as a witch and a heretic before a tribunal of 40 theologians and jurists at Rouen. She stood steadfast and answered clearly all the charges. At one point her accusers took her into the torture chamber to intimidate her. She answered:

> Even if you tear my limbs from each other, and part my soul from my body, I shall not say anything different, and even though I did say something different, I would make it clear that you had forced me to do so by violent means....[19]

Her final judgment was based on 12 points. Among them were a denial of her gift of prophecy and the wearing of masculine clothes.

On May 30, 1431, Joan, now 19 years old, was tied to a stake and burned alive. Not once did she beg to be released, for she was not afraid of martyrdom. She had finished the course and fought the good fight. Her last words were simply the sweetest ones human lips can utter...*Jesus, Jesus.*

Reports are that the English, upon returning to camp, could only mutter, "We are lost! We have burned a saint!"[20]

King Charles VII later reversed the verdict against her and Joan was declared the patroness of France in 1922. Joan, like Jeremiah, did not consider her youth to be an obstacle in the path of her destiny in God. She died having fulfilled the purposes of God for her life in her generation (see Acts 13:36).

Did this story speak to your heart? Perhaps God is calling you to be a Deborah in your generation. There are women in congress right now who are there because they feel a distinct call of God to help change America. Other women in nations all around the world are receiving similar calls. Even if you aren't called to be a Deborah, I would encourage you to study the women of the Bible and find the one(s) you most relate to. God is raising up Esthers and Naomis (godly grandmothers) to bring healing to their generation through their lives!

Notes

1. Edith Dean, *Great Women of the Christian Faith* (Uhrichsville, Ohio: Barbour and Company, Inc., 1959), pp. 240-241.
2. Ibid., p. 242.
3. Ibid., p. 243.
4. Ibid., p. 244.
5. Ibid., p. 244.
6. Ruth A. Tucker and Walter L. Liefeld, *Daughters of the Church* (Grand Rapids: Zondervan Publications, 1987), p. 303.
7. Edith Dean, *Great Women of the Christian Faith*, p. 244.
8. Ibid., p. 246.
9. Ibid., p. 4.
10. Ibid., p. 4.
11. Ibid., p. 5.
12. Ibid., p. 5.
13. Ibid., p. 6.
14. Tucker and Liefield, *Daughters of the Church*, pp. 101-102.
15. Edith Dean, *Great Women of the Christian Faith*, p. 7.
16. Ibid., p. 61.
17. Ibid., p. 63.
18. Ibid., p. 63.
19. Ibid., p. 65.
20. Ibid., p. 65.

Moms and Other Great Handmaidens of Faith

As I have poured over piles of books about great women of the faith, one determining factor has leapt out at me again and again...the influence of godly mothers on their sons and daughters.

Moms of Merit

Many of the greatest leaders, reformers, theologians and thinkers were deeply touched by the lives of their moms who, like Eunice and Mary, the mother of Jesus, believed in their sons.

Motherhood has somehow been considered a secondary calling to many women today. However, I believe nothing could be further from the truth! If the Lord had not called me to preach and travel, I would gladly have stayed home with my children until they were grown. In fact, after I finished my fifth year of college, I quit teaching to stay home with my daughter because I didn't want a woman other than myself to raise her.

Chrysostom's Mom

Even the pagan world has been touched by godly moms. Libanius, a noted pagan orator exclaimed in admiration when he learned of the self-sacrifice and purity of Anthusia, Chrysostom's mother, "Heavens! What women these Christians have!"[1]

Anthusia lived from approximately 347 to 407 in the city of Antioch where Paul began his three missionary journeys. Her son Chrysostom's name was originally John, but he was renowned as a preacher and became known as "Golden Mouthed," or Chrysostom.

Like many women today, Anthusia was concerned about the corruptions in her city. During Chrysostom's formative years, Anthusia taught him to love the Bible and studied it together with him. This gave him a deep love for Scripture, which could later be seen in the many homilies he wrote. As a result of his mother's godly influence, Chrysostom became one of the greatest expository preachers the Church has ever known.

Augustine's Mom

The prayers of Monica (331-387) helped to bring the young Augustine back to the Lord from his life of rebellion. Augustine spoke of his mother, Monica, as "God's handmaid who poured into my ears much about God, none of which sank into me until I was much older. She privately warned me not to commit fornication; but above all things never to defile another man's wife." He went on to say, "But this I knew not, and rushed headlong into such blindness, that amongst my equals I was ashamed to be shameless."[2]

Augustine pursued a life of unabashed depravity. At 16 he took a mistress and had a son by her. Then he entered into the sect of Manicheans, a heretical group. All the while his mother bathed her prayers in weeping. Augustine writes in his autobiography, *Confessions*, of how God "drew his soul out of the profound darkness, because of his mother who wept on his behalf more than most mothers weep when their children die."[3]

Monica's war for the soul of her son was not won overnight.

In fact, he went deeper into sin for nine years—at times seeming to rise, but then falling deep into Satan's clutches once again. He was a prodigal in every sense of the word.

Augustine finally moved from Carthage to Rome and then Milan. His mother, a widow, followed him even though it was extremely dangerous for a woman to travel alone in those days. She, like Paul, even had a vision in the midst of a storm that all would be safe and gave this prophetic word to the sailors aboard the ship.

In Milan, Monica went to see her son and encouraged him to give up his mistress of 15 years. She was delighted when he sent his mistress back to Africa, only to witness him taking another one in her place!

Finally, as a prodigal at the end of himself, Augustine, alone in a garden, entered into an intense struggle between his flesh and his spirit where he admits that he cried out to God:

> "How long, Lord? Wilt Thou be angry forever? Why is there not this hour an end to my uncleanness?" Suddenly, he heard the voice of a child singing in the garden: "Take up and read; take up and read." Quickly he took up a volume of St. Paul's Epistles and read Romans 13:13-14: "Not in rioting and drunkenness, not in chambering and wantonness, not in strife and envying; but put ye on the Lord Jesus Christ, and make not provision for the flesh, to fulfill the lusts thereof." He read no further, for instantly, "All the gloom of doubt vanished away."[4]

Augustine rushed to tell the good news to his mother. A short time later he and his mother decided to return to Africa with friends. They stopped at Ostia, which is at the mouth of the Tiber River, to rest. How sweet it was for Monica to spend long hours talking about the Lord with her son!

Unfortunately, her joy this side of heaven was short-lived, for while she was still in Ostia, Monica became very ill and died a swift death (within nine days) at the age of 56. She had spent many years of her life crying out to God for the prodigal to come home and had been there to welcome him with open arms.

Augustine went on, with the help of Bishop Hippo, to save Christianity when the Roman Empire disintegrated. It often seems that the greater the call of God, the more Satan fights for a person's soul.

Is there a prodigal in your life? If so, I pray that this story will encourage you not to give up praying and fighting for his or her soul. Many times the battle is much longer and fiercer than you think you have the strength for, but if you do not grow weary in well doing, you will win. Your prodigal will turn. Don't look at what your natural eyes see, but intercede with eyes of love that see the destiny God has planted within your son or daughter's heart.

John and Charles Wesley's Mom

Other reformers were greatly impacted by the lives of their mothers. Men such as John and Charles Wesley by their mother, Susanna, whom I briefly mentioned earlier.

Susanna, or "Sukey," was a beautiful woman with silky dark hair and deep blue eyes. The last of 25 children, Susanna was the daughter of a well-to-do cleric and grew up in London, England, in the seventeenth century. During this time when few women were educated, Susanna's father taught her Hebrew, Greek and Latin. She could write as well as any man, and her keen mind allowed her to discuss theology as articulately as any seminary student.

Most men would have been intimidated by Susanna's intellect, but not young Samuel Westley, who later changed his last name to "Wesley." Samuel met Susanna when she was just 13 and they knew each other for seven years before they married.

Susanna and Samuel had a tempestuous marriage at best. He became a spendthrift dreamer who kept them in debt for most of their marriage. They had 19 children together and 9 of them died. Their home was burned to the ground more than once and Samuel abandoned Susanna for long periods of time.

In the midst of all her sorrow, Susanna home-schooled all 10 of her children, teaching them to read Hebrew and Greek and memorize Scripture. She also found time to invest one hour a day with each of her children separately to get to know them and stay in touch with their feelings. A rigorous taskmaster, she set high standards for her children, not allowing them to use coarse language or fail in their studies. Susanna called this her "method" of arranging the day. This term must have had an impact on her children, because two of her sons later called the new move of God "Methodism."

One of her moments of greatest terror was seeing her young son, Jackie, stuck in an upper story of their house while it was awash in flames. Some young farmers stood on each other's shoulders and plucked him out of the fire and saved his life. Jackie went on to become known as the great reformer John Wesley.

Her husband, Samuel, for all his faults, was a firm believer that God wanted to send revival to England, and prayed for it diligently. Susanna loved Samuel all the days of his life in spite of his many failings.

Incredible as it may sound for a woman with so much knowledge of God, Susanna didn't really know Him as her personal Lord and Savior until the very end of her earthly life. She had heard about the inner witness and read how Christ had warmed the life of others' hearts, but didn't really understand until one day when she was taking Communion and came to the realization that Christ died for her personally. What a life-transforming thought! Her heart caught fire with that thought and she was changed eternally.

Susanna died in July of 1742 with her children gathered around her. As she looked from face to face she said, "Please, my children, as soon as I'm released, sing a psalm of praise to God."[5]

Never underestimate the power of a praying mother. Susanna's sons changed the face of Christianity, and today she lives on through the Methodist churches established all around the world.

Making It Personal

It has occurred to me that there may be some readers who, like Susanna, have gone to church most of their lives, but have never had a personal experience with Jesus Christ. Maybe someone gave you this book, and although you have loved God, you don't really know Him.

Why don't you take a minute with me right now to pray, asking Jesus Christ to come into your life. You will then have accepted Him and the price He paid for you on the Cross. He loves you and gave His life for you. Won't you give your life to Him?

Pray this prayer with me:

Dear God,
Today I ask Jesus to come into my heart and be my personal Lord and Savior. Please forgive my sins and wash me from all the wrong things I have done. Be the Lord of my life. Thank You, Jesus, for coming into my heart.
In Jesus' Name. Amen.

Others of you may need to rededicate your lives to the Lord. Perhaps you have a cold heart toward God or you have been living a selfish life and are far from Him. Please pray this prayer of rededication with me:

Dear God,
I realize today that I have been far away from You in my heart. Although I once prayed to receive Jesus Christ as Savior, He really hasn't been the Lord of my life. Lord Jesus, I now enthrone You as King over my heart. Take my life and use it. Make me a woman of destiny like Susanna Wesley.
In Jesus' Name. Amen.

I prayed that last prayer with you in my own heart. My heart burns to do more with my life for the Lord Jesus than I am doing now. Part of my struggle in writing this chapter is the many women of faith I have to leave out. I've been humbled to read of the great sacrifices so many missionary women have made. Many, like Susanna, have lost child after child to sickness and disease. Truly the nations have been evangelized at a high cost to the hearts of mothers.

I would be deeply remiss to make this hall of faith a "white only" chapter, as women of all races and colors have made huge sacrifices to see that the ends of the earth receive the gospel. This next section is dedicated to non-Western missionaries.

Thank God for the Indispensable "Bible Women"

A study such as this would be remiss if it didn't include a section on the "Bible women." This was the title given to Christian female nationals who were employed with very low salaries. In her book *Western Women in Eastern Lands*, Helen Barrett Montgomery wrote, "The Bible woman has become an institution. Her work is indispensable; she multiples the missionary's influence, goes before to prepare the way, and after to impress the truth. One of the humblest, she is at the same time one of the mightiest forces of the Cross in non-Christian lands."[6]

Rosaline Goforth in China
Bible women were represented by many nationalities. Missionaries such as Rosaline Goforth, who was a missionary in China around the turn of the century, worked with Bible women who made contacts for her that she herself could not have made. Bible women also worked independently of women missionaries. These women were extremely hard workers and often had to fight terrible family pressures. This was especially painful in oriental societies and places such as India.

Kieko Yammamuro in Japan
Bible women played a crucial role in the development of the

Christian church in Japan. According to Winburn Thomas, the Bible woman was the "female equivalent of a male evangelist," but because of the low position of women in oriental society, her place in the Church—especially in the early years—was not as secure as was that of the male evangelists. Yet as early as the 1880s, nearly 40 Bible women were employed by seven different missions in Japan.

In addition to Bible women, non-Western missionaries have been extremely courageous in the area of missions, humanitarian service and education. In the early twentieth century, Kieko Yammamuro helped lead the fight against prostitution in her native country of Japan. She directed a Salvation Army home that took in young girls who had been kidnapped and forced to work in the notorious Yoshiwara district. She also established a sanitarium for tuberculosis patients. Kieko often had intense struggles of which she wrote in her diary:

It seems too adventurous perhaps, but God is able. I have no one save the Holy Ghost to rely upon. My weak health and lack of ability seem to deny me success, but when I am weak, God is strong. Depending upon Him alone, I go forward to establish the Sanitarium. To be with the children makes me happy and perhaps some will call me neglectful of my duty as a mother. But though my eyes are wet with tears, I must go forward. Oh Lord, fill me with the Holy Ghost. Give me power to move the people. Amen.[7]

Pandita Ramabai from India

One of the most outstanding Christian educators was Pandita Ramabai from India. Although quite controversial, she succeeded in establishing schools for girls—among them a school for child widows at Pooma. You may remember that even to this day, though much change is taking place, widows are burned on their husbands' burial pyres.

The notion of educating women in Indian Hindu society was quite foreign to the thinking of the writers and their interpreters, who all agreed:

That women of high and low caste, as a class, were bad, very bad, worse than demons, as unholy as untruth, and that they could not get Moksha as men. The only hope of their getting this much-desired liberation from Karma and its results...was the worship of their husbands. The husband is said to be the women's god; there is no other god for her.[8]

Ramabai's work grew, especially during the 1900 famine. More than a thousand girls received Christ during that time, and the work experienced major spiritual breakthroughs. She had a deep longing for revival and loved her country and its culture. Ramabai believed it was her responsibility to make Christianity known to her culture. Although she was a pioneer, and thus might have made some mistakes along the way, God used her in a powerful way in her own country.

Amy Carmichael, a Western Missionary
Although Amy Carmichael is a Western missionary, no chapter such as this would be complete without mentioning her work in India. She was probably the most famous woman missionary of her time. She also wrote 35 books on missions and established a school and home for temple prostitutes called the Dohnavur Fellowship. In 1916 Amy founded the Sisterhood of the Common Life to steer young women, who were called to be single, into single-minded ministry.

I particularly encourage those of you who are single to study her life. She, like Lottie Moon, grappled with the thought of remaining single. Women missionaries of her time were often expected to live single lives as career missionaries at a huge cost. And even though many never had physical children of their own, God gave them many, many spiritual children who considered the women missionaries "mothers."

Amy later related her struggle during her early missionary service in Japan in the following manner:

On this day many years ago I went away alone to a cave in

the mountain called Arima. I had feelings of fear about the future. That was why I went there—to be alone with God. The devil kept on whispering, "It is all right now, but what about afterwards? You are going to be very lonely." And he painted pictures of loneliness—I can see them still. And I turned to my God in a kind of desperation and said, "Lord, what can I do? How can I go on to the end?" And He said, "None of them that trust in Me shall be desolate." That word has been with me ever since.[9]

Amanda Smith, an Ex-Slave

Any chapter dealing with heroines of the faith would be incomplete without honoring the role of African-American women in Christianity. Among the most noted and courageous of these women was the Methodist revivalist Amanda Smith, who lived from 1837 to 1915. Amanda was born a slave in Maryland and had previously worked as a scrub woman.

As I studied her life, I felt great admiration for her as a pioneer who has gone before me to set an example for my generation. I have suffered persecution at times and even hostility, but nothing compared to what Amanda must have encountered. Elliot Wright put it like this:

She was an unusual sight in post-Civil War America—a black woman evangelist, an ex-slave, traversing north and south, preaching to all races and then spending fourteen years evangelizing in England, India, and Africa. She too was part of the Holiness movement.[10]

Amanda Smith's story would not be complete without expressing the godly example of her mother and grandmother. Where would we be without the mothers of the Church?

Amanda received opposition from the Black African Methodist Episcopal Church (the AME) as well as the white people. When the AME held their first general conference south of the Mason-Dixon Line, Amanda decided in her heart that she was going to go. Her appearance caused quite a stir of gossip, even though she says in her own words:

> The thought of ordination had never once entered my mind, for I had received my ordination from Him who said, "Ye have not chosen Me, but I have chosen you, and ordained you, that you might go and bring forth fruit."[11]

Oh, dear Amanda, your sisters down through the ages and those of today respond to your statement with a joyful, "Amen, sister, amen!" If it isn't God who is calling us, then why would we ever want to say yes to being handmaidens of the Lord?

Holy Handmaidens Who Struggled with the Call

As I have studied the women of God down through the centuries, there is one glaring unifying theme: most of them, like myself, were extremely reluctant to become women in ministry, or to accept any kind of leadership role in the Church. It wasn't easy then and, although much has improved since Amanda Smith's time, it still isn't easy today. (We'll discuss this more in later chapters.)

Because so many more women of faith deserve to be in this book, it is with a certain amount of anguish that I close it with a few contemporary heroines. I would encourage you to buy some of the excellent books written today about this subject (see the bibliography) and find yourself in their pages.

I'd also suggest that you read their stories to your sons and daughters. We need examples of mothers of the faith as well as fathers. Pastors need to preach about these heroines from the pulpit and inspire the generations to come with their examples.

The last several women mentioned in this chapter have greatly impacted my life. Each of them has given me something very special and unique in love and nurturing for which I'll be eternally grateful.

Gladys Aylward was an English maid called by God to China under impossible odds. Her story never ceases to inspire me to have faith in God despite the biggest mountains of adversity. Truly there are many of whom the world was not worthy!

Personally, Margaret Moberly and the leaders of Women Ministers International helped mentor me. Great women such as Marilyn Hickey, Jane Hansen and others have touched my life by their friendship. I will be weaving more of their influence on my life as I continue in further chapters.

Freda Lindsay, a Kingdom Giant

One of the giants in God's kingdom who struggled with the call was Mrs. Freda Lindsay. Mrs. Lindsay was born in Canada on a large wheat farm near Burstall, Saskatchewan, and is one of 12 children. Her German-origin parents grew up in White Russia and met and married in the United States, but later heard of great opportunities in Canada. It seems that God had a plan for little Freda to be Canadian! (Do I hear an "Amen!" from the country to the north of the United States?)

Although Freda fervently wanted to go to high school, her father was from the old school that believed women did not need to be educated. Fortunately, the same tenacity that was to stand her in good stead later in her life was apparent when she convinced her mother that she would find a job if her mother would talk to her father about her education. It isn't surprising at all that Freda found that job and was able to move to town to attend school.

Later, Freda visited her sister who told her of a revival meeting in progress held by a young evangelist named Gordon Lindsay. She tells of her struggle to accept the Lord in her book, *My Diary Secrets*:

For want of something better to do, I decided to attend the revival that night. When the invitation to accept Christ was given, although under conviction of the Holy Spirit, I was too proud to go forward, knowing that the people in the church were aware that I came from a Christian family. I deluded myself into thinking they believed I was a Christian. I am sure most of them knew that during my years of working away from home I had left the path of following the Lord.

After the dismissal prayer, I nonetheless made my way to the altar at the front of the church. There the devil told me I would live a dull and drab life if I were to become a Christian (yet now as I read over my diaries, they sound like storybooks), that I would never have any friends, and on and on he went. Nevertheless, with the Holy Spirit tugging at my soul, I surrendered my life to the Lord that night and was gloriously converted.[12]

At the altar that night Freda heard the same Holy Spirit tell her that Gordon would one day be her husband. Five years later they were married.

Gordon was quite a romantic, as his letters showed. Waiting for the wedding day was difficult for the young couple because Gordon was pastoring a church in San Fernando, California. I found one of his letters deeply touching:

> San Fernando, California
> September 3, 1937

Dearest Freda,

It is said of Jacob that the seven years he waited for Rachel were only as days, but you know that these two months seem as years. However, every time I think of how close the time really is, I feel like praising the Lord, for He has surely given me the one girl out of the many thousands I have seen that I can really love. Dr. Jeffries may tie the knot, but you are already knitted to my heart inseparably.

> Your darling sweetheart,
> GORDON

Freda and Gordon's life together has been about as far from boring as a couple could ever imagine. Volumes could be written about their work during the "Voice of Healing" days when they were working with great men and women of God such as William Branham and others. The Lord led them to buy an old night club in Dallas, Texas, and gave Gordon the vision to build a Bible school, Christ for the Nations Institute (C.F.N.I.). My sister and brother-in-law are both graduates, so my own family greatly benefited as did my pastor, Dutch Sheets, and many other friends in ministry.

March of 1973 was, as usual, a busy one for the Lindsays—by then they had three children—two boys and a girl. Toward the end of that month, when they went to the lake, Gordon requested that 1 Corinthians 15 be read for the family devotions. The chapter deals with the resurrection of the dead, which is personally interesting to me because when we went to pick up my dad's effects after his death, the only passage marked in his Bible was this same one.

On April 1, 1973, Gordon Lindsay slipped out to glory while sitting on the platform at C.F.N.I. Freda and Gordon had been married 35 years. *The Voice of Healing* (a magazine dedicated to the revival and miracles that came out of the movement) was started on April 1, 1948.

Freda began to receive prophetic words from respected leaders revealing that Gordon's mantle had fallen upon her shoulders, and one day after the funeral, the board of C.F.N.I. voted that she was to succeed her husband.

The weight of the massive responsibility of that huge work for the Lord came down upon her shoulders, seemingly crushing her small frame. Inside Freda Lindsay, however, lived a big God whom she had served unreservedly since she had knelt at that altar in Portland, Oregon.

Following the funeral, Freda reported:

After friends and family had returned to their own homes, I was left alone with Carole [her daughter]. I started to get out of bed the next morning and found I had no strength even to stand. I lay back down and called Carole into my room. I told her the task was too great—the responsibility of our missionary work that was reaching into over 100 nations was too much...the finishing of the Institute building...the 300 native churches we were at that time helping to build...the Bible school in Zerka, Jordan, that we had just started to build...they were more than I could carry.

Carole said to me, "Mother, let's just pray. And let's just take it one day at a time. The Lord will give you strength for just today." So I crawled out of bed and prostrated myself on the floor. For some time I lay there sobbing out my inadequacy at the immensity of the task when suddenly the Holy Ghost took over.

Then I bathed myself, dressed and went to work. And the Lord has each day provided strength sufficient for all the needs that have arisen.[13]

As of this writing Mrs. Freda Lindsay is 83 years old and still traveling the world over. Christ for the Nations Institute has built 10,000 native churches in third-world countries, has 40 affiliated Bible schools, and 26,000 students have come through the doors of the institute. Some naysayers claimed after Gordon's death that the doors of C.F.N.I. would close within six months. Guess they sort of missed it, don't you think? All because of one little girl born from a family of 12 who gave all of her heart, soul and mind to loving and serving her beloved Savior.

Evelyn Christenson,
a Portrait of Humility and Virtue

When I think of the women I have looked up to throughout the years, at the top of my list is Evelyn Christenson. Few women have done more to mobilize prayer. She is a woman who is as real as anyone you could ever meet. In fact, I called her when I was going through a deep valley and her words greatly encouraged me.

Evelyn found Christ when she was nine years old, and was

called to the prayer ministry in 1967 when the Lord spoke to her through Revelation 3:8:

I know your works. See, I have set before you an open door, and no one can shut it; for you have a little strength, have kept My word, and have not denied My Name.

At first, she thought the Lord just meant He needed her for about six months when asked to conduct an experiment at her church on what actually does happen when women pray. Little did Evelyn know, however, that the time would be extended until today when she has ministered for 30 years.

Evelyn has gone through many trials of the faith with her own family, but has seen the goodness of the Lord through them all. She has come through victoriously by learning to pray the Word. Her teaching on prayer has encircled the globe. Few women have taught the Bible with more depth and passion than Evelyn. Yet, in spite of all of this, she has remained humble and approachable.

One of the greatest contributions she has made to the fulfillment of the Great Commission came through the training manual on Evangelism Prayer that she wrote for the A.D.2000 Women's Track.

Evelyn received a call to minister in India, but it was 30 years before she actually saw the complete fulfillment of it. Her radio show has been broadcast in India in Hindi and English for nearly 18 years, and God has mightily used her to penetrate the nation for Christ.

I believe that this dear heroine of the Lord can easily say to others, "Follow me, as I follow Christ"—although she probably wouldn't say that about herself. Thank God for her example to my generation.

Vonette Bright: His Vision, My Call

Some of God's women leaders received the call to minister through the vision the Lord gave their husbands. I asked Vonette

Bright one day at a Focus on the Family meeting for A.D.2000 and Beyond if God called her independently of her husband. She stopped and thought a moment, reflecting, and said, "Bill received the vision to help reach the world for Christ and to begin on the college campus. We assumed that God's call for Bill was also my call. Afraid of what that meant, I asked God for a heart to respond. Bill calls me cofounder."

Of course, this great woman is not only an author, but was also used of God along with others to call together the great prayer congress in 1984, which some people feel was the beginning, in some respects, of the prayer movement encircling the globe today.

Corinthia Boone

No chapter on heroines of the faith would be complete without honoring Dr. Corinthia Boone, one of the greatest modern-day African-American leaders that I know. She has been a good friend to Mike and me for many years and we greatly admire her.

Corinthia was born in Prince George County, Maryland. Her mother's side was Baptist and her daddy's was Pentecostal. Corinthia had an experience when she was eight years old that was to mark her life forever.

One day while sitting in the back of the church, Corinthia was suddenly engulfed in the presence of God. To tell it in her own words, "God had answered my desire to know Him." A change was evident in her life and she would often be called to the altar to lead in prayer. As usual, the Holy Spirit led in a way that affirmed what would be her first ministry prayer.

The impact of this touch from God was deep and lasting. Corinthia shared with me in her voice, which sings with the joy of the Lord, "After that experience the trees sang and nothing looked the same to me."

A couple of years later, Corinthia began to attend a holiness church where she began testifying, prophesying, singing in the choir and speaking. When I heard this story I thought, *No won-*

der the Lord said, "Let the children come unto me." Children are often underestimated with regard to their abilities.

The Lord led this mighty pioneer of God to earn her bachelor of science in education from Bowie State University, then later

"The testings...have plowed long furrows upon my back, but without those furrows there would be no place for the seed. Without the opening of the seed, it could not fall into the ground and be fruitful."
(Dr. Corinthia Boone)

her master's in administration supervision, a Bible school certificate from Baltimore Bible College, and then at last, a hard-earned doctorate from Union University in philosophy with an emphasis in counseling.

Corinthia worked for years with Bishop Meares at Evangel Temple in Washington, D.C., and helped set up their Sunday School department as well as working in many other areas of the church. She started in the church as an usher, then one day became an ordained elder.

In 1985 Corinthia was appointed unanimously to be the chairperson of the Greater Washington National Day of Prayer. She has founded Together in Ministry International (T.I.M.), a fellowship of pastors finding new relationships, friendships and inspiration in a multicultural setting—an oasis of refreshing through worshipful prayer. Her ministry, the International Christian Host Coalition, is a multiethnic group of leaders who are committed to community transformation. This ministry (I.C.H.C.) is the umbrella ministry for T.I.M. and the Greater Washington National Day of Prayer.

I asked Corinthia if she would share some wisdom with those who read this chapter. She began by quoting Psalm 129:3: "The

plowers plowed upon my back; they made long their furrows."
She went on to explain, "I have learned more from testings than
anything else in my life. The testings I have gone through have
plowed long furrows upon my back, but without those furrows
there would be no place for the seed. Without the opening of the
seed, it could not fall into the ground and be fruitful. Yes, I have
had many testings, but always determined that they will only
cause me to bear more fruit."

Corinthia, my friend, or should I say Dr. Corinthia Boone,
B.S.,M.S.,Ph.D., I commend you for your courage. You are a true
pioneer and heroine of the faith with many lessons for people of
all ethnicities. I salute you for not becoming bitter from the
storms of life. Thanks for your example.

Fuchsia Pickett

Dr. Fuchsia Pickett was born in the rural area of Irishburg,
Virginia. Seemingly all through her life, Fuchsia was one who did
things before her time—true to her prophetic nature. She graduated from high school at age 16 and married her first husband,
George Parrish, right out of high school. At age 17, she gave birth
to her son, Darrell.

Fuchsia was "rocked in a Methodist cradle." She sang in the
choir of the United Methodist Church and was a faithful Sunday
School and Vacation Bible School teacher, but she didn't know
Jesus. Finally, a young Presbyterian friend started praying for her
to be saved. The Holy Spirit touched Fuchsia in a mighty way
while she was singing the hymn "It Is Well with My Soul" for a
revival.

Sometime later Fuchsia had a sovereign visitation from God.
In her own words:

> I was in my room waiting for George to come home from
> work....As I lay in bed, I heard a voice louder than a normal
> tone call my name. I raised up in the bed and answered
> questioningly, "Yes?" As I sat there for a moment, I sensed

that my room was filled with the presence of God.

No one answered my response, so I lay back down. A few moments later I was awakened and I heard that voice call my name again. I decided it must be the people living upstairs in our house. I got up and looked up the stairwell, but I did not hear a sound. There was no one in the house. I went back and lay down on my bed. The third time, I heard my name called aloud. I fell by my bedside trembling. I asked, "God, is this You?"

He said, "Yes, Fuchsia. I want you to preach and teach My Word."

I surrendered to God that night, although I didn't know how or when or where I would fulfill the mandate He placed on my life. I was a wife and young mother. It did not seem likely that I could get the preparation I would need to preach the gospel. But God always provides where He has commanded an obedient heart."[14]

The Lord did provide for Fuchsia's education in Bible college at Aldergate University and graduate work at the University of North Carolina. He made a way where there was no way.

Fuchsia went through many trials. Many of her family members died from a genetic bone disease that also attacked her later in life. The Lord miraculously healed Fuchsia, then used her in a mighty healing ministry.

Dr. Fuchsia Pickett has a deep, intimate relationship with the Holy Spirit. He has given her many powerful visitations and taught her truths that have been a great blessing to the Body of Christ. She has never given up her walk with the Lord, even though her first husband died during surgery. The Lord later gave her Leroy Pickett, who has faithfully stood beside her in ministry for many years.

In 1963 the Lord gave Fuchsia a vision of a hydroelectric power plant from which many streams poured forth into a river of God. It flowed from the Church universal. The river was channeled into great transformers from five geographical points in the

United States. Underground pipes were laid and the Lord told her, "When I get them all hooked up, I will pull the switch."[15]

The Lord had shown her the networking that is taking place today. Underneath the mammoth power plant Fuchsia saw a harvest field stretching throughout the world. The Lord showed her that when the waters from this power plant are released, there will be healing for body, soul (emotions) and spirit.

Finally the Lord showed Fuchsia that the Church must be delivered from prejudice, denominationalism, culture, custom and tradition. This vision is amazingly accurate for the Church today. Barriers are falling between denominations and many are working together on projects to reach the unreached. A move of reconciliation is occurring between the races that will bring great healing to the nations of the earth. Surely the Lord's Hand is getting ready to release a great outpouring of revival upon the earth, such as the people of the earth have never experienced.

Dr. Fuchsia Pickett obeyed the call of God when it was unheard of for a woman to stand in the pulpit. As of this writing, she is in her 80s and still traveling and teaching God's Word with full steam. She has never wavered in the call and is a true heroine of the faith.

I am including two more women in this chapter, not because of their pulpit ministries, but because of the impact they have had on my life. This is not to say that they haven't greatly touched others' lives through their ministries, but each of them has given something unique to me in love and nurturing. The first one I want to mention is Doris Wagner.

Doris Wagner, a Living Legend

Doris Wagner was born on a dairy farm in St. Johnsville in upstate New York. Her father was a German immigrant who had settled just outside this little one-stop-light town with a population of 1,500. (This story proves that we should never despise the day of small beginnings, because one day little Doris would grow up and lead to the Lord a young man getting his degree in dairy farming, whose grandfather had been the country doctor in St. Johnsville.) I wonder if Doris ever dreamed as a teenager of whom she would one day marry. Any daydreaming she might have done would probably never have touched upon the fact that she would eventually help start an organization that would influence the whole world in prayer.

One day Doris went to a farm in another town and saw a young man milking a cow. The year was 1949. This young man was interested in the bright-eyed Doris, but the two of them were worlds apart in their thinking. He was a gambler and a drunkard, and she was a committed Christian who had just given her life to Jesus a week before.

Although Doris witnessed to him, the young man was reluctant to become a Christian, knowing that if he did, he would have to give up the lifestyle he was living in the fraternity house at Rutgers University. This young man had such a brilliant mind that he could factor the odds at draw poker, and was a perpetual winner. In fact, his gambling was providing his spending money at college.

Finally, love and the Lord won in the battle for his soul, and he asked Doris to marry him. However, when asked, she looked him straight in the eye and said, "I can't. I'm a born-again Christian and I promised the Lord I would only marry a Christian."

He replied, "Well, what does it take to be a Christian? Will you show me how?"

"In a moment," she said, "but I must tell you something else first. I have also given my life to God to be a missionary."

"Missionary?" he said. "What's that?" When she explained, he said, "I think I'll be a missionary, too!" So he gave his life to the Lord and became an ex-gambler and ex-drunkard. This was in January of 1950.

Now, I know some of you may highly suspect his motives, but the years have proven that his experience was more than with just a pretty face and dimples. Dr. C. Peter Wagner went with his wife, Doris, to Bolivia where they were field missionaries for 16 years. Then they returned to America to spend the next 25 years at Fuller Seminary, where Doris served as Peter's personal secretary before they launched Global Harvest Ministries.

Global Harvest Ministries was founded to coordinate the United Prayer Track of the A.D.2000 and Beyond movement. In 1996 Doris and Peter moved the ministry from Pasadena, California, to Colorado Springs in order to become founding partners of the World Prayer Center. Doris, in addition to serving as the executive director for Global Harvest, also has an ongoing ministry of deliverance and speaking. She is affectionately known as "Mom" to many around the world.

Doris was my buddy in the early days when I first went to Argentina and stayed busy kicking out demons left and right in order to clear the way for revival in that nation. She is a living legend, and one of God's heroines of the faith.

Many Women Do Noble Things, but You Surpass Them All (Prov. 31:29)

The last, but certainly not the least, of the great women I want to share about in this chapter is my own mother, Eleanor Johnson Lindsey. I dedicated this book to her, because I am what and who I am due to her prayers and belief in me. I went through some dark trials—even though never deep rebellion—and she was always there for me.

Mom met my dad while she was a Presbyterian. When he told her that he was called of God to be a minister, she cried. Being a pastor's wife was not her idea of a fun life, but he wanted to be a *Baptist* minister, which meant she would have to leave the Presbyterian church and be rebaptized. The news was overwhelming.

Mom is a spunky lady, though, and the tears were short-lived. She and Dad went to Southwestern Seminary in Fort Worth, Texas, after Dad graduated from Baylor. I lived on "seminary hill." Times were tight. In fact, the house we lived in was eventually torn down. (It wasn't in the greatest shape even way back then!)

Dad and Mom pioneered churches under the Home Mission Board. Money was always tight, but I don't ever remember hearing Mom complain. She just prayed.

Mom is now a beautiful 71-year-old who still looks young and radiant. She has a list full of people's names from her church and others to pray for, but I know a day never goes by that she doesn't pray through my schedule. Thanks, Mom. I couldn't do what I do without you. You're the best mom in the whole world!

Notes

1. Edith Dean, *Great Women of the Christian Faith* (Uhrichsville, Ohio: Barbour and Company, Inc., 1959), p. 26.
2. Ibid., p. 23.
3. Ibid., p. 23.
4. Ibid., p. 24.
5. Sandy Dengler, Susanna Wesley (Chicago: Moody Press, 1987), p. 201.
6. Ruth A. Tucker and Walter L. Liefeld, *Daughters of the Church* (Grand Rapids: Zondervan Publications, 1987), p. 342.
7. Ibid., p. 351.
8. Ibid., p. 344.
9. Ibid., pp. 305-306.
10. Ibid., p. 270.
11. Ibid., p. 271.
12. Freda Lindsay, *My Diary Secrets* (Dallas: Christ for the Nations Publishing, 1984), p. 14.
13. Ibid., p. 250.
14. Dr. Fuchsia Pickett, *Stones of Remembrance* (Lake Mary, Fla.: Creation House), manuscript.
15. Ibid., manuscript.

Gender to Gender

One day while driving to the store, I began listening to my five-year-old son, who was sitting in the back seat. At first I thought he was talking to himself out loud. Then, as I tuned in further, I came to the realization that most of his conversation wasn't with words; rather he was simply making sounds—such as urrrrr, bang, bang, uh-uh-uh-uh, vroom, vroom, vroom and the like.

Men Who Bark and the Women Who Love Them

Puzzled by this, I wondered if imitating sounds could be a pattern in little boys. I found to my utter amazement that it is. Perhaps this surprise discovery wouldn't have caught his dad off guard at all....I wondered. So I expanded my search to other men in general and my husband in particular. As I listened, I was intrigued to find that even grown men are sometimes prone to this peculiar behavior—not in the same way, of course.

When we first married, I remember watching Mike open the door and bark like a dog to get the various pets rattled in houses up and down the alley of our neighborhood. Mike then would shut the door with a grin on his face as the uproar of responding barks ensued. I realize that not all men would do this and I don't want to

be stereotypical. (I do think that quite a few men would either rel-
ish this thought or at least enjoy it.) However, my husband's friend,
David, who lived directly under our upstairs apartment, loved to do
the same. In fact, occasionally they would bark in chorus! It seemed
to be a form of that mysterious thing called "male bonding."

Born to Be Different

Females, on the other hand, are more prone to words—lots of
them. Little girls dote on long conversations over tea parties.
They talk to their dolls and pets. And when they grow up, the
need to talk grows with them. A noted marriage therapist said
that a wife needs at least one good hour of conversation with her
husband a day.

When teaching about the difference between men and
women to a group of pastors' wives in Latin America, the women
laughed and gently protested that their husbands needed lots of
words. Although this may be true, there is a major difference
between talking and communication. Pastors in general may be
more prone to talking, but it is heartfelt communication on a
more intimate level that women need—not just words. Women
generally have a greater need for this kind of intimate interchange than men do.

The gender gap is so broad that it is even evident in small
children. Books have been written attributing the problem to
men and women having been born on different planets—and if
you have had a problem communicating gender-to-gender, this
certainly may not seem out of the realm of possibility!

A part of the gender gap really is physical in nature. Gary
Smalley and John Trent have this to say about it:

Medical studies have shown that between the 18th and 26th
weeks of pregnancy, something happens that forever separates the sexes. Using heat-sensitive monitors, researchers
have actually observed a chemical bath of testosterone and
other sex-related hormones wash over a baby boy's brain.

This causes changes that never happen to a baby girl. Here's a layman's explanation of what happens when those chemicals hit a boy's system:

The human brain is divided into two halves, or hemispheres, connected by fibrous tissue called the corpus callosum. The sex-related hormones that flood a baby boy's brain cause the right side to recede slightly, destroying some of the connecting fibers. One result is that, in most cases, a boy starts life more left-brain oriented.

Because little girls don't experience this chemical bath, they leave the starting blocks much more two-sided in their thinking. And while electrical impulses and messages do travel back and forth between both sides of a baby boy's brain, those same messages can proceed faster and be less hindered in the brain of a little girl.

Well, not exactly. What occurs in the womb merely sets the stage for men and women to "specialize" in two different ways of thinking. And this is one major reason men and women need each other so much.

The left brain houses more of the logical, analytical, factual and aggressive centers of thought. It's the side of the brain most men reserve for the major portion of their waking hours. It enjoys conquering 500 miles a day on family vacations, favors mathematical formulas over romance novels, stores the dictionary definition of love and generally favors clinical, black-and-white thinking.

On the other hand, most women spend the majority of their days and nights camped out on the right side of the brain. It's the side that harbors the center for feelings, as well as the primary relational, language and communication skills. It enables them to do fine detail work, sparks imagination and makes an afternoon devoted to art and fine music enjoyable. Perhaps you can begin to understand why communication is difficult in marriage....[1]

(I know that some of you women readers will be tempted at this point to get into what we in America call, "male bashing," and make a comment such as, "I always knew that men were brain damaged!" Resist this at all costs or you may create a need for gender reconciliation.)

It All Began in the Garden

Although it is true that men and women have many physical differences, I believe the breakdown in their spiritual communication began way back in the book of Genesis.

In order to understand God's original intention for the genders, we need to recognize one very important point: the only thing God said was not good in all of creation was man's aloneness (see Gen. 1:4,10,12,18,21,25,31; cf. Gen. 2:18). Therefore, it stands to reason that Satan would want to wound the relationships between men and women—not only in the home, but also in the work force and the Church, so that man would once again be in the only state God called "not good." (I want to make it clear to all unmarried readers that this affects you too. You can be unmarried and still not be alone.)

In the beginning God created mankind (or "humankind," as is becoming more common) in His image, male and female (see Gen. 1:26,27). It is a mistaken belief that Adam had both male and female attributes. Although Eve was "bone of my bones and flesh of my flesh" (Gen. 2:23), God put something in her that came straight from heaven, which Adam had not been created with. I believe God looked around and knew in His purposes that something was still missing upon the earth. If He left man in his present state, the full image of who He is as God would not be represented upon the earth; so He created woman. Therefore, the full image of God is not fully displayed through only one gender, but it happens on every level as men and women complement each other, side by side. When this happens, all things created seem to breathe a sigh of relief and somehow express, "This is right. This is good. This is how God intended the earth to be."

Sadly, men and women have so wounded each other that we

see extreme forms of anger displayed. At one end of the pole, women turn to lesbianism and feminism and say to the men, "We don't need you. The only good man is a dead man." Almost invariably at the root of this rage is a father who was abusive. It's interesting to check out this pattern in leading women within the most extreme feminist movement.

On the other hand, men's views can also be distorted concerning women. Many men who are strongly against women in ministry in the Church have often had big problems with a controlling woman somewhere in their lives, and the women they know suffer because of the way their mothers, sisters, lovers or other females have abused them.

This breakdown in communication began in the Garden. Satan's strike against the man and woman seems to have occurred at the tree of the knowledge of good and evil. A fascinating aspect of this interchange between the snake, the woman and the man is that the sin involved the mouth.

Note that Satan approached the woman with food. Perhaps he worked on a natural desire of hers to prepare food for her husband. Here was a different and appealing tidbit they hadn't eaten before. Sadly, if they had partaken deeply enough of the fruit of the tree of life, they wouldn't have had any desire for this forbidden fruit.

Likewise, it is possible that the man was used to receiving food from the woman and this weakened his defenses against eating that which the Lord had said, "You must not." Immediately after they partook, their eyes were opened and death came into their lives. I believe that a veil was placed between them, inhibiting their ability to communicate, because the only way a man and a woman can truly relate is through God. Before the Fall a supernatural anointing existed that surpassed the differences in their brains and gave them oneness of heart.

Created to Complete, Not Compete

Norm Wright has written a fascinating book entitled *What Men*

Want. Chapter 2, "The Dialogue," relates an imaginary conversation between God and a man. It goes like this:

> "So You purposely made them (male and female) different as they are?"
>
> "Yes, I did. You're suggesting it was accidental?"
>
> "Oh, no...no, not at all. But, sometimes...."
>
> "You know the story. Satan clothed in the form of a serpent came to them and spoke to Eve. He convinced her to disobey Me. She invited Adam to join her, and instead of saying, 'No, we need to obey God,' he caved in. This was the first sign of passivity. The man-woman relationship and everything else became disordered. He then began to blame. First he blamed his wife, and then he blamed Me for giving her to him. Ever since Adam's time, men have tended to be defensive. They often interpret innocent questions as accusations. And the blame that started in the Garden....Oh, men have cultivated that ability well! The role I assigned to Adam has been distorted."
>
> "Ah, wait a minute. Men are defensive by nature? I don't think we're so defensive."
>
> (Silence.)
>
> "Well, perhaps some men are, but we do get accused a lot...."
>
> (Silence.)
>
> "All right, we're defensive. OK, please continue, or is that it?"
>
> "There's much more. In the Garden, both Adam and Eve could relate emotionally. They were able to give one another the gift of understanding. Not now. Now, if a woman wants understanding from a man, what does she get?"
>
> "Solutions, answers, advice...."
>
> "A relationship that was meant to be complementary became competitive. Eve's desire was to control Adam.

What I created to be a perfect balance resulted in a deteriorating imbalance and a clash of wills."[2]

Wright goes on to share other deep insights about male-female relationships that resulted from the Fall, such as power struggles, domination, emotional nakedness, lack of trust, fear, anger, control, etc.

It doesn't take a very perceptive person to look at the relationships between men and women today and see that he is right in his assessments. Painfully right.

Satan cannot afford to have Eden restored and man and woman standing together as they did in the Garden. This would bring order to the home and order to the Church.

God looked down through time and already had a remedy prepared: Jesus, the Lamb of God, slain from the foundation of the world. He came and died so that the terrible rip in gender relationships, which came in through sin, could be healed through His own blood on Calvary. Only the power of the Cross can fill the gender gap and create the bridge we so desperately need to restore us to Eden.

Without men and women working side by side, the Church will be ineffective. The complete image of God will only be manifested in its full expression when men and women stand side by side in the Church. Is there any wonder that the devil fights gender reconciliation at all levels? Satan cannot afford to have Eden restored and man and woman standing together as they did in the Garden. This would bring order to the home and order to the Church.

Commissioned to Subdue the Earth and the Enemy, Not Each Other

The Bible says that one day there will be a restoration of all things that God has spoken by the mouth of all His holy prophets since the world began (see Acts 3:21). One of these prophecies was that in the end times, He would pour out His Spirit upon the sons and daughters (see Joel 2:28,29).

Jane Hansen and Marie Powers's excellent book, *Fashioned for Intimacy* (Regal Books), gives us an in-depth study of Creation and the role of men and women. (I highly encourage you to read it, as it will fill in many of the blanks I am not able to cover in this one chapter.) One of the points Jane and Marie make in their book is that humanity was made to have authority upon the earth.[3] This was the job description given to God's image bearers—initially the man, and subsequently man and woman together. At the moment of Adam's creation, an evil force was already loose in the earth that Adam was instructed to guard against in order to protect his sanctuary. Ultimately, Adam and Eve together were commissioned to subdue and be in authority over all the earth. The enemy they were to subdue was God's enemy, Satan.

Satan simply cannot afford for men and women to reconcile on a gender level. I personally believe that no power of agreement on the earth is stronger than a husband and wife who touch heaven together in their prayers. When healing happens on this level, God's created sons and daughters will come into a level of authority that Satan has not had to deal with since the beginning of the world. Therefore, he has built up generations of strongholds to prevent gender reconciliation.

Numbers of Christian leaders today feel that the gender gap is the final pioneer area in need of healing. Much work is being done to bring racial reconciliation. Pastors and leaders are meeting together for prayer, but the genders are separated in the meetings. I would even go as far as to say that I believe a cultural gender bias is at work. Many male leaders who mentally agree that men and women need to work together in ministry show little evidence of their belief by their words and/or actions.

Purging Our Patterns of Denial

Actually, I hesitate to even bring up the topic of denial. However, when a stronghold is exhibited in a culture, the mind-set is often so ingrained that godly people who are caught in its grip have no idea they are participating. I've often seen this form of denial in relation to racial reconciliation. (Which, by the way, is another area where we have a long way to go.)

One day when Mike and I were meeting with leaders in another country, we were discussing the need for racial reconciliation on a national level. These godly leaders looked at us and said, "We don't have a problem with racism in our country."

I quietly turned and looked at a black friend (I might add, the *only* black person in the meeting) and said, "Elan (not his real name), are you always the worship leader and never the speaker?"

Elan looked rather uncomfortable, gazed at the floor, and in a downcast voice answered, "Yes." The white leaders were absolutely shocked and proceeded to plan a time of national repentance.

I bring this up because I have seen similar instances happen with women leaders in meeting after meeting. A number of years ago I attended a prayer breakfast for American leaders on our National Day of Prayer in Washington, D.C. At one point, the master of ceremonies asked all the ministers in the room to stand. As I looked around, not one woman stood up. Why? We were too embarrassed to face the possible criticism our standing might evoke. I personally would stand if asked today, but I simply didn't have the strength of spirit to do so back then.

Another time I spoke at a major meeting for pastors and leaders. At the end of the meeting, the 70 leaders had a discussion about how they were going to take their city for God. The conversation was full of comments such as, "We men have to do this. We guys need to be more united." As I sat quietly on the side, I watched the faces of the three or so women ministers in the group. Their eyes reflected sadness and I felt a deep sense of sorrow for them. The insensitive statements of the male leaders didn't really matter that much to me. I was flying out of the city the next day. They, however, had to remain, feeling extremely marginalized in their call to minister in that city.

A word of caution to women leaders reading this chapter: It is very important that we not allow a root of bitterness to spring up in our souls over this need for gender reconciliation (see Heb. 12:15). You can always identify a woman minister with unforgiveness towards men in her heart—it affects the purity of her message. Little slurs against men will come out in her delivery. This is not healthy and needs to be dealt with.

There may be women readers who need to stop and make a list of the men who have hurt them and simply forgive. Likewise, some men need to make a list of the women who have hurt them. I am greatly concerned about the number of militant female Christian leaders who are making sweeping statements in anger that say, "It's our time, and we are going to do what God calls us to do no matter who we run over." This will only create a bigger breach between the genders.

Mike and I once went to a church where the pastor so hated women that his Mother's Day message was simply a chance to berate women. He finally got so angry that he jumped up and down on one of the metal chairs until it bent! Needless to say, women never preached in that pulpit. I am grateful to report that he has since changed his opinions.

Getting God's Perspective

Why is gender reconciliation necessary? Because God wants us to see clearly in our walk with Him. Matthew 7:3-5 says:

"And why do you look at the speck in your brother's eye, but do not consider the plank in your own eye? Or how can you say to your brother, 'Let me remove the speck from your eye'; and look, a plank is in your own eye?

Hypocrite! First remove the plank from your own eye, and then you will see clearly to remove the speck from your brother's eye."

One day when I was plane hopping in Dallas, to my surprise, my good friend John Dawson was on the same flight. (John is the head of the International Reconciliation Coalition.) We were able to sit across the aisle from each other and the conversation came around to this issue of the need for gender reconciliation. John has often mentioned that he believes gender-to-gender is one of the pioneer areas in need of reconciliation

I shared with him that some men ministers are actually very positive about releasing women into ministry, but they are simply put off by pushy, loud and controlling women. It should not be a mystery to anyone that men hate pushy women.

(As a side note to this, I have often found it difficult with my prophetic gift not to overwhelm a meeting. Many times I have gone away kicking myself for opening my mouth so much. People with a prophetic gift can be pushy whether they are male or female. You need to strike a balance and discern when it is appropriate to share prophetic insight and when it is best to keep your mouth shut. It is an ongoing growth process.)

John grinned and said, "That's interesting. Do you mind if I share that in my meetings?" He then proceeded to explain that men bond through razzing (a mild to not-so-mild form of teasing). I have to admit that lightbulbs went off in my head at that moment! Memories of meetings where I was the only female leader in a crowd of guys poured through my mind. (You see, sometimes I'm the token woman. I really don't mind. They say, "Well, we'd better get a woman, so let's ask Cindy Jacobs." Actually, I take it as a compliment that they love and trust me.)

The point is that there were times when I thought the men were being hostile to me, but they were actually showing that they liked me! I was "one of the boys," so to speak. John proceeded to explain that women bond through affirming one another, while men bond through razzing.

What revelation! What does this mean? When women get together, one of the first things they will say is something like, "Oh, Susie, I really like your dress. Is it new?" or "What have you done to your hair? It looks great." Whereas a man would say something like, "Where did you get that tie, from the garbage can?" or "Hey, old man, I heard you huffing and puffing up those stairs. Getting old, aren't you?" (I personally believe men have a lot to learn from women about affirmation; but then, I think I just got myself into trouble!)

Lord, Help Us to Understand Each Other

Communication breakdown—that snake's intrusion between men and women—has such far-reaching effects today. Saint Francis of Assisi prayed some wisdom on this centuries-old problem: "Lord, grant that I may seek more to understand than to be understood." One passage of Scripture that is particularly applicable to gender-to-gender relationships came from Paul:

> Fill up and complete my joy by living in harmony and being of the same mind and one in purpose, having the same love, being in full accord and of one harmonious mind and intention. Do nothing from factional motives—through contentiousness, strife, selfishness or for unworthy ends—or prompted by conceit and empty arrogance. Instead, in the true spirit of humility (lowliness of mind) let each regard the others as better than and superior to himself—thinking more highly of one another than you do of yourselves. Let each of you esteem and look upon and be concerned for not [merely] his own interests, but also each for the interests of others (Phil. 2:2-4, *Amp.*).

Some excellent resources are available today to help men and women communicate more effectively. And even though many of these books are geared toward marriage, the principles in most cases can be applied to any gender relationship. One of the best books that I have found is *Communication: Key to Your Marriage* (Regal Books) by Norm Wright. Another good source of help can be obtained from Alfred H. Ells of House of Hope Counseling in Scottsdale, Arizona. Ells has both an audio and video series, which are available to help conflict resolution. The following are his "Nine Proven Steps to Resolving Conflict":

1. Don't *stuff* conflict issues—pray about them—then *talk* about them.
2. One person starts by *openly* and *honestly sharing* with the other (see Jas. 1:19; Prov. 15:32; Eph. 4:15,25).
3. The other person is to *listen, understand and respond* to what is being said (see Prov. 18:13; Phil. 2:1-4; Eph. 4:2; Jas. 5:9).
4. Mutual restating.
5. *Stick to the topic* and look for *areas of agreement*, not just disagreement.
6. If the discussion escalates, *withdraw*, but *not before scheduling* the next discussion.
7. Mutually identify a *biblical plan of action* that will resolve the problem and *restore unity*.
8. Humble yourself and take ownership for how you have *accidentally or purposely offended* the other person *or contributed to the problem*.
9. Control your spirit (see Prov. 16:32; Col. 3:12,13).

I found some excellent advice on relationships in an article entitled "Advice You Can Bank On" by Gary Smalley. Although the focus of the article is marriage, the principles can be used across-the-board for genders:

To divorce-proof your marriage [or relationships], be sure you are making more "deposits" to the well-being of your spouse [or other person on some kind of relational level such as family, church, business, etc.] than "withdrawals."[4]

Smalley goes on to say that a withdrawal is anything sad or negative that drains energy from your mate. It's a harsh word, an unkept promise, being ignored, hurt or controlled.

In essence, to keep good accounts in "relational banking," we need to give more positive input than negative. I once heard that it takes 10 positive comments for every 1 negative remark. That is quite probable. This leads me to a point I want to make about releasing what I call a "spirit of affirmation" in relationships.

Accentuate the Positive, Eliminate the Negative

Many times we in the Body of Christ tend to be extremely negative. Some cultures and generations are much more critical than others. I once mentored a young lady who came from a country where people spoke their minds much more freely than we did

We should "fast" from criticism for three days to see if we are capable of refraining from speaking negatively about others.

in Texas. She was always in hot water for things she would say at church. For instance, she would walk up to a lady and say, "You look really fat in that dress." This kind of brutal honesty would be bad in any case, but in our Southern culture, it was almost unpardonable!

We worked and worked with her until she began to see what a critical person—both personally and culturally—she was. Finally the woman became a much more gracious, loving person.

I sometimes think we should "fast" from criticism for three days to see if we are capable of refraining from speaking negatively about others. I've tried before and was amazed at how many critical thoughts I had to slay in my mind so they didn't come out of my mouth. Actually, I work at this regularly, as do many believers.

Releasing a spirit of affirmation is a very important concept for us to understand, for both males and females. It is often difficult for us to verbalize praise for one another, even though we may feel we want to.

Many people in my parents' generation (World War II Era) had the unspoken philosophy that you didn't praise your children to their faces because it would spoil them. I started comparing notes with others my age and found that their parents would compliment them to their siblings, but didn't pass those positive words along to them personally. As I have mentioned this unspoken philosophy to different members of that generation, they usually look surprised at first, but then begin to change this unhealthy mind-set.

Some cultures are not very good at praising people. Their thinking is, *Why should I praise people just for doing what they should be doing?* However, it's important for everyone to receive words of encouragement and gratitude. The Bible has so much to say about thankfulness. Luis and Doris Bush (who have been powerfully used of God in the A.D.2000 and Beyond Movement) are two of the most grateful people I have ever met. In fact, I heard Pastor Ted Haggard of New Life Church in Colorado Springs comment about them one day. Ted had asked Luis to do something for him and said that Luis turned him down in a most gracious manner, while thanking him two or three times for asking him.

We can all learn much from such positive people. Another person who has greatly impacted my life in this manner is Dick Eastman, president of Every Home for Christ. Dick lives with a spirit of gratitude about him.

Women especially need verbal affirmation. This is why men are told four times in Scripture to love their wives. If women are not affirmed enough, especially by their husbands (for those who are married), they can become quite vulnerable to other men.

This is not to say that men don't need affirmation; of course they do. We all do, but women in general have a greater need for affirmation than do men.

When Gender Bonds Lead to Bondage

In studying why people fall into adultery, I have found that Christian women are commonly hooked through the *spirituality* or *sensitivity* of men rather than through physical attraction. This creates a bond in the emotions or soul realm that often leads to spiritual adultery.

Spiritual adultery is when two people, either of whom are married to another person, form a bond in which they think more about another person at their business, church or school than their own spouse. A good test is to check your thought life. How much of your time do you spend thinking about a person of the opposite gender other than your mate?

Years ago I related quite often on a regular basis to a male leader from another ministry. After a few months, I found myself looking forward to his calls. We had so much in common. Each conversation was spiritually and intellectually stimulating. In the meantime, Mike was busy working at a job that took him away from home from 7:00 A.M. until around 8:00 or 9:00 at night.

Please understand, I never held this man's hand, kissed him or even considered it at that stage. However, the pull was strong—very, very strong. I slipped into a mode in my thought life where he filled a space in my emotions that only my husband was supposed to fill.

Mike and I have always had the kind of relationship where we can be open about anything with one another. One day Mike said, "Honey, this guy calls and asks about you when you're on the road. He wants to know if you have arrived safely and how the ministry is going. I think he cares for you a little too much."

At that moment I had a huge reality check. You see, if I had consciously thought that the relationship I had with this ministry leader had gone that far emotionally, I would have pulled out long before. I was blindsided because of the distance Mike's job and our busy lives had put between us, and I was frankly emotionally needy for conversation.

I then shared with Mike that I felt I was somewhat wrapped up with this other man in my emotions and was shocked to come to that realization. We prayed together and I asked God to forgive me. Mike and I then discussed how we could improve our communication.

What I hadn't understood was that intimate conversation breeds intimacy. When having conversations with those of the opposite sex, it's very important to maintain a brother-to-sister relationship. This is especially important with prayer partners. Prayer partners of the opposite sex should never become confidants greater than your spouse. Nor should you have private, one-on-one meetings with them. Phone conversations are OK, but I would limit them and involve the person's spouse as much as possible.

Afterward, I thought it would be quite easy to break the tie I had formed with the other guy. Wrong! Although I stopped talking to this man on the phone, the pull I felt toward him was tremendous. Some days it was all I could do not to pick up the phone and call him. Thoughts of his voice and how he looked haunted my mind.

Finally, one day I cried out to the Lord for help. The Lord gently spoke to me in my spirit that a major reason I was so emotionally entangled with the other guy was that I had lost my first love for Him. The Lord could have kept me emotionally pure and unentangled if I had spent more intimate time in worship and prayer. Wow, was that a revelation!

The Holy Spirit then instructed me to appropriate the fear of the Lord upon my life concerning that relationship. Then, I closed my eyes and imagined myself in the throne room of heaven and gave God all my needs and empty places and asked Him to fill them up with His presence and love. Immediately, I sensed a sweet presence of the Lord, and His answering touch permeated my soul.

What happened next took me by surprise. Suddenly I had a vision of Mike and me dancing together, and a song that was spe-

cial to me when we first fell in love poured from my memo-
ry..."The First Time Ever I Saw Your Face." At that moment, all the
first-love emotions I had for Mike poured through my heart. I fell
in love with my husband all over again.

Spiritual adultery. It sounds really ugly, doesn't it? Actually, it
can happen in other kinds of relationships too. I have even heard
of a Christian leader to whom God spoke that he was in spiritual adultery with the ministry. Things were definitely out of order
in his home.

Soul Ties: The Good, the Godly and the Ugly

Another similar type of bondage is what I call *soul ties*, which
are bonds that form in our emotions. Although they are very
similar to spiritual adultery, they also affect those who are not
married. A soul tie is a bond formed between two people in
some form of covenantal relationship. An example of this in the
Bible would be David and Jonathan. First Samuel 18:1,3,4 tells us
about David and Jonathan's bond:

> Now when he had finished speaking to Saul, the soul of
> Jonathan was knit to the soul of David, and Jonathan loved
> him as his own soul. Then Jonathan and David made a
> covenant, because he loved him as his own soul. And
> Jonathan took off the robe that was on him and gave it to
> David, with his armor, even to his sword and his bow and
> his belt.

According to *Strong's Concordance*, the word "knit" means
"to tie or bind."[5] David and Jonathan's souls were knit together
in covenant. This, of course, can be a wonderful thing. However,
a dark side can surface that binds you in an unhealthy relationship, such as the one I had with the other ministry leader. These
ties can be quite strong, so it is very important that you not enter
into covenant with other people lightly.

Healthy Soul Ties

Healthy, covenantal relationships can be a tremendous strength and blessing. For example, Mike and I have just such relationships with a number of couples. People such as Peter and Doris Wagner, Ed and Ruth Silvoso, Chuck and Pam Pierce, Bob and Susan Beckett, Dutch and Ceci Sheets, Luis and Doris Bush—the list can go on and on. These people are like family to us. We have wept, prayed and endured great crises together. They are *"until death do us part"* type relationships, unless the Lord should tell us otherwise.

In addition to David and Jonathan, another instance of a soul tie in the Old Testament was between Ruth and Naomi. In fact, we sing about their covenantal relationship at weddings: "Entreat *me not to leave you"* (Ruth 1:16, italics added). Their relationship was quite a healthy one between an older and younger woman.

Unhealthy Soul Ties

As I mentioned, unhealthy, dysfunctional soul ties can be dangerous. Counselors might call them codependent relationships. One way these ties are formed in a negative way is through sex outside of marriage. The Bible tells us that in marriage the two shall become one flesh (see Matt. 19:5).

I have often counseled people who, even though they are married, still have thoughts that plague them of former boyfriends or girlfriends with whom they have had sexual relationships. Plaguing memories might happen even though they've asked forgiveness for their sins. Couples often feel deep guilt because of these betraying thoughts and emotions. You see, they are supernaturally tied to those old relationships. Thank God that His power can break these kinds of ties. Other covenantal relationships can be traced to former church memberships where people made vows to join the church but never asked to be released from those vows to go to a new place.

How do you break a soul tie? Well, God might give you a supernatural plan such as He did in the case of my deep emotional tie with the ministry leader, or you can pray the following prayer with me:

Father God, I now ask forgiveness for the sin of breaking covenant and/or forming a tie outside of marriage. Please forgive me. In Jesus' Name. Amen.

A variation of the prayer might be:

Father God, I recognize that I have an unhealthy soul tie with _____. Please set me free today. Free my thoughts and my emotions. I now break any tie that I have had with this person in Jesus' Name. Amen.

I must admit that being so vulnerable about my personal life is not easy. However, after counseling many, many people who have had a problem with spiritual adultery, I felt the best way to truly set you free was to open my own heart and share my experience with you. I pray that the truth will set you free. It could save your marriage, or the marriage of others around you.

The Healing Balm of Human Words and God's Power

Although these truths I've shared can run on many levels, the deepest woundings in need of the healing balm of the Lord's power in most relationships begin with gender issues. John Dawson says in his book *Healing America's Wounds*:

The wounds inflicted by men and women on each other constitute the fundamental fault line running beneath all other human conflict.[6]

A few years ago I sat in the audience of a Women's Aglow International conference in Orlando, Florida, while John Dawson was speaking. Toward the end of his session, John simply and humbly made a confession and asked forgiveness of the nearly 10,000 women representing about 80 nations. John asked forgiveness as a male for the multitude of hurts afflicted on these women by men.

How can I describe what happened? A torrent of tears poured out of many, many women. Most of them, some victims of incest, physical and/or emotional abuse, had never dreamed they would ever hear such words from a male. As I looked around, I noted women holding each other and weeping. The power of forgiveness was at work on a scale that few in the Body of Christ understand.

A supernatural release of God's love and power came from those simple words. Who could ever have dreamed that John Dawson's words would produce such a profound, deep effect on this gathering of women? John stood in the gap for those wounded women to bring them to a place of release from their emotional prisons.

Several years later, I sat down to read the manuscript of John's book *Healing America's Wounds* and was touched once again by memories of that moment when he put his confession into writing:

Dear female reader, I may not be the guy that hurt you but I look upon your hurt with shame and embarrassment, nonetheless. There have been times when I have had to ask forgiveness of mother, wife, sister and female associate. One woman in particular I would beg for forgiveness if I knew how to contact her. I am no stranger to masculine pride and male appetites. Maybe I haven't committed rape or some other loathsome offense, but it is really just a matter of degree.

Some of you were molested by your father, the ultimate parental betrayal. Some of you experienced other forms of incest and you haven't felt whole since. Most of you know what it's like to be the plaything of a teenage boy, emotionally if not physically, and nearly all of you carry some wound of rejection from a broken teen relationship or a troubled marriage.

You know what it's like to be ogled like a side of beef by someone of greater strength; to be condescended to and joked about in the presence of men. You also know what it is like to be treated tenderly but never taken seriously, your gifts spurned and your advice unheeded.

Please forgive me, forgive us. You were never meant to experience these things. They represent a gross distortion of the part of the character of God that was to be revealed to you through father, brother, husband and male friend. These things broke God's heart along with yours.[7]

Possibly John's confession has deeply touched you. If so, I would encourage you not to move on too quickly with this chapter. Why not stop and forgive any hurt done to you, either by a man or a woman. Women can be controlling and dominating and wound the men they relate to. This gender issue is a two-way street and both genders have deep sin issues that need to be addressed. The power of the Cross is here even through the written Word. You might even call a friend and ask for prayer. James 5:16 says: "Confess your trespasses [faults] to one another, and pray for one another, that you may be healed."

I once spoke at a conference in Brisbane, Australia, with John when he decided there needed to be repentance between the genders. We worked on this concept for three days before true confession and repentance fell. A Baptist pastor called the women in the church forward and asked their forgiveness for not releasing them into ministry.

The response was startling. Some of the most reserved, somewhat quiet women fell on their knees and wept almost to the point of wailing. Their pain levels must have been enormous! Later, as I studied the history of Australia, I found out why the women of this country particularly suffer. The first white women who ever came to the shore of this former penal colony were repeatedly gang raped and suffered other unspeakable outrages.

After our visit, Jim Nightingale, Robyn Pebbles and other Australian leaders went to the very place where this atrocity had occurred, and reenacted the arrival of the women in the costumes of the day through a prophetic act. The difference was, instead of being horribly abused, the women were received with a godly welcome and a proclamation of repentance was read to them. I believe that the ax was laid to the root of female abuse that day through a loving prophetic act.

Viva La Difference!

God has purposes not only for the genders, but also racially *within* the genders. Let me explain. When God created the races, He also placed redemptive purposes or strengths within the females or males of different ethnic groups. As I was pondering this one day, I meditated on the fact that God chose a Jewish woman to raise His Son on the earth.

Although Jewish women are often stereotyped as being controlling, smothering females, this is only a perversion of the wonderful gift of nurture that Jewish women have for their children. For those of you who are mothers or nurturers through teaching Sunday School, I believe there is a great possibility that we can learn from the Jewish culture. (Of course, I realize there are great moms in every culture.)

One of my good friends who is Jewish, Hal Sacks of El Shaddai Ministries in Phoenix, Arizona, suggested that the males of the Jewish race have special gifts of faithfulness to wives and family, as well as perseverance in the face of great adversity.

Other cultures have an emphasis on hospitality, such as the Italians and Arabs. Italian women in general can't stand having people come into their homes without feeding them. Italian men seem to me to have a gift of leadership. I have heard of ex-Mafia men who made the best head ushers or administrators for churches. Why? For one, they understand authority.

Much will be gained from healing of genders and races. And this is really a pioneer area we are just beginning to understand in the Body of Christ. I personally believe, as I alluded to earlier, that we are much further along in the area of racial reconciliation than in gender reconciliation. Conferences where the people in leadership are quite comfortable with dealing with the race issue have not even begun to touch the issue of gender.

While speaking at a large gathering for a women's conference, the Lord gave me an unusual prophecy. It went like this:

If my Body begins to release gender-to-gender reconciliation and healing, there will be a day when divorce in the Church will be abnormal. For I desire healing between the male and female. My people have bought into a lie that there will always be large numbers of people divorcing. I desire to heal those broken through divorce and those who were victims, but I also desire to break down the walls that have caused relational breakdowns and divorce. Only believe, says the Lord, for all things are possible if you will only believe.

The next several chapters took me quite a long time to write as I have read stacks of books and poured through many translations of the Bible. I've also been working with some theologians who have been prayerfully studying the Greek and Hebrew concerning the question of women and the Church. Actually, what I've found is quite exciting, and I am believing that it will cause a great release of women into many areas of ministry in the Church.

Notes

1. Gary Smalley and John Trent, *Why Can't My Spouse Understand What I Say?* (Colorado Springs: Focus on the Family, November 1988), p. 3.
2. H. Norman Wright, *What Men Want* (Ventura, Calif.: Regal Books, 1996), pp. 14-15.
3. Jane Hansen with Marie Powers, *Fashioned for Intimacy* (Ventura, Calif.: Regal Books, 1997), page 36.
4. Gary Smalley, "Advice You Can Bank On," *Focus on the Family*, (Feb. 1997): 3-4.
5. *The New Strong's Exhaustive Concordance of the Bible* (Nashville: Thomas Nelson Publishers, 1984), #7194.
6. John Dawson, *Healing America's Wounds* (Ventura, Calif.: Regal Books, 1994), pp. 246-247.
7. Ibid., pp. 246-247.

The Woman Question

God is calling many women in this hour to follow Him and use all their talents, gifts and abilities. For many of these women, how to do this in a biblical way that pleases the Lord is stressful and confusing.

As I've intimated earlier, I was amazed to read the accounts of women ministers from a century ago whose struggles paralleled those I wrestled with in the early '80s when I finally submitted to the call of God. And amazingly, I still hear these same unresolved issues voiced by young women today.

But Lord, What Is a Woman to Do?

What are the reasons for the trepidations in the hearts of women called by God? Although they are varied, the following are the most frequent:

Women in General

1. What about those difficult passages? (Doesn't the Bible say women should be silent in the Church?)

2. Is God really calling me?
3. What is He calling me to do?
4 How will saying yes impact my family or relationships?
5 What will my pastor and/or church think?
6. Am I having grandiose hallucinations in thinking that God wants me to be a woman minister?
7 How do I find the answers to all these questions?

Married Women

1. How do I relate to my husband as a woman in leadership?
2. What about submission?
3. How will I handle my duties at home if I go into ministry? (Who will wash the clothes and go to the grocery store?)
4 What will my husband think? Will he be mad, supportive or think I've lost my mind? ..Have I lost my mind?

Single Women

1. If I accept the call, will the man I fall in love with be happy about it?
2. How will I financially support myself if I go into ministry on a full-time basis?
3. What will people think of a single woman ministering without a husband to cover her?

These questions can tend to buzz around and around in your brain until you are brought to a point of desperation and tears. Believe me, I've been there and lived it! Many voices bombard a woman trying to sort out her place, not only in ministry, but also in life in general. For the woman sensing a call of God, the decision-making process is greatly compounded by the fear of missing His will for her life, as well as the fear of being labeled unbiblical.

If the woman is raised in a part of the world where women

are repressed or oppressed, or the culture frowns upon women doing any kind of work outside the home, a compound fracture often occurs that can cripple her ability to hear the Voice of God.

Restoring God's Truths About Women

So how do you answer these questions and find God's will for your life? I wish I had all the answers. I can only tell you that I have personally sorted through volumes of resources, met with highly respected theologians and listened intently to the Holy Spirit's leading as I researched this subject.

Major prophetic voices are prophesying all around the world that this is the time to find a way to release women into the ministry.

Of one thing I am certain: *God is calling women today in a greater way than He ever has before.* Major prophetic voices are prophesying all around the world that this is the time to find a way to release women into the ministry. The different prophesies say things such as, "God is raising up a new generation of women ministers in the anointing of an Esther or Deborah." Others announce, "Make way for the women, for God is pouring our His end-time anointing on His handmaidens."

Dr. Bill Hamon often talks about what he calls "restored truth," or the fact that God emphasizes certain truths at different times down through the ages. Luther's ringing affirmation that "the just shall live by faith" was a restored truth which began the Protestant Reformation, but today even Catholics agree that Luther's insight was valid. Part of the role of the prophet is to announce to the Church the truths that God is restoring, or that have been neglected. Such is the case with the role of women in the Church.

One Commission for Two Genders

No issue in the Church today is more controversial than the roles of women in ministry. A good friend of mine who is the editor of a major Christian magazine said, "Just put 'woman' and 'minister' in the same sentence and you won't believe how many angry letters we receive."

One extremely insightful comment came to me from Pastor Gary Kinnaman of Word of Grace Church in Mesa, Arizona. During breakfast with Pastor Kinnaman and his wife, Marilyn, one morning, he brought up Galatians 3:28. "Cindy," he said, "the Body of Christ has come a long way in recognizing that there is neither Jew nor Greek, neither slave nor free, but we haven't begun to understand that there is neither male nor female."

I have written a whole chapter on the gender issue, but I felt I needed to write this chapter as a foundational stone upon which I will build the remainder of the book. Many leaders believe bringing resolution to the conflict over gender roles in ministry could be likened to the "final frontier" for the Church. Some prophets have even gone so far as to say they believe that in five years many of us will feel as though we were in the Dark Ages concerning women in ministry.

Vonette Bright of Campus Crusade made the following statement in an address to both men and women at the Latin American 2000 meeting in Panama, which drew about 4,000 delegates:

There are not two commissions—one for men and one for women.

She went on to describe how Bill (her husband), the founder and president of Campus Crusade for Christ, has always treated her as an equal partner in the ministry. She wanted only to be Mrs. Bill Bright, but he urged her to develop her capacity for leadership. As a result, she has often been a peer with men on committees and was one of three women on the original 50-member Lausanne Committee. Her views have changed through the years as she has traveled the world and seen how often women were pushed down. Her voice rang out so that all could hear her warning clearly:

> I feel that God may judge some men for limiting women and not allowing them to develop their leadership skills.

Vonette shared evidence of how women's perspectives enhance committee decision making by preventing a masculine tunnel vision focused entirely on results, without consideration of how the results will help and hurt people.[1]

The Woman Question: Determining Your Position

As I've studied the so-called "difficult passages" about women, I have concluded that the differing interpretations are rather like that of teaching on end-time eschatology. Throughout the years I've heard excellent sermons on just about every position, all using Scripture, and all sounding as if they had merit! When this kind of impasse happens, we must arrive at a position through personal study, prayer and seeking God's face.

I have had to work through my own cultural and denominational grids in order to discern what is from the Holy Spirit and what is simply my "own stuff." A couple of my personal filters are:

1. How is my cultural or denominational background coloring my beliefs? (I was raised in a Texan and Southern Baptist culture. Regardless of our backgrounds, we all have cultural biases, whether we want to admit them or not.)
2. How is my personal "baggage" causing me to refuse to look at Scripture in a new way? (For example: Am I biased against men or women because of my family of

origin, or because of fears of being in error or disloyal
to my denomination?)

As I have considered my own background, I have had to ask
myself: *Have I ever sincerely studied the opposing view while
prayerfully seeking the Lord to give me His heart and mind on the
matter rather than simply relying upon what I have been given?*

When God began to deal with me about preaching the gospel,
as I wrote in chapter 1, I had to move from the extreme position
that it was unbiblical for women to preach at all, to saying yes to
becoming a woman minister.

Many women throughout history and today are bringing great
blessing to the Body of Christ through their teaching ministries,
missionary work or pastoring of churches. Jesus said, "By their
fruit you will recognize them" (Matt. 7:20, *NIV*). One of the ways
to judge whether God is working through a person's ministry is
by measuring its fruitfulness and blessing. Women in numerous
different ministries teach both men and women and are produc-
ing godly, lasting fruit for the Kingdom. Would that be happening if their work wasn't sanctioned by God? Wouldn't their ministries simply be dead and lifeless if God were not anointing
them? This question alone should compel us to rethink some of
the traditional positions the Church has taken regarding women!

Truth Does Not Change, Beliefs Do

Many times throughout the years, the Lord touched my life
through an experience that went beyond my theological beliefs
and caused me to do a serious searching of the written Word. I
remember when I didn't believe that God spoke to His children
other than through Scripture (I had been taught that the Bible
was a "closed canon" and that God did not speak anymore as He
did in Bible days). Now, my understanding has so changed that
I've written a whole book about how to hear the Voice of God.

My pastor father, who has been with the Lord since 1973,
helped me immensely in my spiritual journey. I once asked him,

"Dad, what would you do if you found that what you believed wasn't the truth?"

He looked me straight in the eye and replied, "Honey, I'd go where the truth was taught." His answer was very freeing to me. It has allowed me to examine and judge the doctrine I may be hearing from the pulpit in light of Scripture. Dad always wanted me to have a *personal* rather than a secondhand relationship with Jesus Christ, and *personal* rather than secondhand understanding of truth.

Why have I explained all of this? For this reason: If you are not willing to reexamine your belief system and allow the Holy Spirit to expose any motives that may be causing you to be unfairly biased, this chapter will probably be a waste of your time. Please realize that I don't want to thrust my conclusions upon you, as I am aware that I can be influenced by my own biases. You may read my conclusions and come away with your same belief system. However, I would like us together to ask the Lord to help *us come to His mind on this.* Before we continue, please pray the following prayer with me:

Dear Father,
Give me eyes to see and ears to hear the truths that may be different from my own thinking. I ask You by the power of Your Holy Spirit within me to help me be open to new truth. Show me where my culture and/or religious biases may be affecting my willingness to be open to what the Spirit is saying to the Church today.
In Jesus' Name. Amen.

We are about to grapple with the two most controversial issues surrounding women in ministry: (1) whether a woman should teach men in the Church and (2) whether in teaching men, women can still be in submission. These are *extremely* sensitive areas to address. In fact, many of my friends have grinned and said, "Cindy, I'm so glad God hasn't asked me to deal with the woman question." I've prayed that the Lord will help me present the different sides of the issues so each of you can pray individually and find the answers that bring peace within your own heart.

Formulating Your Bias for Interpretation

While researching this subject, I was given a paper entitled *Gender and Leadership* by Robert Clinton of Fuller Theological Seminary. This paper reveals Robert Clinton's own journey concerning women in leadership, one that led to his paradigm shift (a change from one model of explanation to another) concerning women in ministry. His shift came partly as a result of personally receiving a blessing from the Lord from the ministry of women leaders.

In this insightful paper, Clinton states that he has some axioms (i.e., established rules or principles of self-evident truth) he has learned throughout his years of Bible study. These axioms, he points out, form part of his framework for doing biblical interpretation. Let's consider them together:

1. Interpret unclear passages in light of clear ones—not the other way around.
2. Major doctrines should flow from what is clear.
3. Controversial passages lacking consensus from godly people of different persuasions usually mean that the passages are not clear enough to resolve with certainty. Therefore we must be tolerant on different views on those passages.
4. Cultures play a strong part in how an interpreter views some of these difficult passages—more than most think. Vested interests in maintaining dominant male roles in society influence much more than we realize.
5. Always examine a passage in its full context. It is part of a larger whole and must be interpreted in light of what it contributes to that whole.
6. Recognize transference cautions. That is the tendency

to project our own present understandings in interpreting something from the past.[2]

Adding to Clinton's starting points, several facts are clear to
me from Scripture:

- God used women to further the spread of the gospel.
- Women were used by God in leadership positions in
  both the Old and New Testaments.
- God chose women as leaders in the Old Testament,
  which put them in roles that affected the whole nation
  of Israel (such as Deborah, Esther and Miriam). In the
  New Testament, we could liken this choosing to that of
  leadership in the Church if we think of ourselves as
  "Jews inwardly" (see Rom. 2:28,29); "the Israel of God"
  (see Gal. 6:1-16); and a "chosen," "royal" and "holy
  nation" (see 1 Pet. 2:9-16, cf. Deut 7:6). There is never
  any indication in Scripture to say that using women in
  leadership will "pass away" in New Testament times.
- Both the Old and New Testaments tell us that God is
  going to "pour His Spirit out upon His handmaidens as
  well as the servants" (see Joel 2:28,29; Acts 2:17).

Deborah and Esther:
Called to Save Their Nations

Now, I realize that a segment of the Body of Christ will disagree
with me; however, an even larger segment will agree. Using
Deborah and Esther as examples, these two women leaders had
high governmental positions that affected the entire nation (by
God's choosing, of course, but would we want it any other way?).
Deborah *ruled* the nation as the senior judge of all the judges
(see Judges 4:4,5; compare with Deut. 16:18-20; 17:9-12). She was
the top authority. She instructed, and prophesied, and even commanded Barak to go to war (see Judges 4:6,7). There is even a hint
of rebuke when she said the honor would be given to a woman,

not to Barak for the victory (see v. 9). Some people today would accuse Deborah, as a woman, of being totally out of her place by instructing a man. Perhaps she would even be branded as a Jezebel!

Esther called a whole nation to a Solemn Assembly to fast and pray to save God's people (see Esther 4:16). I have heard people say that this is "only one exception." However, calling Esther's action "only one exception" reflects a bias against women. Why not say that it was "precedent setting"?

Aren't we all "exceptions" in one way or another by the grace and calling of God? I certainly believe that I am, because I see my own weaknesses and frailties, oftentimes like neon signs flashing before my eyes.

A Closer Look at the
Roles of Women in Scripture

Dr. A. J. Gordon was a Baptist pastor in the 1880s and '90s who advocated women in ministry. He was a historical mentor for Robert Clinton. I was fascinated to study his article on "The Ministry of Women" written in December of 1894. It is so relevant to today that I was amazed it could have been written more than 100 years ago! One of the reasons this paper is so important (as pointed out by Clinton) is that Gordon's arguments cannot be disqualified because he was biased by the Women's Liberation Movement. On the contrary, Gordon's arguments are firmly grounded in Scripture and guided by the same interpretational principles that traditionalists use. I will quote from Gordon later in the chapter and am including his entire article in the appendix.

Let's take a look at ways women were used of God in Scripture. I am aware that even in this area disputes may arise, so what is clear to me may not be clear to you. (Remember that prayer we prayed earlier? Even if something makes you angry, read to the end and then prayerfully seek God about it.)

We discussed the view Jesus had of women in general and how He elevated the societal status of women. Now we will examine the ministry of women in the New Testament and the Early Church to help lay a foundation for moving from those passages which are clear (or more clear) to those passages that are unclear.

Deacons

According to Romans 16:1, Phoebe was classified as a "servant" or "minister"[3] of the church at Cenchrea. The word used to describe her, *diakonos*, is a masculine form. I found a number of different explanations regarding her office. Dr. A. J. Gordon's paper "The Ministry of Women" was particularly enlightening to me:

> The same word, *diakonos*, here translated *servant*, is rendered *minister* when applied to Paul and Apollos (1 Cor. 3:5), and deacon when used of other male officers of the Church (1 Tim. 3:10,12-13). Why discriminate against Phoebe simply because she is a woman? The word *servant* is correct for the general unofficial use of the term, as in Matthew 22:10; but if Phoebe were really a functionary of the Church, as we have a right to conclude, let her have the honor to which she is entitled. If "Phoebe, a minister of the church at Cenchrea" sounds too bold, let the word be transliterated and read, "Phoebe, a deacon," a deacon, too, without the insipid termination "ess" of which there is no more need than that we should say teacheress or doctoress....It is wonderful how much there is in a name! "Phoebe, a servant" might suggest to an ordinary reader nothing more than the modern church drudge who prepares sandwiches and coffee for an ecclesiastical sociable. To Canon Garret, with his genial and enlightened view of women's position in apostolic times, "Phoebe, a deacon" suggests a useful co-laborer of Paul "traveling about on missionary and other labors of love."

Of interest is the fact that the ending of the word *diakonos* when it describes Phoebe's office is masculine. Yet, Phoebe is clearly a female. It seems that there are occasions in Scripture where the "offices" in the Church are given male endings, even though the person filling the office may be a woman![4]

Charles Trombley provides some insight concerning what Romans 16:2 says about Phoebe:

Paul uses an interesting word concerning Phoebe in Romans 16:2. The *King James Version* used the word *succorer* in this verse, but the word *prostatis* isn't translated that way anywhere else in the Greek Scriptures. It was a common, classical word meaning "patroness or protectorship, a woman set over others." It's the feminine form of the masculine noun *prostates*, which means "defender" or "guardian" when it refers to men. In 1 Timothy 3:4,5,12 and 5:17, the verb *peritoneum* is used of the qualifications for bishops and deacons when Paul charged the men to "rule" well their households, which included caring for their needs. Whatever it means for men, it must mean the same for women. Whatever these bishops and deacons did for their households, Phoebe did for the Church and Paul. The positions were identical.

If we refuse to admit that Phoebe "ruled" or "led" or was a "defender" or "guardian," then we must reduce the male deacons to whatever level Phoebe was ministering. If Phoebe just *succored*, then that's all the male deacons did. It's quite inconsistent to translate the word as "ruler" when it refers to men and *succorer* when it refers to women.[5]

Another place where the role of women as deacons has apparently been minimized is in the English translation of *gunaikas* ("women" or "wives") in 1 Timothy 3:11. Paul has just outlined the requirements for bishops and deacons (see vv. 8-10). Many translators have assumed that "likewise, *gunaikas*" in 1 Timothy 3:11 could only refer to the "wives" of the male leaders; to support their translation, they added the word "their" to the text. However, in 1 Timothy 3:11 there is no definite article in the sentence construction, nor are the possessives used. Furthermore, identical language is used for both the deacons and the women who "likewise" must be "grave" (see vv. 8,11). Therefore the translation "their wives" must be rejected. Paul is clearly referring to women in important leadership positions.

Clearly Paul held Phoebe and other female fellow-workers in high esteem. In fact, of the 29 people Paul greets in Romans 16, 10 are women (if we count Junia, which I do).[6]

Another source for the importance of women in leadership in the Early Church is from the testimony of a governor of Bithynia, called "Pliny the Younger" (A.D. 52 to A.D. 113). He also indicates that women were deaconesses in the Early Church. In a letter seeking advice regarding how to handle the large numbers of all classes and genders turning to Christ, Pliny states:

> I thought it the more necessary to inquire into the real truth of the matter by subjecting to torture two female slaves who were called *deacons* (italics mine), but I found nothing more than a perverse superstition which went beyond all bounds.[7]

Even though women were recognized as leaders in the first-century church, during the second century, women's positions in leadership began to fade. An early third-century writing called the *Didascalia* (teaching) said that persons being baptized came up from the water and were received and taught by the women deacons, so such women were still teaching during the third century. However, by the time the Council of Orange convened in 441, the office of women deacons had been almost completely abolished. The Council directed, "Let no one proceed to the ordination of deaconesses anymore."[8]

I often wonder about the adding of the *"ess"* —the ministry terms that we use to describe a woman's function in the Church. Often it applies a standing less than that of a man who is doing the same job. In fact, historically, when the change was made from deacon to deaconess, that is exactly what happened.

Apostles

For some, the thought of a woman ever being among the highest levels of authority in the Church is simply too big of a stretch. However, let's take a look at a woman whom many believe was an apostle and then see if, experientially, we can validate that God is anointing women to do the work of apostles in more recent times.

I like the statement David Cannistraci begins with in the section of his book, *The Gift of Apostle* (Regal Books), entitled "Can Women Be Apostles?" He says:

> This is a truly complicated question, but as Gilbert Bilezikian has pointed out, "Every generation of Christians needs to examine its beliefs and practices under the microscope of Scripture to identify and purge away those worldly accretions that easily beset us, and to protect jealously the freedom dearly acquired for us—both men and women—on the hill of Calvary."[9]

There are times when we have to look around and say, "If God is using women in such powerful ways in the Church, maybe we need to reevaluate our thinking, *for they are either tools of the devil, or blessed by God* to fulfill a place that I didn't think they could in my paradigm."

I discussed this point with a theologian friend who stressed the point that people sometimes have imperfect motives, but God blesses their efforts anyway such as when Moses struck the rock (see Num. 20:10-16). However, just because a woman feels called to minister, does that mean she is doing so out of impure motives? The ones I know certainly do not. They feel a genuine call to preach, and display the character and nature of Christ in their motivation.

In the Romans 16:7 passage we looked at earlier, Paul mentions Junia and Andronicus as being "of note among the apostles."

There is much controversy as to whether the name should be the female "Junias."[10] The reasons I believe Junia was a woman are (1) Andronicus and Junia were likely a married couple. The context suggests they were married: Junia's name is paired with a masculine name and the only other pairing of a female and a male in Romans 16 is Priscilla and Aquila, whom we know to have been married (see Acts 18:26), and (2) John Chrysostom, an Early Church father, praises Junia, the woman apostle.

Trombley summarizes:

> John Chrysostom (337-407), bishop of Constantinople, wasn't partial to women. He said some negative things about women but spoke positively about Junia. "Oh, how great is the devotion of this woman that she should be counted worthy of the appellation of apostle!" Nor was he the only church father to believe Junia was a woman. Origen of Alexandria (c. 185-253) said the name was a variant of Julia (see Rom. 16:15), as does *Thayer's Lexicon*. Leonard Swidler cited Jerome (342-420), Hatto of Vercelli (924-961), Theophylack (1050-1108), and Peter Abelard (1079-1142) as believing Junia to be a woman.
>
> Dr. Swidler stated, "To the best of my knowledge, no commentator on the text until Aegidus of Rome (1245-1316) took the name to be masculine. Apparently the idea that Junia was a man's name is a relatively modern concept but the bulk of the best evidence available is that Junia was indeed a woman, and an outstanding apostle."[11]

This passage is fascinating indeed. It includes three prominent Early Church fathers, *Thayer's Lexicon* and three medieval theologian Christian writers who all agree with the premise that Junia was a woman. Surely we've accepted other stances in Scripture to be true with much less supportive historical evidence than this one. Then why the struggle? For one, because the office of apostle is believed to be the highest spiritual authority of those listed in Ephesians 4:11. If Junia was a woman, then the whole theology barring women from ministering in leadership roles in the Church would have to be changed. The paradigm shift would be massive.

Incidentally, some of my friends and I have a saying about our spiritual journey in the last few years. It goes like this: We have made so many fast paradigm shifts that it has stripped our gears five times! Probably our brakes too! However, we are quite recovered as of this writing. Who knows how many more paradigm shifts we might make if the Lord tarries?

So we see the question about whether Junia was a woman, although vigorously debated, is part and parcel of the bigger controversy in the Body of Christ about the roles of women in the Church and home. The Church is in a major transitional time in our thinking on this subject, and we are all in process and doing the best we can before God to state our beliefs.

I discovered a fascinating tidbit of information in a note from the book *Woman in the Bible* (InterVarsity) by Mary J. Evans concerning the English translation of Chrysostom's *The Homilies of Saint John Chrysostom*, Volume 11, page 555:

It is interesting that in spite of Chrysostom's clear statement, the editors of the English translation of his works felt bound to add a footnote pointing out that Chrysostom must have been wrong on one of the two points for 'it is out of the question' for a woman to have been an apostle!

The Body of Christ is fortunate to have leaders such as Dr. Bill Hamon and Dr. C. Peter Wagner who believe that couples working together as "apostolic teams" are certainly a wave of the future and an excellent scenario for married couples.

Dr. Hamon has the following to say about what he foresees as a restoration coming to the Body of Christ with apostle-prophet teams:

Immediately after the birth of the Prophetic Movement a multitude of prophets began prophesying in the nations.

As a result the Berlin wall was torn down, the Iron Curtain ripped apart and the mountain of Communism was leveled. Many dictators throughout the world were dethroned. While God was shaking the dictatorial "one man rule" in the nations, He was also working in the Church. The day of the "one great man" ministry started coming to an end. God began to emphasize the *"team ministry"* (italics mine) principle as never before since the first-century church. The apostle-prophet teams were restored. The husband and wife teams were activated so that the wife, instead of just serving as a helper to her husband, became a co-laboring minister. We at Christian International Network of Churches ordain the husband and wife equally. If one of the mates does not know his or her calling, then we believe for it to be made known in the prophetic presbytery that we give with each ordination. *This is the day and hour when God is bringing forth His women to be the ministers that God ordained them to be. Husband and wife teams are one of the highest orders of team ministries.* The activation of "team ministry" is definitely a work of the Holy Spirit for this day and hour (see Rom. 12:3-8; 1 Cor. 12:12-31; Lev. 26:8; Deut. 32:30).[12]

This is certainly the case among some of the Latin American churches I have observed. Vision de Futuro in Argentina, one of the largest churches in the world with a membership of about 90,000, has a practice of placing couples in the ministry as a team. Reverend Omar and Marfa Cabrerra, who lead the church, are an excellent example to their young leaders.

Elders

As mentioned in an earlier chapter, many have felt Jesus would have chosen a woman in the original Twelve if He wanted to establish that women could be apostles. Trombley's answer to this objection is that:

Christ ministered primarily to the house of Israel (see Matt. 15:24). He preached to Jews who were governed by both civil and religious matters.[13]

Although the original Twelve were male, we need to keep in mind that Jesus took the radical step of having female disciples. And even if the early women disciples were not explicitly named as "apostles" or "elders," this does not mean they were not functioning as teachers or exercising authority in the Early Church. Many apostles and elders in the Early Church were unnamed.

Traditionalists may argue that "elders" were always male. However, from the book of Hebrews, we see that at least sometimes the term "elders" could also include women. In Hebrews 11:2 we read, "This [faith] is what the ancients were commended for" (*NIV*). The word "ancients" comes from the Greek word *presbuteroi* (plural of *presbuteros*) and has traditionally been translated into English by the terms "elders" (*KJV, NKJV, ASV*) and "men of old" (*RSV, NASB*). Yet among these "elders" mentioned, we find Sarah (see vv. 11,13); Moses' mother (see v. 23); the women among "the people" who crossed the Red Sea (see v. 29); Rahab (see v. 31); possibly Deborah, one of the judges who "administered justice" (see v. 33); possibly Esther "whose weakness was turned to strength" and saved her people from destruction by foreign armies (see v. 34); the woman of Zaraphath (see 1 Kings 17:17-24) and the Shunnamite woman (see 2 Kings 4:8-36) who received back their dead, raised to life again (see Heb. 11:35).

In addition, the phrase "others were tortured and refused to be released, so that they might gain a better resurrection" in Hebrews 11:35 strongly reminds us of the mother of the seven brothers martyred by Antiochus Ephiphanes during the Maccabean rebellion (see 2 Maccabees 7). This woman urged her sons to be courageous in light of the resurrection to come, and ultimately was martyred herself.

These "elders" are the same ones who surround us as "the great cloud of witnesses" in Hebrews 12:1. Clearly, in biblical usage the term "elders" does not always exclude women.

In fact, because the Old Testament was the Bible for the New Testament Church and thus, precedent setting, it certainly would not have seemed unusual for women to hold responsible positions of eldership such as did Moses' mother, Rahab and Deborah.

We also find the feminine form of *"presbyter"* or "elder" *presbytera* occurs in nonbiblical early Christian literature. The word is often translated simply as "old woman"; however, at times the term refers to women who were part of the clergy. For example, the Cappadocian father, Basil the Great (A.D. 330-379), apparently uses *presbytera* for a woman who is head of a religious community. Also applied to women is the term *presbutis*, "older woman" or "eldress." This usage of the word for "eldress" appears in Titus 2:3 and is often translated here as "older woman."

A troublesome passage that often limits women's ministry in the Church is 1 Timothy 3:1: "This is a faithful saying: 'If a man desires the position of a bishop, he desires a good work.'"

At first reading, it would seem clear that a woman cannot be a bishop because the text reads, "If a man...." In fact, Christian tradition has leaned heavily in the direction of male bishops throughout history. However, the word translated "man" is actually the Greek word *tis*, a gender neutral pronoun meaning "anybody" or "anyone." Thus this verse should read: "If anybody or anyone desires the office of a bishop...." This seems to leave room for a bishop being a woman.

Archaeological evidence also supports the position of women in leadership in the Early Church. According to Dr. Catherine Kroeger, fresco work from the Priscilla catacomb in Rome shows one of many *"orant"* (praying) women depicted in the catacombs. Kroeger points out that this is an amazingly authoritative stance, such as that of a bishop. The shepherds on either side may represent pastors, in which case the woman may be in the role of bishop, blessing pastors in her charge.[14]

Modern-Day Apostles
In order to apply the title of apostleship to modern-day leaders, it is important to examine the criteria for apostleship. Cannistraci gives the following seven demands that define apostles:

1. Apostles are required to have a definite and personal call from God in their lives.
2. Apostles are required to have a special intimacy and acquaintance with Jesus Christ. In 1 Corinthians 9:1, Paul qualifies himself as an apostle by citing his contact with Christ: "Am I not an apostle? Am I not free? Have I not seen Jesus Christ our Lord?" Clearly, personal acquaintance with Christ was considered a requirement for apostleship among the Twelve (see Acts 1:21-25). Although today's apostles are of a different category, we can be sure that intimate knowledge of Christ is vital for fruitfulness in apostolic ministry (see John 15:4,5).
3. Apostles are elders and must meet the biblical qualifications of an elder.
4. Apostles are ministers and must function as such. The work of a valid apostle will always be in the areas of equipping, training and leading others into mature ministry.
5. Apostles are required to have the recognition and confirmation of peers.
6. Apostles must have specific fruit to which they can point to demonstrate their apostleship.
7. Apostles must maintain their apostleship by complete submission to Christ, or they will fall from apostleship and lose their office as did Judas (see Acts 1:25).

Cannistraci ends this section by giving the following definition of apostleship:

An apostle is a person who is called and sent by Christ and has the spiritual authority, character, gifts and abilities to successfully reach and establish people in Kingdom truth and order, especially by founding and overseeing local churches.[15]

This definition is broader than what probably would have been given by a leader from Cannistraci's church background a number of years ago. He is a "New Apostolic" leader, to use a term coined by Peter Wagner. The New Apostolic Movement consists of churches that are not affiliated with a certain denomination, but rather have relational covenants with other churches of like beliefs. My own church, Springs Harvest Fellowship, is a "New Apostolic" church, and we are a part of a federation of churches that are autonomous but relate together in yearly apostolic meetings.

We are still learning about the role of the apostle in the Church today. In general, the New Apostolic churches would be in consensus that someone who holds the office of "bishop" in the Church is also an apostle. Not all apostles, however, are bishops. Bishops are usually thought of as people who have more than one church under their leadership.

Today, apostles are beginning to be recognized in such areas as prayer, worship networks, evangelism, etc., which certainly interface with the local churches. But their work affects a much broader base than, for instance, one particular denomination.

Women of Uncommon Callings

Let's consider some women who have greatly affected the face of the Church.

Aimee Semple McPherson

In the light of this information, I propose that Aimee Semple McPherson certainly was an apostle, being founder of the Foursquare denomination. Although traditionalists may have a problem with her because she had no apparent male covering, history records that God did a work through her that affected her generation and generations following. The doctrine of the Foursquare Gospel which she proposed is followed by thousands of people around the world.

Catherine Booth

I also believe that Catherine Booth (1829-1890) was an apostle, who, along with her husband, founded the Salvation Army. Indeed, when her husband had to stop his work due to a complete break-down in health, Catherine took charge of the entire ministry.

As one biographer notes: "It was she, and not William Booth, who laid the first stone of the Salvation Army." Though Salvation Army letterheads and news stories today declare "William Booth, Founder," the title of her biography is more accurate: *Catherine Booth, the Mother of the Salvation Army*. Before her death in 1890, she had preached to millions.[16]

Henrietta Mears

There are other women who would not have thought themselves to be apostles to the Church, but who, to my thinking, fit the definition given earlier of an apostle. One of these is Henrietta Mears (1890-1963). Miss Mears is the founder of Gospel Light Publications, the company that owns Regal Books (who, by the way, is the publisher of this book).

Some of Miss Mears's most outstanding accomplishments occurred during the time she was the director of religious education at First Presbyterian Church in Hollywood, California. Within three years of her arrival, she had built a dynamic Christian education program with a Sunday School enrollment rising from a fairly respectable Presbyterian 450 to an absolutely awesome 4,500; it was the talk of the West Coast. In the class she taught for college students, weekly attendance ran to 500 men and women who were devoted to "Teacher," as she was called. Her enthusiasm for the Lord Jesus Christ was contagious.[17]

Miss Mears had a profound impact on Billy Graham when he was a speaker at the Forest Home camp she founded. At the time Reverend Graham was a 30-year-old college president who was having deep personal struggles with the inerrancy of Scripture (i.e., that the Bible was inerrant and written under the inspiration of the Holy Spirit). Miss Mears talked personally with Billy and prayed with him until he experienced a tremendous break-through in faith concerning God's Word.

Graham gives insight into her quick wit, humor and transparency in his book *Just As I Am*. He shares how he invited her on a moment's notice to a very fancy dinner held in his honor in England. She accepted. When he went to greet her along with his wife, Ruth, they both commented on how lovely she looked. In his own words, "She smiled and pulled us closer. 'I didn't have a formal thing in my suitcase and had no time to shop,' she whispered. 'I'm wearing my nightgown!'"[18] Miss Mears was not at all religious. She was as real as can be and displayed a genuineness in her personhood that few have reached.

I wrote in my book *The Voice of God* how Henrietta Mears's biography has affected my own life. She led both Dr. Bill Bright and his gifted wife, Vonnette, to the Lord. Bill and Vonette lived with Miss Mears for 10 years of their married life. Bill Bright says, "Her life was one of spiritual multiplication."

Former chaplain of the United States Senate, Dr. Richard C. Halverson, had the following to say about this great saint of God:

> In my mind, Henrietta Mears was the giant of Christian education, not only in her generation, but in this century. She was an extraordinary combination of intellect, devotion and spirituality; an administrative genius, a motivator, an encourager and a leader.
>
> I thought of Henrietta Mears as *a female Apostle Paul* (italics mine); in fact, I often referred to her as the "Epistle Paul." There is simply no way to exaggerate her effectiveness as a teacher, communicator and inspirer.
>
> In a very real sense Miss Mears is responsible for my family. Not only had she been counselor to Doris and me through the years, but she introduced us in her office. I understand that she predicted the introduction would turn out the way it did. There is not an area of my life that her influence has not touched with great significance. Philippians 1:3 expresses my sentiments perfectly concerning her.[19]

While I believe Miss Mears to have fulfilled the work of an apostle, she also exemplifies that of a teacher, so her name could be placed in the next section as well. I realize she would have been more comfortable there because so many of her beloved students addressed her as "Teacher."

Teachers

As far as I could find, the most powerful example of someone teaching another person the way of Christ is that of Priscilla. Although the Bible speaks of the office of a teacher in Ephesians 4:11, I could not find a better model for someone who could be called a teacher than Priscilla. We are told that Priscilla, along with her husband Aquila, taught the great orator Apollos (see Acts 18:26), and in spite of 1 Timothy 2:12, there is no indication that this was in any way seen as wrong either by Luke the author of Acts or by Paul.

Some fascinating issues swirl around Priscilla and Aquila. When Paul first met this couple, Luke recorded the meeting by stating Aquila's (the husband's) name first, and then Priscilla's (the woman)(see v. 2). However, by Acts 18:18, Paul reversed the order when recording their names. Why? It was customary in Paul's days to give the name of the one who was the more prominent of the two first.

Ben Witherington III says:

We can now discuss Priscilla's part in these matters. It is stated that both she and Aquila instructed Apollos and that her name is mentioned first, so that if anyone is indicated by Luke as the primary instructor, it is Priscilla. By "more accurately" (see Luke 18:26, *RSV*), Luke depicts Priscilla as expanding the matter further than basic Christian teaching, or at least in a way that involves the whole panorama of Christian teaching, so that the piece of the part would be seen in relation to the whole. Apollos is depicted as already having a correct framework and knowledge about "the things concerning Jesus." Further, Apollos is not just any convert to the faith, but a man "well versed in Scripture" and this presupposes that Luke wants his audience to see that Priscilla and Aquila were also knowledgeable enough about Scripture to teach Apollos in such a fashion that he would accept it from both a woman and a man.[20]

Chrysostom said of Paul's listing Priscilla first, "He did not do so without reason: the wife must have had, I think, greater piety than her husband. This is not simply conjecture; its confirmation is evident in the Acts."[21]

Note that the order of translation from the Greek is *reversed* in the *King James Version* as well as the *New King James Version*. According to Dr. Bruce Metzger, eminent scholar of New Testament textual criticism, this is only one of the places where there is a blatant tampering with the original text by scribes with a bias against women.[22] Both the *New International Version* and *New American Standard Bible* show the correct translation.

Another place where a clear mistranslating concerning women appears, because of a cultural bias, is in Psalm 68:11. The *New American Standard* version says, "The Lord gives the command; the *women* who proclaim the good tidings are a great host" (italics added).

Both the *King James Version* and the *New King James Version* leave out the word "women" altogether: "The Lord gave the word; great was the company of those who proclaimed it" (*NKJV*).

Why was this done? Any good translator can tell that the Hebrew is referring to women by using the feminine gender. If one puts the translation of the *King James Version* in its A.D. 1611 context, it isn't too hard to figure out. The translators simply could not believe that women could publish the good news, so they "doctored" the passage according to their paradigm or worldview.

Bushnell suggests another way of looking at 1 Corinthians 9 in *God's Word to Women*. She brings up the premise that Paul is addressing critics who not only disputed his right to be called an apostle (see 1 Cor. 9:1), but also criticized him because he traveled in the company of women (see v. 5). He answers their question in this manner: "Have we not power to lead about a sister, a wife, as well as other apostles, and as the brethren of the Lord, and Cephas?" (*KJV*).

It's interesting that the *King James Version* leaves in the word, "sister." The *New King James Version* and the *New American Standard* simply say, "believing wives." Bushnell believes that the "sister" in this passage was Priscilla, who was traveling with him along with her husband, Aquila. If you recall the worldview the Jews had on women, you can imagine how distasteful it would have been to the Judaizers (those who wanted to put Christianity back under the legal system of the law) for a woman disciple to be in Paul's company.

Who in modern times is fulfilling the role of a Priscilla? I personally feel that one of the best examples is Kay Arthur. Her *Precepts* course is used in 110 nations and 22 languages throughout the world. She has even edited a Bible called *The International Inductive Study Bible* (Harvest House Publishers).

Pastors

As I began to meditate on women pastors, it occurred to me that it might be interesting to find out who the *men* pastors were in the Bible.[23] I decided to call a few friends who have seminary degrees and pose the question to them. After I asked the question the first time, silence fell for a moment on the other end of the line and then, "Well, I don't know. Was Timothy a pastor?" Actually, no. He was an apostolic legate. Timothy represented the apostle Paul and did apostolic work himself, appointing elders and establishing church order in Ephesus and Asia Minor.[24]

It's amazing how many people are pastors but, for the most part, have just learned about pastoring from mentors or seminaries without thinking about what was probably going on during New Testament days.

This really started me thinking. I pondered, *Who were the New Testament pastors? How did they function? How were they structured?* Although this book is not meant to go into these issues in depth, it is pertinent to our study to think about them.

The churches during this time period were "house churches."

The basic social and economic unit at the time of the Early Church was the *oikos* (Greek for "house" or "household"), or extended family, which consisted of husband, wife, children of that marriage, and might also include grandparents or other relatives, in-laws, apprentices and/or artisans connected to the economic basis of the house, and servants and their wives, children or relatives. Obviously the *oikos* was very different from what we know as a "nuclear family" of husband, wife and children from that marriage. The lives of the people in an *oikos* were connected in many ways; they saw each other every day and knew each other very well. The Early Church spread like wildfire "from house to house" (see Acts 2:46; 5:42; 20:20). If the head of the household believed and got baptized, often so would the whole household, as in the cases of Cornelius (see Acts 10:2,25-27,44-48), the Philippian jailer (see Acts 16:31-34) and Crispus, the synagogue ruler (see Acts 18:8). Sometimes, as appears to be the case with Lydia, the head of the household was a woman (see Acts 16:13-15).

Dr. C. Peter Wagner says the following in his commentary on Acts:

> It is easy for us in the twentieth century to forget that no such things as church buildings, as we now know them, existed in the Early Church. Bradley Blues says, "The gathering of Christian believers in private homes (or homes renovated for the purpose of Christian gatherings) continued to be the norm until the early decades of the fourth century when Constantine began erecting the first Christian basilicas."[25]

Mary J. Evans has the following to say about New Testament pastors in her book *Woman in the Bible*:

> In dealing with the subject of pastors in the Bible, it is important to note that we have, in fact, very little information about the precise relation between "office" and "function" in the New Testament Church. The Pastoral

Epistles make explicit what is apparent elsewhere, that there were those who were appointed to a specific office. However, while we learn much about the characteristics required in those who aspire to office, we are told very little about the particular responsibilities and tasks assigned to the holder of any individual office. For example, some, but not all, elders labored in preaching and teaching (1 Tim. 5:17) and certainly not all preachers and teachers were elders (cf. Col. 3:16; 1 Cor. 14:26, etc.). There is no clear distinction made between regulated offices and unregulated ministry by those with no official position in the New Testament.[26]

Dr. Gary Greig, associate professor of Old Testament at Regent University School of Divinity, makes this interesting point: "As far as I can see from studying and praying through the evidence in the New Testament and from the popular and scholarship books and articles on the topic, the Early Church 'elders' were like senior pastors or bishops, and the 'deacons' like associate ministers."[27]

Therefore, among others, male "deacon" ministers would have been Stephen, Philip, Nicanor, Timon, Parmenus and Nicolas (see Acts 6:5) and the most evident female "deacon" ministers would have been Phoebe and possibly Priscilla and Lydia.[28]

The "caregivers" of the Church, or what we would think of as being pastoral, could very well have been the presiding elders of the local house churches. No men or women are actually referred to as pastors, per se, in the Bible; however, they functioned as shepherds or pastors.[29]

The strong possibility that the "elect lady" of 2 John 1 is, in fact, the gatekeeper of orthodoxy for a house church, means that we cannot be absolute in our assumption that these kinds of leadership positions were never held by women. That John, the "elder," is writing to the "elect lady" who led a house church is supported by the fact that John did not write to the "elders" or other male leaders of the house church, but to her. As the person responsible

for orthodoxy in her house church, she would have been responsible for at least some teaching and exercising of authority in the
Church. It is unlikely that the "elect lady" was merely a lady with
a big family, because "children" is a common New Testament term
for "disciple," especially in John's writings.[30]

Peter Wagner has some excellent points about the gift of pastor in his book *Your Spiritual Gifts Can Help Your Church Grow*
(Regal Books). Although he is not arguing pro or con about the
ordination of women in the book, he believes the gift of pastor
is given to both men and women. He says:

> I believe that the gift of pastor is given to both men and
> women. My lifetime observation of churches in many cul-
> tures leads me to believe that this is usually another of the
> gender-biased gifts. More women, I think, have the gift of
> pastor than men do. Take as a starter, Yonggi Cho's Yoido
> Full Gospel Church in Seoul, Korea. It is the largest local
> church in the world and has more than 700,000 members.
> More than 80 percent of the pastoral work in the church is
> done by women.[31]

Dr. Cho often tells that he wasn't able to mobilize workers for
his cell ministry and the Lord spoke to him to go to the women;
they would do the work. When he did not see the breakthrough
in Japan that he desired, he sent a woman pastor to establish the
church. God blessed tremendously and a powerful church was
raised up under her ministry.

His Anointing, Her Willingness

This brings me to an observation I have made about the spread of
the gospel in the book of Acts. A great possibility exists that Paul
placed women over many of the house churches just as Cho did
because he knew they would get the job accomplished. He could
rely on them. (I'm not saying that men cannot be relied upon,
but the female gender does have a more natural nurturing that

lends itself to hospitality as well as discipleship. This combination works well in the establishment of house churches.) Even

Even when they are not naturally suited to be leaders, the Holy Spirit will sometimes use those who may not seem as gifted but are more willing.

when they are not naturally suited to be leaders, the Holy Spirit will sometimes use those who may not seem as gifted but are more willing. After all, it is His anointing that works in and through us to accomplish His purposes.

Presiding Elders

Given the social standing that heads of households had, we can reasonably assume that often the "presiding elder" (a modern name some churches give their senior pastors) of a house church was also the head of the household where the church met. Lydia and Mary, the mother of John Mark, and others very possibly functioned as "presiding elders" (or at least the deacons) of the churches in their houses. In fact, if this is so, most of the house churches listed in Scripture were "pastored" by women! It is quite probable that some of the leaders of these house churches began as deacons and progressed to being "presiding elderlike" figures. Either way it is highly likely there would have been women at the "Pastors and Elders Seminar" held by Paul, as mentioned in Acts 20:16,17.

Team Ministry: The Call to Couples

Priscilla and Aquila must have left Paul at some point and established a church in their home because 1 Corinthians 16:19 says,

"The churches of Asia greet you. Aquila and Priscilla greet you heartily in the Lord."

Note that in this passage, Aquila's name is mentioned first. It's quite possible that he had a higher anointing to lead a local house church than she did and her gift was used more in teaching, or perhaps even in a traveling ministry.

I have already stated my hope that the example of Priscilla and Aquila (or "Aquila and Priscilla," depending on whether they were in the local house church or traveling) working together as team ministers is going to be the norm one day rather than the exception. One example of this is Marilyn and Wally Hickey. Although she has the more visible ministry, he is the pastor of the church. Therefore, the presentation of their names would be according to their setting.

Even though the person with the strongest anointing and public ministry gifts may be the visible leader, the combined strengths of both are needed to fulfill the work God has called them to in order to complete the purposes of God for their lives. It is certainly this way with Mike and me. Many people do not realize the extent of the ministry of Generals of Intercession and the amount of work it takes, not only administratively but also in other ways, to fulfill the vision of God. As of this writing, the *GI News* is distributed to 42 nations, and we are working to assist numerous organizations in setting up their prayer structures.

This is an excellent example of team ministry, which I spoke of earlier. In the future, churches will call both the husband and wife to pastor the church. The one with the strongest anointing will be the prominent one, but both will be necessary for the church to function as it needs to. Many men who have only involved their wives with ministry to the women of the church will seek their wives' counsel and begin to work as teams. For some, while their children are small, this may be on a limited basis, but will increase as their children get older. Others will function together even when the children are small, as do the ministers in Argentina. Some wives may not feel comfortable with a visible role or vice versa, but each will be valuable for insight and counsel.

I have observed different churches that are already taking this step by setting in the wives as pastors of the church. Among these are Dr. James Maracco, who bestowed on his wife, Colleen, the title of pastor. She now serves on the church staff with 12 other pastors. Another is Bob Beckett of Hemet, California, who ordained his wife, Susan, to be a pastor of The Dwelling Place Church.

How did the people of the church respond? They were utterly delighted. Each of these women had functioned in their roles for some time before they were officially recognized as such, so the people already loved them and looked up to them. Their ordinations were like celebrations and it was easy to begin to call them "Pastor Colleen" and "Pastor Susan." I will elaborate more on the differences in these roles in later chapters.

Although many leaders would say that "experientially" they see women in leadership, they stumble over those difficult passages. In the next two chapters we will look at different interpretations of the Scriptures regarding women in the Church. Pray hard, keep your mind and heart open and let's plunge in together!

Notes

1. *Women of Vision 2000* (Newsletter of the A.D. 2000 and Beyond Movement Women's Track: 1st quarter, 1997), p. 4.
2. Dr. J. Robert Clinton *Gender and Leadership* (Barnabas Publishers, 1995), pp. 18-19.
3. The *KJV, NKJV, NASB* and *NIV* all describe Phoebe as a "servant." However, see *A Greek-English Lexicon of the New Testament and Other Early Christian Literature*, ed. by Walter Bauer, William F. Arndt, F. Wilbur Gingrich and Frederic Danker (hereafter *BAGD*) (Chicago: The University of Chicago Press, 1957; revised edition, 1979), p. 184, 2b, citing early second-century Latin texts which translate the Greek *diakonos* with the Latin word "minister."
4. Dr. A. J. Gordon quote is taken from a paper written in 1894 and published in Dr. J. Robert Clinton's *Gender and Leadership*.
5. Charles Trombley, *Who Said Women Can't Teach* (South Plainsfield, N.J.: Bridge Publications, 1985), pp. 194-195.
6. According to the *Theological Dictionary of the New Testament*, edited by Gerhard Kittel and Gerhard Friedrich (Grand Rapids, Mich.: 1964) vol.

2, p. 93, an order of deaconnesses quickly arose in the Early Church. Also, we have seen that Paul called Phoebe a "deacon," a lofty term in the New Testament. It is significant that Philip also was a deacon (in Acts 6:2, "to serve" is the same verb used for serving as a deacon in 1 Timothy 3:10,13). Notice that as a deacon, Philip preached, healed, taught, baptized and church planted in cross-cultural missiological settings (see Acts 8:4-25), always in accountability to the Jerusalem elders (see Acts 8:14ff.). It is therefore clear that "deacons" could and did exercise tremendous leadership and authority.

7. Quoted in Charles Trombley, *Who Said Women Can't Teach?*, pp. 195-196.
8. Quoted in Charles Trombley, *Who Said Women Can't Teach?*, p. 197.
9. David Cannistraci, *The Gift of Apostle* (Ventura, Calif.: Regal Books, 1996), p. 86.
10. Such as John Piper and Wayne Grudem, *Recovering Biblical Manhood & Womanhood*, p. 80.
11. Charles Trombley, *Who Said Women Can't Teach?*, pp. 190-191.
12. Dr. Bill Hamon, *Apostles and Prophets* (Shippensburg, Pa.: Destiny Image, 1997), pp. 115-116.
13. Charles Trombley, *Who Said Women Can't Teach?*, p. 191.
14. Dr. Catherine Kroeger, *Christian History* magazine, Issue 17 (taken from the caption of a picture).
15. David Cannistraci, *The Gift of Apostle*, pp. 90-91.
16. L. E. Maxwell, p. 107 (taken from an unpublished manuscript *The Ministry of Women of Salvation Army Principles*, November 26, 1977), p. 1.
17. Billy Graham, *Just As I Am* (Harper San Francisco, Billy Graham Association, 1997) p. 137.
18. Ibid., p. 213.
19. Taken from the endorsement of *Dream Big*, the story of Henrietta Mears's life (Ventura, Calif.: Regal Books, 1990).
20. Ben Witherington III, *Women and the Genesis of Christianity* (Cambridge: The Press Syndicate of the University of Cambridge, 1990, reprinted 1995), p. 220.
21. Katherine C. Bushnell, *God's Word to Women* (self-published through Bernice Menold, 10303 N. Spring Lane Peoria, Ill., 61615 and Cosette Joliff 408 Clybourn Peoria, Ill., 61614. Original book last published in 1923), paragraph 195 (no page numbers in book).
22. Bill Metzger, *A Textual Commentary on the Greek New Testament* (Stuttgart: United Bible Society, 1971), pp. 466-467, referring to Acts 18:26. Most textual critics think the manuscripts of the Western tradition of the Greek New Testament later reversed the order of the names because of a bias against women.
23. No one is called "pastor" or "shepherd" by name in the New Testament except Jesus (see John 10:11,14; Heb. 13:20; 1 Pet. 25).

24. See Acts 19:22 and 1 Tim. 1:3. Also see G. F. Hawthorne's article "Timothy" in the *International Standard Bible Encyclopedia*, Vol. 4 (Grand Rapids: William B. Eerdman's Publishing Company, first published 1915, reprinted 1988), pp. 857-858.

25. Dr. C. Peter Wagner, *Blazing the Way* (Ventura, Calif.: Regal Books, 1995), p. 196.

26. Mary J. Evans, *Woman in the Bible* (Downers Grove, Ill.: InterVarsity Press, 1984), p. 110.

27. Paul and Peter tell elders to "pastor/shepherd" the flock of God (see Acts 20:28 and 1 Pet. 5:1,2). Elders were clearly responsible for pastoring those under their care, but clearly both men and women were involved in the function of pastoring....A "pastor" was not necessarily a paid Christian professional leading a local congregation; more likely a "pastor" would be the leader of a house church (see Eph. 4:11)....Priscilla and the Marys who followed Jesus were not called "pastors," but there can be no doubt that they pastored. "Deacons" were not at all limited to simply serving physical needs as many "deacons" are today.... "Elders" were not the decision-making committee for a local congregation. The biblical term "elder" seems to mean a man who has oversight over a church or group of churches in a city or in a geographical location (see Acts 14:23; 20:17,28; 1 Tim. 5:17-19; Titus 1:5-9; 1 Pet. 5:1,2). Taken from personal correspondence with Dr. Gary Greig and Bayard Taylor.

28. Although the text of the New Testament does not explicitly call Priscilla and Lydia "deacons," they functioned as such.

29. The elders of Ephesus called together by Paul in Acts 20:17 were told to "shepherd" the Church of God (see Acts 20:28). These elders would have represented at least some of the "elders" mentioned in Ephesians 4:11. In 1 Peter 5:1,2, Peter also says that elders are to "pastor" God's flock. Therefore, at least some elders were pastors.

30. See John 13:33; 21:5; 1 John 2:1,12,13,18,28; 3:7,18; 5:21; 2 John 1,4,13; 3 John 1.

31. C. Peter Wagner, *Your Spiritual Gifts* (Ventura, Calif.: Regal Books, 1979, 1995), p. 137.

Domestic Authority
(Headship and Submission)

Years ago I studied extensively about end-time eschatology, and would listen with fascination to Bible prophecy teachers. When we joined different churches, each had slightly differing end-time views and each believed they were absolutely right.

Because this study was so interesting to me, I attended seminars and avidly read the passages and interpretations given by the teachers. They used words such as "pre-trib," "mid-trib," "post-trib." Amazingly they all seemed to have degrees of validity. My father used to say he was a "pan-millenialist," which meant he believed everything would "pan" or work out in the end. I know this must sound appalling to those who are very sure about what they believe about the end times!

As I've done research for this chapter, I have felt much the same at times: each position I've studied seems to have strengths. One reason end-time prophecy teaching is not absolutely across the board the same is that the Bible simply isn't totally clear. Of course, we have our interpretations of the symbolism and typology used and can have strong opinions, but this alone leaves an openness for me to believe that when we get to heaven, none of us will have had perfect interpretations.

Earlier in this book, I alluded to the fact that I have felt much the same way as I have studied the "difficult passages" concerning women at home, in the Church and in related topics. I wrote in chapter 8 about women and the Church to hopefully establish some precedents that Paul enlisted women in many and various aspects of the New Testament Church. Although this chapter will deal mostly with domestic issues, some bleed over occurs between domestic (i.e., home-related) and spiritual (i.e., Church-related) issues dealing with authority structures.

This chapter will deal with passages that are much disputed today related to women and the home. I'll call this subject "domestic authority." Then, the next chapter will deal more with spiritual authority outside the home. I have, hopefully, done some distilling for you on this subject. Whole books have been written about these passages of Scripture. Therefore I can only provide a snapshot or condensed version. I'll list many of the books I've used in my research for your further study. Many of the books have greatly divergent viewpoints.

We Are All One in Christ Jesus

In studying these difficult passages, there are foundational scriptures that have affected the way I look at the other verses we'll examine.

Galatians 3:26-28:

For in Christ Jesus you are all sons of God through faith. For as many [of you] as were baptized into Christ [into a spiritual union and communion with Christ, the Anointed One, the Messiah] have put on (clothed yourselves with) Christ. There is [now no distinction] neither Jew nor Greek, there is neither slave nor free, there is not *male* and *female*; for you are all one in Christ Jesus (*Amp.*, italics added).

There are words used in this passage (chosen by the writers under the inspiration of the Holy Spirit) that we need to think about. First, *all* believers, men and women, are called "sons." Why was the word "sons" used instead of "daughters"? If we explore the setting of this writing, we understand that culturally the sons inherited, not the daughters. What a strong and powerful message! We are all inheritors. Not that He looks on all of us as the male sex, but as having the rights and privileges attributed to an adopted son at that time.

Then, we see a very wonderful statement about those who are baptized into Christ: "there is neither *male nor female.*" This will be particularly important as we delve into the matter of headship and spiritual authority versus domestic authority. For in the Church, there is neither male nor female but, of course, in the marriage relationship, gender is an issue. We do not stop being male and female when we become born again.

Galatians 3:26-28 has been referred to by writers such as Jessie Penn-Lewis as the *Magna Carta* for women. Webster defines Magna Carta as "a document constituting a fundamental guarantee of."[1] Essentially, although we have been given this wonderful Magna Carta, a couple of practical issues still have to be discussed. I'll divide these into two basic categories: *Spiritual Authority* and *Domestic Authority.* Let's begin our study with the issue of headship and submission. It is probably one of the most controversial subjects I can think of in the Church today.

My Viewpoint

As I've explored these categories, I have tried to delve into them with an open mind and heart regarding my adherence to the theology of women in the Church and home that I have believed as a minister. I have read ultra-traditionalists (who believe that women should not teach adult men in the Church or hold governmental responsibilities) to egalitarians ("biblical feminists" whose stance is that there is neither male nor female in function in the Church or home).[2]

After researching both positions, I find that I don't fit into either category. I have demonstrated in the previous chapter the biblical precedent for the principle that in the New Testament, men and women function according to *anointing and spiritual gifts* rather than merely according to *gender*. However, domestic authority in the home is delegated to the headship of the husband. (I'll define both of these more later in this and the following chapter.)

As I've prayerfully threaded my way through this subject, I've had numerous dialogues with theologians including Dr. Gary Greig from Regent University. We have been challenged and stretched as we've studied, sought the Lord and reexamined our belief systems.

Heirs to a Corporate Destiny

In order to more fully understand headship and submission, it is important to revisit what happened in the Garden of Eden and the Fall. In doing so, we'll take a look at the role of the couple in the Garden, the subsequent Fall and its effects on gender and the Church.

God created the man and woman to be a team....The two becoming one flesh causes them to be able to accomplish something higher than each of them could do alone.

As I wrote earlier, for man to be alone was the only thing that God declared as being "not good." What made the situation good or complete was the formation of the woman from his side (the Hebrew word *tsela*[3] [see Gen. 2:21-23]).

The woman was to be a "helper" (Hebrew: *ezer kenegdo*) to

her husband. "She was an *ezer kenegdo*—a helper exactly parallel to him (see v. 18)—not an exact replica of him, but a perfect complement to his imperfect reflection of the image of God. She had equal rational capacities to the man, as shown by the fact that she understood and was held fully accountable for her sin by God (see 3:2f, 16). Whatever else she was, she was not inferior to the man."[4]

God created the man and woman to be a team with a corporate destiny bigger than both of them separately. This was God's intent for marriage. The two becoming one flesh causes them to be able to accomplish something higher than each of them could do alone.

My husband, Mike, says that when he grew up, the general belief was that male headship meant the woman was supposed to basically pour herself totally into her husband's destiny, regardless of her own giftedness. The thought that the woman had a role as "helper" such as described in the Garden was relatively unknown.

Adam and Eve's first role was team work in ruling the earth (see Gen. 1:26-28). And yet, commonly team work is a missing ingredient in today's marriages. For years while Mike pursued his career with American Airlines, he lived with traditionalist expectations regarding male headship and women in ministry. To embrace the ministry God had given me required a significant shift on both of our parts, especially his. But as great as the adjustment has been for both of us, the peak years of Generals of Intercession ministry only came as we began to learn how to work as a team in our destiny. (More about this in the next chapter.)

The Fall: The Cause of the Mighty Gender Bender

The introduction of sin and the fallen nature of the human race has brought a polarization not only to married couples working together, but also to males and females relating in the Church.

Genesis 3:16 records the results of this fallen nature:

"I will greatly multiply your sorrow and your conception; in pain you shall bring forth children; your desire shall be for your husband, and he shall rule over you."

Katherine C. Bushnell (1855-1946, medical doctor, missionary and advocate for women's rights) challenged the prevailing traditionalist interpretation of this verse (and others—see *God's Word to Women*[5]), namely, that the woman's "desire" for her husband was sexual or psychological (or both), and that the man was to subjugate the wife under him. She argued, based upon early translations of the Hebrew Bible into Greek, Syriac, Latin, Coptic, Armenian and Ethiopic that the word "desire" (Hebrew: *teshuqah)* should have been translated "turning" (Hebrew: *teshubah,* a difference of one letter).[6] According to Bushnell, Genesis 3:16 explained that the woman's "turning" is "toward" her husband. In other words, she "turned away" from God for fulfillment, meaning and direction, and instead would "turn toward" the man.

Although I agree with Bushnell that women have often inappropriately "turned toward" men instead of God for fulfillment, meaning and direction, the word "desire" (*teshuqah)* here is found in two other passages that give a clearer picture of the meaning in Song of Solomon 7:10 and Genesis 4:7. Although Song of Solomon 7:10 used "desire" in a positive way, in Genesis 4:7 we see sin's desire to entirely control Cain and cause him to do evil. Genesis 3:16 also bears this negative meaning in the woman's desire to influence and control her husband. Both Genesis verses, closely related by grammar and context, indicate inappropriate desire.[7] Essentially the woman's fallen nature will desire to control the man.

The next phrase of Genesis 3:16 then says that the fallen nature of man shall *rule* over the woman. It is important to understand this word "rule" (Hebrew: *mashal).* Coming from opposite sides of the fence, both traditionalists and egalitarians (biblical feminists) have understood the term to mean "rulership" or "mastery."

Bushnell strongly objected to the idea that man "must rule" over woman in an authoritarian way. I agree with her. This verse has been used for centuries as a club against women, either to totally subjugate them or to severely restrict their gifts and talents. And when "rule" is misunderstood as "authoritarian mastery" it makes for big trouble in marriage. Why?

The spirit of competition between the husband and wife will be huge because the sin nature of both will want to control the relationship. The sin nature sets up a cycle of judgment as each person in the marriage desires to "rule" out of selfishness. This is why both submission of the woman to her husband *and* mutual submission are so very critical in a marriage (see Eph. 5:21-25). Without both kinds of submission, there is World War III. (Have any of you noticed that?)

There is a much better way of understanding the word *mashal* than the dead end of subordination and domination. The immediate context of Genesis 1 and 2 provides us with several good operating definitions of *mashal:*

- The man was to *abad,* "work, serve" and *shamar,* "watch, guard, protect" the Garden (see 2:15). In this case, the highest being of all creation, the one created in God's very image, was to serve, protect and care for the lowest of the Creation, the plants.
- The man was to enjoy the fruit of the Garden (see v. 16), but there were definite limits to what he could and could not do (see v. 17). He was never an absolute, despotic lord.
- The man was to gratefully receive the gift of a wife (see vv. 23,24), someone who stands on equal footing with him. Together they were to bring glory to God by "ruling" the earth (see 1:26,28).

In addition, the Bible teaches that God "rules" over creation with gentleness, humility and servanthood (see Psalm 104:10-32; 105; 106; 107). His "rule" is not despotic or authoritarian. Jesus Himself, the Son of God, could have ruled as a dictatorial leader, but did not (see Phil. 2:6-8). In short, Adam was to "rule" with gentleness, humility and servanthood, just as Christ loved the Church and gave Himself up for it (see Matt. 20:25-27; Eph. 5:25).[8]

Not Every Man Is Over Every Woman

An important point I'd like to make here is that Ephesians 5:21-31 concerns a married couple, not every male and female. This point is so critical. Not every man is over every woman. For instance, my husband (not every male I meet) is my head. If every man had headship over me, the effects would be far reaching and devastating.

The fact that not every woman is under every man's authority is important to every married woman minister.[9] How could a woman minister operate in her anointing if every man in the listening audience had a greater authority over her than, let's say, her husband or pastor? Her hands would be tied as to the release of her gift.

If she is single, to ensure her completeness (so she will not be in the condition of being alone), it is good to have those she relates to in spiritual authority (either male or female, by anointing, not gender). She is not, however, under every man in the Church. If she is married, she will be under her husband's authority at home and they both should be under the authority at Church. This doesn't negate, but enhances the domestic authority.

Saying that there has been much misuse of authority in the Church against women is an understatement. Whole movements, such as the *Discipleship* or *Shepherding* movement, were particularly abusive to women in general. This movement sprang up in the '70s and finally seemed to break up in the '80s. One teaching and practice of the movement was that a woman could not marry unless the men elders of the church said they had heard from God prophetically as to who her mate was to be. Some of it was more rigid than others, giving their husbands such sweeping rights as to refuse a woman the right to buy a dress unless chosen by her husband. This sounds like the profile of a cult.

I know a number of women who were deeply wounded by

this movement and its abuses. It largely affected the charismatic community. This is one area where a great need for gender reconciliation still exists. In fact, many Christian women today simply cringe when they hear the word "submission" because of all of the negative connotations it has for them.

Women readers who have been through the more extreme forms of religious abuse associated with distortions of headship and submission, please make sure you have prayed and forgiven those pastors, your husband or ex-husband, boyfriends, etc., so you can read this chapter as a whole person.

Also, men, please take a moment to reevaluate your heart to see if you have any issues regarding controlling or manipulating women. I'm going to talk about some pioneer areas concerning submission that will require these areas of pain to be healed so you can *respond* rather than *react*. This will allow you to rethink some ways you might have had of relating to your wife as well as women in general.

Mutual Submission in the Fear of God

So with the understanding that this issue is surrounded by much woundedness from both genders, let's look again at Ephesians 5:21-31 and 1 Corinthians 11:3. I'll key off of the Ephesians passage in this chapter:

> Submitting to one another in the fear of God. Wives, submit to your own husbands, as to the Lord. For the husband is head of the wife, as also Christ is head of the church; and He is the Savior of the body. Therefore, just as the church is subject to Christ, so let the wives be to their own husbands in everything. Husbands, love your wives, just as Christ also loved the church and gave Himself for her, that He might sanctify and cleanse her with the washing of water by the word, that He might present her to Himself a glorious church, not having spot or wrinkle or any such thing, but that she should be holy and without blemish. So

husbands ought to love their own wives as their own bodies; he who loves his wife loves himself. For no one ever hated his own flesh, but nourishes and cherishes it, just as the Lord does the church. For we are members of His body, of His flesh and of His bones. For this reason a man shall leave his father and mother and be joined to his wife, and the two shall become one flesh (Eph. 5:21-31).

This passage on submission begins with the idea of mutual submission. The word for "submitting" here is *hupotasso,* which means "to subordinate, to obey, to be under obedience, submit self unto."[10] It's amazing how little the Church focuses on a married couple submitting *one to another.* Much has been preached to the women about submitting to their husbands, but when was the last time you heard a sermon pointing out that husbands loving their wives as Christ loves the Church means *placing oneself under* to serve as Jesus did when He washed the disciples' feet (see John 13:4-9)? Or when was the last time you heard a sermon asking husbands the question: *Are you submitting to your wife in the fear of the Lord?* In fact, it has been so little emphasized that it almost sounds like heresy!

The Issue Is Love, Not Submission

In preparation for this chapter, I've polled some very close friends with good marriages. I posed this question to them: "Does the subject of submission come up in your marriage?"

Each of them said an emphatic, "No!" My sampling ranged from a couple in their 60s, one in their 40s, another in their 30s and the last in their 20s. While each of them believe in not only mutual submission, but also the headship of the husband in the home, it seems that each of them in a practical sense submit to each other's strengths as well as roles in marriage.

The Gradys
For instance, my good friend Lee Grady shared how he believed

his wife, Deborah, was the home manager and knew more about the day-to-day needs of the children. She, in fact, has chosen to home school their children. He shared that although this was a mutually agreed-upon decision, the brunt of the work rested upon his wife and that she was with the children more, so she naturally knew more of their needs. Of course, they prayed about the decision together, but ultimately she was left to decide. My theory is that the best marriages function this way.

The Duncans

Kyle Duncan, the associate publisher of Regal Books, and his wife, Suzanne, are very much a couple of the '90s. They split the household chores and work together as a team. In fact, this seems to be the direction the generations are taking. The young married men of this generation for the most part don't feel it lessens their masculinity to help their wives around the house. (Of course, some parts of the United States and the world are very macho and would not adhere to this. However, I have friends in Argentina of this age group who mutually share in the housework, so even this is changing.)

The Wagners

I have watched C. Peter Wagner and his wife, Doris, whom Mike and I have, for years, considered to be our spiritual parents. They have one of the best marriages I have seen. Even though Peter is clearly the head of the house, he is so secure in his identity and position that it is totally nonthreatening to him to have Doris suddenly yell across the house, "Peter, would you please take out the trash?" He usually hops right up and goes and does what she has asked, knowing that it doesn't threaten his manhood to mutually submit to his wife's needs. Nor does it take away from his position as head of the wife. However, at the seminary (where Dr. Wagner works with Doris) you don't see this kind of thing happening. The Holy Spirit has clearly worked out the sense of competitiveness with which so many young (and not so young) couples struggle.

The Sheetses

I also talked to my pastor, Dutch Sheets, about this subject of headship and submission. One of the points he made that I think is tremendous is that even though he is the head of his wife, he doesn't make a decision until they have mutual consent. By this, he means that if they can't agree upon a decision, even if he knows he is right and his wife is wrong, he takes time and prays with her and by himself until they reach a compromise. He said that the Lord has never failed to bring them into agreement.

The Jacobses

As for Mike and me, we lead an extremely complicated life as you can well imagine, so these issues can get quite complex. I'm going to discuss our struggles and some of the things we have experienced in the next chapter called "Anointed to Serve" when I deal with submission in a marriage where the woman is the more visible leader.

Modern-Day Foot Washing

I stumbled upon a fascinating piece of insight while researching for this book that may get me into big trouble with the men readers. However, please don't skip over this section because I know you want to be a servant like Christ is to the Church.

When Jesus washed the feet of the disciples, He was making a huge societal statement. You see, only women and slaves ever washed anyone's feet. This is why Simon Peter objected so vigorously to Jesus wanting to wash his feet. Jesus was taking the lowest possible position and essentially doing women's work. To gain the full impact of this, you'll need to read the last chapter entitled "The Cultural Reformation." Women were near the bottom of the list in society—right near slaves.

How does this translate in modern-day society? Your wife might need you to mop the floor or dust the furniture or offer to baby-sit one night a week so she can go out with the girls (now that's certainly modern-day foot washing).

(I'm chuckling as I write, because immediately after I studied this, I called one of my good friends, Cheryl Sacks, to share this tidbit and she started laughing. Evidently she had just asked her husband, Hal [who networks the pastors in Phoenix, Arizona], if he would help her mop the floor! He groaned when she coached me into telling him what I'd learned, but he was good natured about the whole thing.)

While I very much believe in the special place of responsibility God has given the husband in the family, it seems that this kind of working together is what our Creator envisioned in the Garden. It is our fallen nature that refuses to submit and wants to compete and control.

Headship: Servant Leadership, Not Subjugation

Moving along in Ephesians 5:22 and 23, we come to the passage pertaining to the wife's submission to her husband, the "head" of the wife. (Note that Scripture doesn't say that he is over the household here, but that he is head of his wife. I believe it pleases the Lord when the couple works as a team to raise their family when they have children.)

> Wives, submit to your own husbands, as to the Lord. For the husband is head of the wife, as also Christ is head of the church; and He is the Savior of the body.

Our understanding of the word "head" (Greek: *kephale)* will have significant impact on our understanding of submission. Two main interpretations regarding the word "head" are being advanced today: "authority" and "source."

Gilbert Bilezikian has argued well for the "source" interpretation in his survey of nonbiblical writings, the Greek translations of the Old Testament and the New Testament. Bilezikian found that *kephale* used as a metaphor for "ruler, authority" in the New Testament is illegitimate because of scarcity of evidence in first-century Greek writings.[11] "Source" or "source of life," he argues, is the idea it conveys in texts such as 1 Corinthians 11:3 and Ephesians 5:23. Katherine Haubert summarizes Bilezikian's conclusion that *kephale* is used metaphorically in the New Testament "in a variety of settings that give it some conceptual flexibility, but always with the notion of serving the Body in a creational, nurturing or representational dimension."[12]

When used figuratively, the word *kephale* or "head" means "fountainhead or life source."[13] Therefore "mastery" and "dominance" are simply not included in the idea of headship; and subordination, subjugation and being ruled are simply not included in submission. Rather, these kinds of distortions come from the fallen nature of humanity. However, the concept of the authority of the husband in the role of servant leadership as Christ is for the Church comes shining through in this whole passage (see vv. 21-31). What does a good head do? He protects, nurtures and releases his wife to become everything God created her to be and do. A husband can either be a fountainhead of life and encouragement to his wife or bind her from reaching her full potential.

One time I was being interviewed over the radio in Argentina. When asked about men and wives submitting, I answered with a rather strong statement: "I believe God is going to hold some men accountable on Judgment Day for holding their wives back from fulfilling their destinies." The interviewer looked shocked! This certainly was not in the Latin American male mind-set. I must say, however, that some major strides have been made in Latin American since that time.

A missionary friend who was in a country in South America told me how he was once in a pastors' meeting where the discussion turned to whether it was all right to beat your wife. He said that the general consensus was that it was permitted as long as no one knew. Bible collector Duwayne Chapman, who has produced a video entitled *The Amazing History of the Bible* (Gospel Light), owns an original copy of *The Wife Beater's Bible*. Of course, I find that few godly counselors would suggest that a woman stay in a home where she is being beaten, but I am still amazed at how many women are afraid of their Christian husbands.

Two Brains, One Head

Years ago I had the false impression that I could not disagree or have my own opinion about anything Mike wanted to do because he was the head. This thinking, however, got us in big trouble from time to time, as I would have a balancing opinion, feel greatly disturbed over his decisions and never say anything.

One time my silence even caused us to lose quite a bit of money! A man asked us to lend him what was to us a lot of money. I felt terribly uneasy about it, but felt I couldn't give my opinion. We loaned him the money without as much as a signed paper on his part that he would repay us. To this day we've never received that money. Sadly, we suffered financially because of it, and I dealt with hurt and anger when we had no money to pay for necessary items. What a hard lesson. I had not been a good *helper* to Mike by my silence.

Florence Littauer has written an excellent book entitled *Wake Up Women! Submission Doesn't Mean Stupidity*, which can help you discern whether or not you are in an abusive situation in your home.

Some women are angry at the thought of proper headship in the home and want to take away leadership responsibility from their husbands. However, I feel more fulfilled, protected and released than stymied because of Mike's headship. I shouldn't be any more upset that God made me a woman and my husband the head than the fact that He made me five feet two and three-fourths inches tall and Mike six feet one inch!

I do believe that my husband is responsible before God for being a spiritual leader in our home. This does not in any way negate my role as a spiritual leader. It does, however, mean that Mike needs to make sure he is right before God in his decisions and actions on our behalf.

Mostly, I find that women *want* their husbands to take more of an active role in praying with and for them and, if they have children, teaching them the Word of God. Somehow the passivity of men that began in the Garden still holds true today.

I personally do not believe it is biblical to call men "the priests of the home." While I understand the positive connotations intended, in actuality there is only one high priest and mediator between God and His children, and that is the Lord Jesus Christ. Each of us can come to Christ alone to hear Him and we don't need a husband to approach God on our behalf.

In studying books both by traditionalists and egalitarians (biblical feminists), I find many points on either side that I heartily agree with. John Piper and Wayne Grudem have written an extensive response to Evangelical Feminism in their book, *Recovering Biblical Manhood and Womanhood.* Although obvious differences exist in what we believe concerning the role of women in the Church, they have much to say that is excellent. Piper and Grudem clearly believe that headship involves authority and that the word "head" does mean "source" in a few passages, but it means "authority" in others.

Piper has an interesting insight in his chapter entitled "A Vision of Biblical Complementarity":

> If I were to put my finger on one devastating sin today, it would not be the so-called women's movement, but the lack of spiritual leadership by men at home and in the Church. Satan has achieved an amazing tactical victory by disseminating the notion that the summons for male leadership is born of pride and fallenness, which in fact pride is precisely what prevents spiritual leadership. The spiritual aimlessness and weakness and lethargy and loss of nerve among men is the major issue, not the upsurge of interest in women's ministries.[14]

The pastor in one church we attended said to me, "We are going to push you back in your gifts so your husband can come forward." It seems to me that instead of trying to suppress the gifts the Lord had given me of prophecy, etc., he should have said,

"Cindy, I see the Lord wanting to increase your husband's ability to flow in his gifts and I'm going to work with him to see that it happens." (Of course, that situation gave me a great opportunity to grow in forgiveness and grace.)

Dennis Lindsey is president of Christ for the Nation's Bible Institute in Dallas, Texas, where he teaches a class on marriage. He says that the wife submits to the God-given position of the husband while the husband submits to the person of his wife. He also makes the following comments on submission or subjecting ourselves to one another:

> It is the art of learning to lose when you could easily win. One of the best illustrations of subjection in everyday experience concerns boats. The crews subject themselves to the commands of the captains. But there is another rule that is being observed. The craft that receives the greater advantage of maneuverability must give way to the craft with the lesser. A fishing boat with a motor must give way to a sailboat, for power gives way to sail. Aircrafts do the same, the more power and maneuverability a craft has, the less right-of-way it has. Christians, like sailors and pilots, should learn to give way to one another to avoid collisions in their life together.

I remember my dad writing me a letter about marriage when I was dating Mike. He said, "Honey, you must give 100 percent of yourself to Mike and he must do the same for you. If you do this, each of you will have 100 percent of your needs met."

Somehow I don't think any of us has this subject of headship and submission totally figured out. Dr. Gary Greig once said to me, "Cindy, there is such a need for gender reconciliation in the Body of Christ that I am not sure any of us will see this subject clearly until the Lord does a deeper work in healing the woundedness both in men and women."

I have to say, "Amen, Gary!" to that. And a day may come when the Lord shows me that even what I've written in this chapter is not exactly right—I am very open to that; but He knows I've studied hard, prayed and done the very best job at expressing what I've determined to be the heart of God on this issue.

Although this chapter dealt mainly with passages of Scripture relating to the home, the next one will delve into the issues stemming from women functioning inside the Church and in full-time ministry.

Notes

1. *Webster's Ninth New Collegiate Dictionary* (United States: Merriam-Webster, 1991), p. 716.
2. Note: I am aware that these are broad definitions and are not by any means inclusive of the theological stances of those who are in either of these categories.
3. Note: The word *tsela* has been translated "rib" in some versions; however, to do so tends to marginalize her creation from man as being from an insignificant part. *Tsela* is used 41 times in the Old Testament and is only used as rib here in Genesis 2:21-23.
4. Dr. Gary Greig and Bayard Taylor. Taken from personal communication on the word *ezer*.
5. I highly recommend the reading of *God's Word to Women*. Katherine C. Bushnell, *God's Word to Women* (self-published through Bernice Menold, 10303 N. Spring Lane, Peoria, Ill., 61615 and Cosette Joliff 408 Clybourn, Peoria, Ill., 61614. Original book last published in 1923). Katherine Bushnell was a remarkable woman who traveled as an evangelist and social crusader with the Women's Christian Temperance Union. In addition, she was a medical doctor and was famous in the Christian community for her work against white slavery and prostitution. As far as I could tell the works are a compilation of Bible lessons taught in the 1920s. Although the work is amazing for its time, I felt that I had to call in some modern-day theologians to study some of her work, such as on the word *teshuqah* because of my inability to read the Bible in its original languages. The personal communication I am referring to is a response to my questions from her book. Dr. Gary S. Greig (Ph.D., University of Chicago) is associate professor of Old Testament at Regent University School of Divinity, Virginia Beach, Virginia. Bayard B. Taylor (M.Div., Trinity Evangelical Divinity School) is senior editor of Biblical and Theological Issues at Gospel Light Publications, Ventura, California.
6. Katherine C. Bushnell, *God's Word to Women* paragraphs 103-133.

7. Personal correspondence with Dr. Gary Greig.

8. As we can see, *mashal* in the earliest pages of the Bible and when it refers to God's rule meant "servant leadership." This meaning eventually became influenced negatively by its association with the "rule" of human kings and princes who were not servant leaders, but despotic, arbitrary, domineering, authoritarian, greedy, cruel and vain (for examples see Gen. 37:8; Exod. 21:8; Judg. 8:23; 14:4; 15:11; Prov. 28:15; 29:12; Isa. 14:5; 52:5; Joel 2:17).

9. For example, Priscilla was not under Apollos's authority when she and her husband Aquila instructed Apollos "more accurately" about Jesus in Acts 18:26. And the "elect lady" of 2 John 1 was not under the authority of itinerant male teachers; she had to discern false teaching and remove false teachers (see 2 John 10,11).

10. James Strong, *The New Strong's Exhaustive Concordance of the Bible* (Nashville, Tenn.: Thomas Nelson Publishers, 1990), #5293, see also BAGD pp. 847-848.

11. The evidence: (1) Greek lexicons do not agree whether *kephale* as a metaphor means "source, origin" or "authority." (2) Of 180 occurrences where the Hebrew Bible uses *ro'sh* in a figurative way to denote "ruler, leader," the Greek translations of the Hebrew Bible (the Septuagint) avoids using *kephale* at least 90 percent of the time. In only five passages does the Septuagint use *kephale* to translate *ro'sh* as "ruler, leader" (see Judg. 11:11; 2 Sam 22:44, which is the same as Psalm 18:43; Isa. 7:8-9 [four times]; and Lam. 1:5), and in each of these cases the translation *kephale* depends on Hebraisms or Massoretic marginal notes incorporated into the Greek text. (3) The contexts of the New Testament passages that allegedly use *kephale* as a metaphor for "ruler, leader, authority" (see 1 Cor. 11:3-16; Eph 1:10; 22-23; 5:23; Col 1:18; 2:10; 2:19) can all be shown to point toward "source, origin" as the meaning. See Bilezikian's appendix in *Beyond Sex Roles: What the Bible Says About a Woman's Place in Church and Family* (Grand Rapids, Mich.: Baker Book House, 1991).

12. Katherine M. Haubert, *Women as Leaders* (Monrovia, Calif.: MARC, a division of World Vision International, 1993), p. 40.

13. Bilezikian, *Beyond Sex Roles*, p. 137.

14. John Piper and Wayne Grudem, *Recovering Biblical Manhood and Womanhood* (Wheaton, Ill.: Crossways Books, 1991), p. 53.

Oh, Those
Difficult Passages

Several years ago my husband, Mike, was interviewed by
Charisma magazine about the Generals of Intercession ministry
and me. When asked how he achieved peace concerning God's
call upon my life, Mike replied, "Barring all the theological questions, it came down to the basic question of whether Cindy had
an anointing from God or not. Once I recognized that she did, I
had the responsibility to trust God with it. He's the One who put
it there."

I wish that just such a statement could settle issues of controversy concerning whether a woman can be in spiritual authority or teach men. Recently a male leader told me, "Experientially
I have received greatly from women ministers, but theologically,
I just can't see it in the Scripture."

Other groups are really struggling with these issues. Pastors'
associations are grappling with the woman question, and women
leaders have been deeply wounded by the male leaders who on
one hand say that the Church will never advance until it is in
unity, but on the other hand refuse to invite women leaders to
pastors' and leaders' summits.

A friend called recently after a discussion about whether women leaders should be invited to a prayer summit in her state. She said the group was torn about whether women ministers should be invited to the meeting. (What made it especially disturbing was that the issue was about who could come to pray.) This same group no longer stumbled over the fact that leaders in the group had been divorced, or how they believed about the rapture.

Of course, I realize it is highly important for men and women to meet separately to deal with issues that particularly relate to gender issues. The bonding and feeling of belonging that develops in gender specific meetings promotes personal and relational growth. Two important examples of these kinds of meetings are Promise Keepers for the men and Aglow International for the women.

Bill McCartney, founder of Promise Keepers, takes a strong stance in their meetings against sexual sin in ways that would cause both the men and the women to be uncomfortable in a mixed setting. The meetings simply would not be as effective with wives or other women in attendance.

Likewise, while men do come to Aglow International conferences, the primary emphasis of this organization centers around women's issues. I have been very involved at the international level with Aglow and have experienced the thrill of worshiping God with women from 60 or more other countries. We have different nationalities, yet as women, we all face common struggles.

Building on Common Ground

Some of you may have heard about what has happened regarding Christian unity in my city, Colorado Springs—the home of 80 plus ministries and many different kinds of churches. Last year when the Evangelical Association held its prayer summit, pastors and their spouses, along with men and women *servant ministry leaders* (we prefer this to "parachurch," which sort of sounds like parasite), were invited. Great blessing pours out from this kind of unity.

Pastor Ted Haggard of New Life Church in Colorado Springs (with membership around 6,000) has written a book entitled

Primary Purpose (Creation House) in which he gives the principles the city leaders have agreed upon to bring such a move of unity. Two of those principles are central to a number of the points I'll be making in this chapter:

1. **Focus on the absolutes.** We all agree that Jesus of Nazareth is the Messiah and that He came in the flesh to destroy the works of the devil (see 1 John 3:8). We know that through Him we have access to the Father and, therefore, eternal life (see Eph. 2:18). In addition we all believe the Bible is the primary source of information about God, and it is the standard we use to judge spiritual experiences and teaching (see 2 Tim. 3:16).

2. **Appreciate one another's respected interpretations of Scripture.** Ted calls them "respected interpretations" because heresy would not be tolerated.[1]

Why do I believe these points are central? Because unity is built around those verses of Scripture that are clear in their interpretations.

Some churches believe women can teach in the church; others don't. Both types of churches may strongly adhere to focusing on the absolutes while also respecting others' different "respected"

Scripture presents the prophetic promise in Acts 2:17 that God will pour out His Spirit upon the women as well as the men. Surely Satan wants to stop this end-time move any way he can....

interpretations of Scripture. Yet, at citywide leadership meetings women leaders are often excluded both physically and verbally (by verbally I mean that the nouns and pronouns used by the leadership are all male, i.e., "We *men* are going to take this city!").

It seems the major divisive issues such as tongues, healing, divorce, how to baptize and other related points of doctrine no longer stop us from coming together in unity. The main issue of division today is "Can a woman teach?"

In spite of the wall of division in the Church about women leaders, Scripture presents the prophetic promise in Acts 2:17 that God will pour out His Spirit upon the women as well as the men. Surely Satan wants to stop this end-time move any way he can— even to the point of using well-meaning Christians who put human limits on the Holy Spirit, who can use whomever He chooses in whatever way He chooses for His purposes at any time He sees fit. God may chose a Deborah or Esther as well as a David or Daniel.

With God's sovereignty and His prophetic promises in mind, we need to look at more of those difficult passages before the chapter about women who feel God is calling them into full-time ministry. The two passages that have brought the greatest confusion and restriction of women's ministry in the Church are 1 Corinthians 14:34,35 and 1 Timothy 2:11-15.

As we delve into these passages, I'll weigh various interpretations I have studied and present comments about what I think the passages are not saying.

Four Rules for Interpretation

While studying the verses in question, allow me to give you four essential principles for interpreting Scripture. For you nontheologians, like me, I've tried not to make this so heavy and boring that you won't enjoy reading it. Instead, I've endeavored to "fillet" and distill piles of research for you in terminology that is user friendly. The four principles are:

1. Determine the author's intent.
2. Determine the context within the chapter, the book and the rest of the Bible.
3. Determine the historical or cultural setting at the time it was written.
4. Interpret unclear passages in light of passages that are clear.

Using these rules for interpretation, let's begin with 1 Corinthians 14:34,35:

> Let your women keep silent in the churches, for they are not permitted to speak; but they are to be submissive, as the law also says. And if they want to learn something, let them ask their own husbands at home; for it is shameful for women to speak in church.

How this passage is interpreted often depends less upon what Paul meant by "keep silent" and "not permitted to speak" than upon the reader's belief system regarding the scope of what a woman can do in the Church. This passage has been read by some groups to mean that women should not be allowed to so much as talk out loud in church; other groups have used this passage as a blanket admonition that women should not be allowed to preach. Neither interpretation adequately takes into account Paul's practice of using women in ministry or his intent in this particular context.

Content Must Be Examined
by Cultural Context

Of course, most groups would not agree that women should not talk at all in church. (This would probably severely limit women's interest in going to church because we women, as a rule, love to talk.)

We see that Jesus went against the cultural grain and encouraged women to "go tell"—from the Samaritan woman who preached to the whole city (see John 4:28-30) to Mary who was sent with the words "He's alive" after His resurrection (see Matt. 28:1).

Similarly, both Paul's letters to the Corinthians and to Timothy address specific problems within the churches. Paul's two letters to Timothy deal quite extensively with false teaching and teachers who were leading women astray. And Paul's two letters to the Corinthians are intended to correct serious breaches of moral conduct and order. These problems were causing serious confusion in the Church, as we can see in 1 Corinthians 14:33:

> For God is not the author of confusion but of peace, as in all the churches of the saints.

What was the problem in Corinth? We know that Paul established the church at Corinth in about A.D. 50, that some prominent Jews were among the first believers (see Acts 18:4,8) and that probably most of the church had come out of paganism and were lower class (see 1 Cor. 1:26). Also, at the time, most women were illiterate and hadn't had the privilege of an education. One of the most amazing things about this passage is that women are told to learn. Most of us today do not understand the impact of this statement because our cultural standards do not prohibit a woman from having an education. However, this was a groundbreaking statement during Paul's time.

Rebecca Merrill Groothuis gives the following insight in her book *Good News for Women*:

> The context of this passage concerns the maintenance of order in the worship service. The same word used of women's silence is commanded of those who would speak in tongues without an interpreter. Paul's intent is evidently to silence only disruptive speaking. The particular type of disruptive speaking that is mentioned with respect to women probably has to do with interrupting the public speaker with questions—a practice that was common at this time. Paul says that women should save their questions to ask their husbands after they get home (1 Cor. 14:35). This indicates that he is primarily concerned with women interrupting teaching, not women engaged in teaching. Apparently, women had been asking questions out loud and disrupting the order of the church service.[2]

The word "silent" has the connotation of "holding one's tongue" (see *BAGD Greek-English Lexicon* #749d, 1b; see also

Strong's concordance #4601), which fits in with this interpretation. The word "women" (Greek: *gune*) in this passage isn't "women" in general, but "wives" because 1 Corinthians 14:35 specifically mentions husbands (see *BAGD*, p. 168b, 1; see also *Strong's* #1135). Another word in this passage translated "shameful" means "disgraceful" (see *BAGD* 25b; see also *Strong's* #149) or not conforming to what is right or fitting for the situation.

It is very easy to misread what was happening in the Early Church through the filter of our own modern-day church buildings and auditoriums. But the Early Church meetings were mostly in home settings because, as I mentioned earlier, basilicas or church buildings were not built until the fourth century. Even if the homes were large, it would still be quite disruptive for wives to be talking out loud during the meetings. If the practice of men sitting separately from the women had been followed (as still is practiced in many churches outside of the western world), the problem would only have been amplified.

Defining "The Law"

An interesting perspective on this passage comes from Katherine Bushnell's *God's Word to Women*. She begins her section (Lesson 25) mentioning that women were only to be veiled when praying or prophesying; therefore, women were clearly not silenced from doing these things (see 1 Cor. 11:4,5). On this point, even many traditionalists agree that women can pray and prophesy in the Church, while at the same time forbidding women to teach men.

Bushnell then quotes 1 Corinthians 14:34 where Paul writes, "for they [the women] are not permitted...as the law also says."

This leads to an interesting question: Where does the law say that women were not allowed to speak? The Old Testament says absolutely nothing from Genesis to Malachi about forbidding women to speak. No such "law" can be found anywhere in the Bible forbidding women to speak in public, unless it be this only one utterance here by Saint Paul. Besides, we know perfectly well the Old Testament explicitly permitted women to speak in public (see Num. 27:1-7). Jesus also encouraged women to speak without rebuking them (see Luke 8:47; 11:27; 13:13).[3]

Bushnell continues her objection to the notion that women were not to speak by saying we do not even know if men were allowed to interrupt a speaker with questions. Bushnell also points out that not all of the listening women would have been wives; some would have been singles, widows, divorced or with Jewish or pagan husbands. (Interesting point for all you singles who are so often left out in church-related issues.)[4]

Some traditionalist theologians say that the "law" against women speaking in public was given in Genesis 3:16, where Scripture says "your desire shall be for your husband, and he shall rule over you." Some, but not all, interpret this restriction on women's speaking to mean that every male has rule over every female in the Church. As I have said before, applying the restriction to all women misses the point. This passage is talking about domestic authority in the home and not spiritual authority in the Church, because the wives with husbands are being addressed, not women in general.

So what could Scripture mean by "as the law says"? Bushnell goes on to explain beginning with 1 Corinthians 7:1. Paul was working from a list of questions the Corinthians had previously sent. When each new question came up, Paul would either name their question or quote from their letter, then give his response.[5]

Bushnell believes 1 Corinthians 14:34,35 was a new question that Paul was addressing and that his answer comes in verse 36 with:

"What? Came the word of God out from you? Or came it unto you only?" (KJV). What follows to the end of the chapter gives guidelines concerning all prophesying and speaking in tongues.[6]

Bushnell believes the Judaizers were trying to put the Church back under the extra-biblical Jewish traditions, which clearly stated that a woman was not allowed to speak in the synagogue. Paul would have actually been rebuking the Corinthian church for not releasing the women and putting them back under the legalism which the Judaizers were trying to put on the Church.

The Question About Women in the Church May Come from Women's Questions in the Church

To repeat, I believe the strongest interpretation is the one concerning disruptions in the Corinthian church caused by women asking questions during the services. I do not believe Paul meant women were not to speak at all because 1 Corinthians 11:5, Acts 18:26 and 21:9 make it clear that they did. I do, however, realize that reasonable people may come to differing conclusions.

Dr. Jim Davis and Dr. Donna Johnson raise some interesting points on the ambiguity of these passages in their new book *Redefining the Role of Women in the Church*:

> It is always difficult to identify the historical context into which Paul was writing. He wrote to address problems in the churches. Without knowing the local situations it is difficult for us to understand his responses. We cannot always be certain whether Paul's teaching applies only to that particular local church situation or whether it is to be applied universally.
>
> Second, the passages about women are full of ambiguous expressions and sometimes contain words which are difficult to translate. In 1 Corinthians 11:10, Paul writes, "For this reason, and because of the angels, the woman ought to have a sign of authority on her head." What does this mean? Why does he mention the angels? Is he referring to the role of the angels in worship? In 1 Corinthians 14:34, he writes, "Women should remain silent in the churches."
>
> Why did Paul not make it clearer? What exactly did he mean? One would suspect that it is not more clear because it was not that important in the Early Church. It is unlikely that the first-century church shared our preoccupation with ecclesiastical structures and status. Undoubtedly, they were too busy spreading the gospel to be concerned about precise job descriptions for women in their churches.[7]

This last statement is an extremely powerful one. As I have traveled around the world and seen great revivals in places such as Colombia and Argentina, I have seen churches in major revival so busy trying to get the converts discipled that they are happy for laborers—either men or women! One young pastor in his 20s in Bogota, Colombia, moaned to Mike and me that he was hardly doing any service for the Lord because he alone was responsible for 130 or so cell groups. Amazing, isn't it?

I find it interesting that 1 Timothy 2:11-15 and 1 Corinthians 14:34,35 cause us so many problems when other obscure passages in the Bible don't bother us even though we don't completely understand them. For instance, most Christians don't spend lots of time trying to interpret the verse that deals with baptism for the dead (see 1 Cor. 15:29).

I believe a day is coming when we will look back at the controversy over women teaching in the Church and simply shake our heads in wonder that it ever was such a big issue. I don't want any young women leaders to have to deal with rejection of their ministries based solely upon their gender. Actually, as I alluded to in the introduction of the book, this is one of the major reasons I'm writing about this subject.

Years ago when I was lonely and struggling with how to be a woman leader in the midst of rejection and misunderstanding, I made a vow to the Lord that I would do what I could to see that other young women leaders didn't have to suffer as I had. This is why the next chapter will be one of practical sharing from my heart to those women (and the people that love them) with a call of God on their lives.

Pagan Practices That Prompted Puzzling Passages

Probably the most controversial and puzzling passage concerning women in the Church is 1 Timothy 2:11-15:

Let a woman learn in silence with all submission. And I do not permit a woman to teach or to have authority over a man, but to be in silence. For Adam was formed first, then Eve. And Adam was not deceived, but the woman being deceived, fell into transgression. Nevertheless she will be saved in childbearing if they continue in faith, love, and holiness, with self-control.

In my study of this passage, I have found Richard and Catherine Clark Kroeger's book *I Suffer Not a Woman* (Baker House) was particularly enlightening for understanding the historical and religious setting of Ephesus at the time 1 Timothy was written. Their study reveals a world of idolatrous paganism based upon a matriarchal society and goddess worship.

The city of Ephesus, the fourth largest in the Roman Empire, lay on the western coast of modern Turkey, in ancient Asia Minor. It was not an easy place in which to bring the Christian message. In pre-Hellenistic times, a famous shrine was built to the great mother goddess, and tradition held that the original image had been brought by Amazons, women warriors from the land of the Taurians on the Black Sea. This idol was placed in an oak tree but was later removed to a sanctuary, about which the rest of the temple grew.[8]

The great mother goddess later came to be revered as Artemis, or Diana of the Ephesians. Her crown represented the walls of the city. Countless pilgrims made their way each year to worship her in this city, and they poured so much wealth into her treasury at the Artemisium that it became an enormous banking and finance center for all of Asia Minor.

William M. Ramsay insists it was no coincidence that the virgin Mary was first called *theotokos* (bearer of God) at Ephesus where Artemis herself had earlier borne the same title.[9]

Another important aspect in our study is understanding the predominant reason Paul was writing to Timothy: heresy infiltrating the Church. We see that three people are mentioned who opposed sound doctrine: Hymenaeus, Alexander and Philetus (see 1 Tim. 1:20; 2 Tim. 2:17; 4:14). The Kroegers suggest that at least one of these individuals was a woman and that 1 Timothy 2:12 forbids her to teach a heresy which was creating serious problems in the Church.[10]

The heresy causing problems was an emerging philosophical and religious system called "Gnosticism" (taken from the Greek word *gnosis* meaning "knowledge"). Gnosticism is a particularly wicked deception that taught, among other things, that Eve was the "illuminator" of humankind because she was the first to receive "true knowledge" from the Serpent, whom Gnostics saw as the "savior" and revealer of truth. Gnostics believed that Eve taught this new revelation to Adam, and being the mother of all, was the progenitor of the human race. Adam, they said, was Eve's son rather than her husband, a belief reflected the Gnostic doctrine that a female deity could bring forth children without male involvement.[11]

The "Silence" of a Teachable Student

Now, let's look back to 1 Timothy 2:11-15 in light of the historical and religious background. We see a similar admonition for women to learn in silence as we did in the 1 Corinthians passage. This time, however, the Greek word used is different from the 1 Corinthians 14:34 word translated "be silent." Although in the Corinthian passage "silent" means "to hold peace," this word "silence" (Greek: *hesuchia*) in 1 Timothy means "stillness" or "quietness" or even "agreement." It expresses the attitude of the learner.

This teachable attitude is the same attitude of humble submission that any male rabbinic scholar was to have in that day. What a beautiful thought! Paul was saying to these women who were never allowed to be taught in a scholarly way in the Jewish synagogue system that they could be full-fledged disciples.

Why was this especially important for women? Their culture worshiped Diana or Artemis and was greatly influenced by the emerging Gnosticism. These women needed to know the truth so they would not be influenced or deceived by false teachers and so they could separate themselves from the deception of the society all around them.

Translators' decisions to render the Greek word *hesuchia* as "silence" in the *King James Version, New King James Version,*

Revised Standard Version and *New Revised Standard Version* is another place where a clear anti-woman bias exists. When *hesuchia* is used of women, the translators chose "be silent." When the same word was used concerning men, the translators chose "quietness" (see 1 Tim. 2:11; 2 Thess. 3:12).

Not to Teach, or Not to Teach Heresy?

So what could this passage mean? Rather than a complete prohibition of women teaching, it is possible that what they were not to teach was heresy. After all, it was in the very same city of Ephesus that Priscilla, along with her husband Aquila, both well known to Paul (see Rom. 16:3), taught a male Christian leader named Apollos in Acts 18:26. Other admonitions in 1 Timothy suggest that women were going from house to house (or perhaps house church to house church) leading others astray. Paul writes about this in 1 Timothy 5:13 where they are described as "busybodies," saying things which they ought not. In verse 15 Paul warns that some have already turned aside after Satan because of the error of their teaching.

It is interesting to note that the word "busybodies," which seems like women who are only gossiping, is actually referring to persons doing something that could be considered a form of witchcraft. The Greek word for "busybodies," *periergos*, is the same word that is translated "practiced magic" in Acts 19:19. These so-called "busybodies" were dispensing something much more deadly than old wives' tales.

David Joel Hamilton has written an excellent master's thesis for his course work at the University of the Nations (Youth With A Mission University in Kona, Hawaii). He also suggests that Paul was not addressing all women in general, but a particular woman who was teaching heresy, because Paul is speaking in the plural in 1 Timothy 2:9,10, switches to "a woman" in 1 Timothy 2:11-15a and then to women (plural) again in 1 Timothy 2:15b.[12]

One of the most difficult sections of this passage is the next verse, 1 Timothy 2:12, because it seems to say that allowing women to teach men would "usurp authority," or take the teaching positions that only men should have. Part of the difficulty arises because the Greek word *authentein* occurs here and nowhere else in the New Testament. Let's look at this word *authentein* to try to determine its possible meaning.

There are main interpretations of *authentein*. One says *authentein* means "to dominate." Traditionalists use this passage to demonstrate that women should not teach men because they would be dominating or "usurping authority over men." John Piper and Wayne Grudem have written from this viewpoint in their book *Recovering Biblical Manhood and Womanhood*. However, there is remarkable inconsistency in how traditionalists treat the prohibition of women teaching. For example, Piper gives a list of the ministries he believes a woman can participate in, which includes teaching up to college-age groups.[13]

Other traditionalists say that a woman as a missionary may serve as a leader and teacher, but she may not pastor a church. Some allow a woman to "share" testimonies of great moves of God seen on the mission field as long as the woman doesn't stand in the pulpit. Therefore, the prohibition is not violated because the woman is not "teaching" but "sharing." Other traditionalists say a woman is teaching when she actually opens the Bible to read a scripture along with her speaking time. The line between "teaching" and "sharing" can become very gray indeed.

Those who propose this kind of drawing of artificial lines around certain types of teaching and authority are doing "hermeneutical gerrymandering," making distinctions in levels of authority in ministry that are not delineated in Scripture.[14]

Furthermore, the traditionalists' viewpoints that limit the setting and to whom a woman can teach do not seem consistent with other Pauline writing. For instance, Priscilla clearly taught or instructed Apollos who was not just an ordinary man, but a Christian leader (see Acts 18:26). Another consideration that some may not have considered is the testimony of Mary Magdelene to the Resurrection (see Luke 24:10). Men everywhere have been taught the glorious fact that *He has risen just as He said*, from the testimony of this former prostitute. Clearly, the Holy Spirit trusted a woman to give this message in a trustworthy fashion, knowing that men everywhere would learn from it. God knew what He was doing and the precedent it would set for the Church thereafter!

Another problem with the traditionalists' position is that it is sometimes assumed that Timothy and the New Testament Church knew about a prohibition against women teaching men. Groothuis has the following to say:

> Paul does not state the prohibition in the form of a reminder, and it is not mentioned elsewhere in the New Testament. How can traditionalists be so certain that it was "Paul's position in every church that women should not teach or have authority over men," and that he was giving "explicit teaching on the subject here simply because it has surfaced as a problem in this church"? Craig Keener observes that what is most significant about the wording of the passage is that Paul does not assume that Timothy already knows this rule....Paul often reminds readers of traditions they should know by saying, "You know," or "Do you not know?" or "According to the traditions which I delivered to you." But in this case, there are no such indications that Paul is merely reminding Timothy of an established rule that Timothy would already have known about. Moreover, there are no parallel texts in the New Testament to support the view that New Testament churches normally denied women teaching authority. Since this passage is related so closely to the situation Timothy was confronting in Ephesus, we should not use it in the absence of other texts to prove that Paul meant it universally.[15]

If Paul did not mean for these texts to universally prohibit women teaching men, then what could he have been saying in these passages? What else could he have been trying to correct in the Church? In order to find this out, we need to study the meaning of the word *authentein* at the time of the first century. Words can take on different meanings even within one generation. Imagine how they can change down through many centuries!

A Closer Look at Gnostic Heresy

What did *authentein* mean at the time of the writing of Paul's letter to Timothy? While it has been translated by the word "authority" in nearly all the English Bibles, *authentein* is not the same word as *exousia*, the word used for "authority" in other passages. Studies of the use of *authentein* in the literature of the day show that originally the word *authentein* meant murder. By the second and third century A.D., its connotation had changed to "having authority over." *Authentein* was also used in connection with sex and murder. Women were known to curse men to death through the use of "curse tablets."

Evidence exists for another possible meaning of *authentein* from that time period—that of "originator." Gnostic heresy during this time period taught that Eve was the first virgin, the one who had no husband and the originator of all life. She was the "illuminator," full of all wisdom, and Adam was actually given life when she saw her colikeness lying flat upon the earth, whereas she commanded him to live. When he saw her, he said, "You will be called 'the mother of the living' because you are the one who has given me life."[16]

This Gnostic myth is, of course, heresy. The Bible clearly states that Adam was created first and then Eve. The idea that *authentein* may have the meaning of "originator" instead of "usurp authority" seems to fit in light of the rest of the passage:

For Adam was formed first, then Eve. And Adam was not deceived, but the woman being deceived, fell into transgression (1 Tim. 2:13,14).

This passage could very well have been written to attack the Gnostic heresy that Eve was the creator. Then, a further blow is dealt against this error in verse 14 which clearly says that Eve was deceived. The Eve of Gnostic heresy could never have been deceived because she was the illuminator and all wise. Second Timothy 2:14 sets the record straight. Only One is all wise and that is God Himself.[17]

As a result of this interpretation, the passage could be translated:

> I am not allowing (present tense for that situation) a woman to teach or to proclaim herself the originator of man (*authentein*). Adam was formed first, then Eve.

In light of the prevailing mother-goddess heresy and emerging Gnosticism in First and Second Timothy and Titus, it seems clear that Paul was bringing correction in 1 Timothy 2:11-15. He was correcting women or possibly "a woman" or even "a wife" who was teaching some kind of heresy. (The word for "women" here can also mean "wives.")

Even if one grants the traditionalists' interpretation that *authentein* means "to usurp authority/dominate," this passage would apply to *the attitude* of the one doing the teaching. No godly Christian woman (or man, for that matter) should ever be controlling, manipulative or domineering. In other words, it could be addressing the *attitude* of humility as she teaches that would be the focus rather than a complete prohibition not to teach men at all.

Spiros Zodhiates, Th.D., editor of the *Hebrew Greek Key Lexicon Bible*, says of 1 Timothy 2:12:

> This problematic text contains two Greek words: *gune*, which means both a woman or a wife; and *aner*, which means man both as a male or a husband. As far as 1 Timothy 2:12 is concerned, it should not be interpreted as a prohibition by Paul for any woman to teach, but only for a wife whose teaching may be construed by those who hear her to think that she has the upper hand insofar as the relationship between her and her husband is concerned.[18]

This explanation is one that Kay Arthur of Precepts Ministries, one of the most noted women teachers of our time, gives to those who ask her about her right to teach in the Body of Christ as it relates to this difficult passage.

Katherine Bushnell suggests yet another interpretation of this passage. She points out that this letter to Timothy, the bishop of Ephesus, was written about A.D. 67 after the awful martyrdom of the Roman Church under Nero in A.D. 64.[19] Nero put thousands of believers in Rome to death after he blamed them for the burning of the city, even though Nero himself had supposedly ordered the burning. Nero was exquisitely cruel in the means he used for their martyrdom. Some were covered with skins of wild beasts and left to be devoured by dogs, others were nailed to crosses and many were covered with inflammable matter and set ablaze to serve as torches during the night.[20]

In his book *The Early Days of Christianity*, Archdeacon Farrar says:

> Christian women, modest maidens, must play their parts as priestesses of Saturn and Ceres, and in blood-stained dramas of the dead....Infamous mythologies were enacted, in which women must play their parts in torments of shamefulness more intolerable than death.[21]

In light of these traumatic and distressing events, Bushnell suggests that 1 Timothy 2:11-15 was not an admonition that women stop teaching for all time, but simply to lay low and be cautious during this season of persecution. I find Bushnell's speculation unconvincing. For one, it is based upon an argument from silence. Against it also are Jesus and Paul's strong words to all believers. Jesus didn't say only men should take up their crosses and follow Him (see Mark 8:36-38). Paul didn't say that only men should put on the full armor of God (see Eph. 6:10-18), or that women should not seek to have the same attitude as Christ, who became obedient to death (see Phil. 2:8). Further, this interpretation doesn't explain the rest of the passage and lacks the strength of the one I previously presented.

In summation, I believe there is definitely room for non-traditionalist interpretations of this passage. If the admonition for women not to teach was universal, it would have been strengthened with other passages. Instead, we find many passages to show that women did indeed teach men and held significant places as leaders in the Church (see Acts 18:26; 21:9; Rom. 16:1,3,7; 2 John 10). The Old Testament, which was the Bible of the Early Church, offers clear precedents for women teaching men in a variety of settings in Micah 6:4; 2 Kings 22:14; and Proverbs 1:8; 31:26.

I believe the Lord is clearly speaking to the Body of Christ today about the need to reexamine our belief system concerning women teaching. We must open our eyes to the fact that when God anoints women with the gift of teaching, He is releasing great revelation and blessing to the Church through them.

I pray that this chapter has brought grace and understanding to the many women and men who see the hand of God upon their lives to be everything that God has called and chosen them to be in this last and greatest hour of harvest before the return of the Lord Jesus Christ for His bride.

The next two chapters will build and prayerfully sew up some loose ends for the book. Chapter 11 is subtitled "Spiritual Authority" and will delve deeper into women in Church government and give practical applications for women ministering in the Church.

Notes

1. Ted Haggard, *Primary Purpose* (Lake Mary, Fla.: Creation House, 1995), pp. 55-56.
2. Rebecca Merrill Groothuis, *Good News for Modern Women* (Grand Rapids, Mich.: Baker Book House, 1997), p. 203.
3. Dr. Katherine Bushnell, *God's Word to Women* (Bernie Menold and Cosette Joliff self-published this book to bring it back into print. Address may be obtained at the back of the book. There are no page numbers in the book.)
4. Ibid., paragraph 203.

5. For possible examples, see 1 Corinthians 7:2; 8:1; 10:23; 12:1; 14:34,35; 15:12; 16:1,12.

6. Dr. Jim Davis and Dr. Donna Johnson, *Redefining the Role of Women in the Church* (manuscript page 35).

7. Richard Clark Kroeger and Catherine Clark Kroeger, *I Suffer Not a Woman* (Grand Rapids, Mich.: Baker Book House, 1992), p. 47.

8. Ibid., p. 54.

9. Ibid. pp. 59-60.

10. Don Rousu, *Spread the Fire*, "The Truth About Women in Public Ministry" (October 1997): 5.

11 David Joel Hamilton, "I Commend to You Our Sister" (master's thesis 1996), p. 271.

12 John Piper and Wayne Grudem, *Recovering Biblical Manhood and Womanhood* (Wheaton, Ill.: Crossway Books, 1991), p. 59.

13. Rebecca Merrill Groothuis, *Good News for Women* (Grand Rapids, Mich.: Baker Book House, 1997), p. 211.

14. Kroeger and Kroeger, *I Suffer Not a Woman*, pp. 212-213.

15. Ibid., p. 99.

16. Ibid., p. 121.

17. Don Rousu, *Spread the Fire*, "The Truth About Women in Public Ministry" (October 1997): 6. Don Rousu, who suggests this interpretation, goes on to say that this statement directly contradicts the notion that Eve was the "illuminator" and carrier of new revelation.

18. Spiros Zodhiates, Th.D., editor of the *Hebrew Greek Key Lexicon Bible* says, "But I suffer not a woman (*gunaiki*, which should be translated as a wife or a woman in her relationship as a wife) to teach (*didaskein*, the pres. inf. of *didasko*, to teach, indicating continuity of teaching), which may be interpreted as lording it over her husband." If this were a prohibition of a woman teaching men, it would have said *authenteo*, "to usurp authority over" *andron*, the pl. gen., instead of the sing. gen., men. Instead of *andros* in the singular meaning "over man," referring to her own husband.

"Paul is anxious to make very clear here that no woman through her teaching should give the impression that she is the boss and lording it over her husband. If any such impression is given at any time, then she should keep quiet. The relationship expressed in 1 Timothy 2:13 is not that of Adam and Eve as man and woman, but rather as husband and wife."

19. Bushnell, *God's Word to Women* (Peoria, Ill.: Cosette Joliff), paragraphs 313-314

20. Ibid., paragraph 314.

21. Ibid., paragraph 322.

Anointed to Serve

(Spiritual Authority)

A few years ago a young minister asked, "Cindy, what has it cost you to serve God as a woman in ministry?"

I didn't have to think a second before I answered, "Everything. It has cost me everything. Death to my own desires, wishes, time—giving up those precious moments with my family and children that any mother wants to participate in." I could have gone on and on. The question elicited memories of nights spent in lonely hotel rooms when it seemed as though every demon in hell had my address.

I paused for a moment as a greater wave of emotion hit me. I then went on to say, "But do you know what I have gained? Everything."

"Is it worth it?" you might ask.

As I ask myself that same question, I see mental images of hundreds of people coming to Christ in nations all around the world, tears streaming down their faces. I ask myself, *What price is one soul rescued from an eternity of hell?* Then I realize anew and afresh, *Yes, it's worth it. For one such soul, I would follow*

*Him in the call again and again. That's why I do what I do and it
is my greatest and highest reward.*

His Grace Is Sufficient for Every Obstacle

This chapter will be a mentoring one for women called by God
to ministry. It will also be useful, however, to *all* readers by providing a window into the special and unique challenges of
women in full-time Christian service (and all the women in ministry reading this chapter are probably chuckling and saying,
"Amen, Cindy, amen!").

As a woman traveling and teaching about prayer and spiritual
warfare, I have faced a number of obstacles. In fact, one day I told
the Lord (actually I was complaining to Him), "Lord, it's hard
enough that You called me to be a woman minister without having me teach on this controversial subject of spiritual warfare.
Couldn't I teach about 'color typing' or something more social-
ly acceptable for a woman?"

Of course, you can see how impressed He was with my comments—my next new topic was this one on women and the
Church, which, as you know, is more than a little bit controversial! It serves me right for complaining, doesn't it? So, the lesson
from this section is: Never, never complain to the Lord! Just tell
Him, "Yes, Lord, I'd be glad to do it. Anything you ask of me,
Lord, whenever you want."

"God, You Stole My Wife!"

One initial obstacle Mike and I faced was that while Mike agreed
with his head that I should preach, his heart was having quite a
struggle. I guess you could distill it down to the statement, "God,
You stole my wife!" You see, being the good Southern wife that
I was, I had waited on Mike hand and foot. He had never polished
his own shoes, washed the car or ironed his own shirts. He didn't
know how to cook and had only washed the dishes once or twice
in our nine years of marriage. In fact, he hardly knew how to use

the microwave, and using the washing machine was totally out of the question! (Our friends in their 20s find this hard to believe!)

During those early days I would often offer to quit the ministry, but Mike would always protest, "No, I know that is what God wants you to do with your life."

Another major problem was that our children were still quite small. Daniel was two and Mary was five. I had a number of intense wrestling matches with God over the issue of childrearing. I begged God to let me wait until they grew up to start ministering, but each time I went to Him the answer was the same: *Take up your cross and follow Me now.*

I often wondered why God required this kind of sacrifice from me while allowing others to stay at home until their children had grown. I now believe it was because of the subjects—prayer, the healing of nations and spiritual warfare—He had called me to teach about. Although I have certainly not been the only one teaching on these subjects, I do know that our ministry, Generals of Intercession, has been used to pioneer these messages in many countries throughout the world. We receive regular letters from leaders sharing how they have set up national prayer initiatives using the materials the Lord has given us.

In light of the high personal price it has cost me as a wife, mom and woman, I can see why God doesn't call more women at the age He called me to travel around the world teaching. But if God is making it clear that this is His will for your life, don't be afraid to say yes to the Lord. His grace is sufficient.

Another challenge I faced as a young woman minister was that I didn't know any other women who were doing what I was doing at the age I was doing it. I would go to meetings where plans would be made with women who, for the most part, had almost grown or adult children. They had more freedom than I, so I repeatedly declined volunteering for the organizations because I wanted to be home more with my children. I teasingly said that I needed God's confirmation in triplicate on my bedroom wall before I would go out and teach.

Have I ever missed God and gone when I could have stayed home? Yes, I believe so. Although I can't think of any specific instances, I'm sure at times in my youthful zeal I occasionally missed it. My husband, Mike, was a good balance for me. He would pray with me when I had any doubts about whether I should go somewhere to teach. If both of us were unsure, we called our pastor, and later, our board of directors for advice.

I'll never forget the day I heard "via the grapevine" (or gossip line) that some of the men and women of our church were saying that I wasn't properly submissive to my husband. Those words hurt me so badly that I felt as though someone had knifed me in the heart. These were people I had prayed for and I thought were my friends.

Later that night, Mike noticed I was walking around with a sad face and asked me what was wrong. After I briefly shared what had happened, he gathered me in his arms and said, "Why didn't they come to me and ask me if you were submissive? After all, I'm your husband, and believe me, would I have told them a thing or two!" What a wonderful release. Mike was covering and nurturing me in just the way I needed and it didn't matter what those other busy-bodies said!

Peer Points and Pressure Points

One of the most difficult subjects Mike and I had to sort through was submission. At times, we would be on the same committee as ministers and would relate on an entirely different authority level than when we were at home. By this I mean that we were dealing in areas of spiritual authority where there is neither male nor female, rather than with issues of domestic authority (family issues of husband and wife).

As I shared earlier, we've had some rather intense discussions and struggles around these issues. Keeping the house clean was relatively easy to settle. Because my travel schedule left me consistently behind in household chores, we simply believed God for the money to hire someone to clean house for us once a week. We didn't have the finances at first, but once we leapt out in faith, God provided the funds weekly.

The problem of shirts was solved by sending them to the cleaners. We learned that rather than becoming stalemated on an issue, we could look for a creative alternative that would meet both of our needs.

One big revelation was recognizing our need to identify each other's roles when we had a conversation. People often unconsciously confuse their roles. For example, they may have one level of authority at their jobs and another at church and yet another on a certain board of directors. They flow in and out of those roles all the time. We realized when we were talking minister-to-minister that we were in the area of spiritual authority where there isn't any male or female. Then, the next moment, we might switch to the subject of Daniel (our son) or our home and transition to the domestic level of authority.

Even when we recognize our roles, things can get murky. We've had to learn to flow together minister-to-minister, even though we are still male and female. As such, we have specific gender needs even though we are in the area of spiritual authority. I talked a little about this earlier as I described how men relate by razzing or teasing, and women relate by affirming one another.

An intense moment came when my feelings had been hurt through some false accusations. Mike was still working at American Airlines and rushing to get out the door. I had been trying to talk to him about how hurt I felt by a pastor who accused me of having a spirit of divination (in those days not many people understood the prophetic, therefore anything that was forth-telling was thought to be divination). Being in a rush, Mike related to me more like a man would do to a man and said, "Cindy, you're just going to have to stop being so sensitive!" (Of course, as prophetic woman intercessors, we do tend to be more sensitive than other people.)

As he was shutting the door to leave, I looked at him and said in a crushed voice, "But I'm a woman too, as well as your wife!" (Life can get complicated at times.)

He shut the door and left. I flung myself against the door crying when all of a sudden I looked up to find Mike standing there with his arms open, beckoning me to come. I ran into his arms and he hugged me tightly and said, "I'm so sorry, honey. I was treating you like I would another man." I think he saw me as being so strong that he thought I could take anything!

Mike and I have found that we relate best when
we keep our identity in Christ and not in who
we are or what we are doing in life.

Throughout the years Mike has learned to be a good covering for me both spiritually and domestically. I almost feel sorry for someone who would try to come against me because he would be on the phone with that person immediately to set him or her straight. On a few occasions I have asked him not to intervene because I thought it would just make the situation worse, and after thinking a few minutes, he would agree.

Mike and I have found that we relate best when we keep our identity in Christ and not in who we are or what we are doing in life. For Mike, it has often been hard. He held an extremely responsible position at American Airlines, but often when he would travel with me, people would teasingly refer to him as "Mr. Cindy Jacobs." I can't tell you how much it would hurt me to hear people say such things. It especially hurts today because he is a cofounder of the ministry and is essentially the nuts and bolts of the organization. Mike is far from being a Mr. Cindy Jacobs. Generals of Intercession would not be able to function without him. He is the CEO of the organization and takes care of the audits, budgets and chairs our board meetings. As a businessman Mike keeps G.I. an organization of integrity.

Inevitably, situations arise concerning the ministry about

which Mike and I don't agree. Usually we pray and reach a viable compromise, or one or the other will give in on the issue. If we do reach an impasse, however, we turn to the board of directors of Generals of Intercession for advice. (Our board is a ruling board and is by no means a "yes" board. Board members are not at all afraid to give us wise, corrective counsel, and on numerous occasions have done so.) We each share our opinions as we poll the board and have never failed to come up with a consensus of advice from them.

When dealing with marriage issues that bleed over into the ministry, we have sought the counsel of our pastor, Dutch Sheets. His wisdom has been a great blessing to Mike and me. Most domestic authority issues don't require outside counsel, but I would suggest to any married couple that they be willing to go for mediation if the issue is important enough to greatly impact the life of one or the other of the marital partners.

If you have read the other books I've written, you know how strongly I feel about the subject of being under the spiritual authority in a local church. Many who have traveling ministries make a big mistake by not relating on a personal level with their pastors. Some are even afraid of this kind of authority. Mike and I, however, have never found it to be anything other than a major blessing. If you don't have a pastor you can relate to, pray and ask God to show you what church would be a good covering for you, your ministry if you have one, and if married, for you and your spouse.

I've had some major identity struggles in trying to figure out the role of a woman in full-time ministry. For one, I had a hard time calling myself a minister. Even after I was traveling and speaking quite often, it was still hard for me to admit that I was a woman minister. Finally, the Lord spoke to me and said, "Cindy, you have accepted the call of God on your life but you have never embraced the call. You don't like being a woman minister. In your heart, you'd rather be something else in life."

Wow, that was really hard to hear, but true—very, very true! He went on in a gentle voice to say, "If you don't love who I made you, you don't love yourself, and if you don't love yourself, then how can you love others? I have made you a woman minister and you will always be a woman minister."

At that moment I embraced the call. "Lord, forgive me for not wanting to be who You destined me to be. I choose to embrace the call today." From that moment I was free and could easily tell people I was a minister with great and abundant joy.

Changed by the Challenge

This book has been quite a journey for me because of the input from my special friends. My good friend and prayer partner, Quin Sherrer, who coauthored *A Woman's Guide to Spiritual Warfare* along with my other friend, Ruthanne Garlock, encouraged me to write about my ordination so people would have insight into the challenges of a woman minister. So here goes...

To begin, I had quite a challenge finding anyone who would ordain me at all. I had been licensed for nearly five years when I felt it was time to seek ordination. (By the way, I had received my license in rather an odd-hand way. After a service, I was handed the licensing card, even though male peers had been given a commission.) Anyway, I asked my pastor if he would ordain me and, as you know, he ordained Mike instead.

Later, I again approached him because I wanted the impartation that I knew came from being ordained. He agreed that we would have the service during a prophetic conference Mike and I were conducting at the church. Shortly before the ordination was to take place, the pastor told me he was canceling it. When I asked him why, he murmured, "Oh, there won't be time. It will crowd the meeting."

I was crushed and embarrassed. I had invited my friends to come for the ordination, and there wasn't enough time to cancel; so when they arrived, there wasn't one! The Lord was gracious to me, however. The night before the conference was to start, I was washing dishes when an angel briefly stood beside me and said, "Cindy, everything will be all right." Incredible peace flooded my soul, and he was right—everything was all right.

Later, the pastor asked my forgiveness and told me he hadn't realized he had a problem with ordaining women in the ministry.

About a year later, the new pastor at our church, Reverend Don Connell, discovered what had happened concerning my ordination and stopped me one day after church. "Cindy," he said, "we'd like to ordain you here at the church. I'm sorry for how you've been treated." Were those ever healing words! By that time I was traveling all around the world speaking to thousands of people. I knew God had ordained me by His Spirit, but I also understood that a powerful anointing comes when one is set aside for service during ordination and laying on of hands.

It is a true saying that good things come to those who wait. My ordination service was a glorious celebration. We had special singers, worship and a beautiful processional. My ordaining committee included C. Peter Wagner, Dutch Sheets, Elizabeth Alves, Eric Belcher, Don and Bernadean Connell and Mike. It was marvelous beyond words. The group did a prophetic presbytery and everything was wonderful until an African man came forward and started so-called "prophesying." He said I was to kiss my husband's feet and call him Lord and other such things. I couldn't believe what was happening. It was rather like a bad nightmare.

Thank God for the committee, who one by one took him aside and corrected him for the false prophecy. They explained to him that he was mixing his cultural understanding with his own emotions. Then they told him that American women don't kiss their husbands' feet! The Lord turned the end of the ordination around and brought a powerful impartation through the laying on of hands and ordination address.

During the prophetic presbytery the Lord spoke through Dutch Sheets that I was a Deborah whose name meant "a bee" and that there would be times when my words would be sweet to the taste and times when they would carry a sting. Eric Belcher of Christ for the Nations also addressed Deborah as a prophetess to the nations.

Let's Talk Ordination

Some people wonder about women being ordained. As I've studied ordination, I have found that quite a bit of ecclesiastical trapping is wrapped around the subject of ordination. I've discovered that ordination is simply setting aside a person to the call of God and impartation through the laying on of hands. Spiritual authority comes through the recognition and affirmation of this setting aside a person to the gospel.

I am amazed at the glass ceiling that still exists concerning ordination of women. Many leaders who purport to be champions of women in the ministry do not ordain women as pastors in the same way they do men. In many cases, the problem is a cultural bias against women. Although ordination is not absolutely essential for ministry, a double standard should not exist. If one ordains a man for a certain position in the Church and a woman is filling a similar-level job, then the woman needs to be ordained also. Women have even told me that their male pastors have chuckled and said, "I'd ordain you if you were a man." Most men don't realize how painful these comments are to women.

I believe it is just as important to ordain those in traveling ministries as it is those who are pastoring. Often, there seems to be an unspoken feeling that those who travel as itinerant ministers are "second-class" citizens and that only those people who pastor should be ordained. Let's consider the message this sends. Is there more than one Church? Are those who travel in ministry "outside" of the Church, and those who speak locally "inside" the Church? Although this may not be the message intentionally being sent, it still amounts to the same thing. There is only one Church and we are all part of the Body of Christ.

Ordination may one day be handled in a completely different way than it is now. Some people do not even believe ordination as currently practiced is valid for today. I personally do, but I also think that if we really believe there is neither male nor female in the Spirit and that God poured out His Spirit on both the handmaidens and the servants at Pentecost, the double standard should not exist in the Church.

For those women who have gone through some difficult times, please make sure you don't allow a root of bitterness against men (see Heb. 12:15). We do not wrestle against flesh and blood, but against principalities and powers of darkness (see Eph. 6:12). Use the hard times as a character-building experience (see Rom. 5:1-5).

If You're Not Called, Don't Enter the Battle

Let me say a personal word to you who feel a call to full-time Christian service as a woman minister. Make sure that you are *called.* So many challenges exist for women in leadership that you must "know that you know" that you are following the will of God and not your own personal desires. God is able to make His call abundantly clear to you. When it is His call, it will be burned deep within your heart. If you are not sure, you will be swayed by the storms swirling around this controversial subject, and you will certainly be sifted and found wanting.

Ann Graham Lotz, daughter of Billy Graham, tells her story in *Christianity Today:*

I began my career as an itinerant minister in response to God's call in my life which was confirmed by Acts 26:15-18. I knew from His Word that I was to be His servant and a witness of Jesus Christ that would involve evangelism and discipleship around the world. One of the invitations I accepted was an opportunity to address approximately 1,000 pastors and church leaders. But when I stood up to speak, some of the men in the audience rose, reversed their chairs, and turned their backs to me.

I went home and prayed, "Lord, you know that address-ing an audience that includes men has not been a problem for me. But it is obviously a problem for them, and I can't continue to stand in the pulpit and ignore this."

As I searched the Scriptures for an answer, God seemed to remind me from John 20 that, following His resurrection, Jesus had commissioned Mary of Magdala in a similar fashion. God also seemed to speak to me from Jeremiah 1:7-8, commanding me to be obedient to my call, unafraid of "their faces"—or their backs. He reinforced this in verse 17, clearly commanding me to "get yourself ready! Stand up and say to them whatever I command you. Do not be terrified by them, or I will terrify you before them." In other words, I was not accountable to my audience, I was accountable to Him.[1]

Other women have suffered similar public persecution when they were speaking by the invitation of conference committees. Jill Briscoe, lay advisor to the Women's Ministry at Elmbrook Church in Brookfield, Wisconsin, where her husband, Stuart, serves as pastor, tells how this happened to her when she was addressing a convention of 3,000 young people:

> I introduced my subject and opened the Scriptures and read them and began to explain them. At that point, a pastor stood up and told me, "Stop, in the name of the Lord!" and said that I was out of order. He then rebuked my husband, saying that he should be ashamed to allow his wife to usurp his authority. He then took his young people out, and several other people followed.
>
> The good thing was that 3,000 rather bored kids suddenly became very attentive. But it left me feeling vulnerable and shocked.

These are only a few of the horror stories I have heard from women leaders in the Church. I was told that a fellow woman minister in Texas was "unordained" by her pastor after a certain apostolic group came through her city. Another friend went to church on a Sunday morning with her family after being on the road speaking and was publicly excommunicated in front of the church for traveling too much. Thank God that His gifts and callings are irrevocable (see Rom. 11:29) and we can't be unordained in the kingdom of God. (This is not to say that God doesn't reprimand His children, but these women were disciplined unfairly according to cultural boundaries rather than biblical ones.)

Because I'm being totally honest and open with you, I will have to admit that I have closeted myself away at times to forgive both acquaintances who have hurt me and people I have considered friends. Somehow, God has blessed me with enormous favor and I seem to bounce back. However, I am sad to say that not everyone I have known has fared the same.

Marilyn Hickey, a Role Model for My Generation

Many of the pioneers in the Church today are women. I wrote about some of them in the chapter "Heroines of the Faith" as well as in "Moms and Other Great Handmaidens of Faith." I wanted to include one of them in this chapter because I admire her both as a woman and role model for my generation. Her name is Marilyn Hickey.

I called Marilyn the other day to see if she'd give me an interview for this book. I always enjoy talking to her. Even though her television program is viewed by more than 65 million people a day and she has traveled and ministered in 77 countries of the world, Marilyn is always humble, warm and caring.

Marilyn's husband, Wally, was called before she was. She said that he would always compliment and encourage her for any step she took as she used her gift of teaching. Marilyn started teaching in a home Bible study for their church which quickly multiplied to 20. During that time, she was encouraged to start a 5-minute radio show that went to 15 minutes a day. Later, God called her to television.

When I asked Marilyn if she copastors the Orchard Road Church (formerly The Happy Church) along with Wally, she said, "No. Although I'm very involved with the church, I feel my primary call is to be a missionary evangelist and teacher. God has called me to cover the earth with His Word."

You may know that Marilyn, like myself, has had books written against what she teaches (or what she supposedly teaches). Curious, I asked, "Marilyn, do you ever read any of the critical things that are written about you?"

"No," she replied, "I have so many things to study and read that I have found I don't have time to stop and read those kinds of things."

What touched me most is how unscathed she sounds in spite of some of the persecution and misunderstanding she has suffered. It caused me to get a glimpse into the heart of a great woman who has paid the price and yet remains tender and compassionate in her calling.

LaNora Van Arsdall, Associate Pastor

Another of my friends who works as a team with her husband is LaNora Van Arsdall. LaNora's husband, Dan, is the pastor of The Sanctuary in Mesa, Arizona. Dan is the senior pastor and LaNora is the associate pastor of the church.

LaNora shared with me that she started out as copastor, but her *primary* anointing really isn't for pastoral work. And it seemed that people were playing them off one against the other. Because of this, she is now the associate so people will know where the ultimate authority lies. This also gives her more freedom to travel and minister without the day-to-day decisions a copastor would be called upon to make.

The Facts

As I was in the process of writing this book, I became curious about women pastors in America. The following are a few interesting facts I discovered:

1. They are paid less than their male counterparts—$5,000 per year less on average. This came out in a study of 15

Protestant denominations. (Source: EP News Service, May 2, 1997.)

2. According to George Barna, men represent 97 percent of all senior pastors. Relatively few women reach that status, even though more than one-quarter of the students enrolled in Protestant seminaries are women and increasing numbers are seeking to become senior pastors.[2]

3. Most of the women who reach senior pastor level do so in mainline churches—Presbyterian Church (U.S.A.) (UPCUSA), United Methodist Church (UMC), United Church of Christ (UCC), Episcopal Church (EC) and Evangelical Lutheran Church in America (ELCA). For theological reasons, many of the Baptist and evangelical denominations prohibit women from becoming senior pastors.[3]

4. Women who make it to the top in a local church tend to be older than their male counterparts, have spent fewer years in full-time ministry and probably entered the professional ministry later in life, serve in older churches and are more likely to lead congregations that have fewer than 100 people.[4]

5. Women also preach shorter sermons, on average, than do their male counterparts. They are every bit as likely as male pastors, however, to have attended a seminary and to be the only full-time professional on the staff.[5]

According to an article in the September 27th edition of the *Denver Post*, ordained women tend to want to share leadership, be more democratic than many church traditions allow and break down hierarchical ways of doing ministry.

Bill Behrens, director of leadership support for the Evangelical Lutheran Church, says that women bring fresh skills to the age-old task of ministry. They nurture the young and care for the old. They challenge the smug, preach the gospel and, above all, build community.

The article goes on to say that last year, more than 27,000 students were preparing for ordination at 230 seminaries accredited by the Association of Theological Schools, according to Nancy Merrill, the association's communications director. Nearly 8,000, or 28 percent, were women, a significant jump from less than 5 percent in 1972.

According to Reverend Lynn Scott, director of Clergy Women's Concerns for the United Methodist Church in Nashville, roughly half the students at Episcopal, Methodist, Presbyterian and Lutheran seminaries are women.[6]

The fact that so many women are going to seminary and seeking ordination should be a loud statement to us: God is calling women today in huge numbers to preach the gospel and be in full-time ministry. The wonderful assurance we have is that the same God who called will open the doors of utterance for us.

Vinson Synan, dean of the School of Divinity at CBN's Regent University in Virginia Beach, Virginia, says that as of 1991, the Assemblies of God counted 4,604 women with ministerial credentials—the most of any denomination in the United States. This amounts to 15 percent of all ministers in the American A/G church. Of these, some 322 are listed as "senior pastors." The percentage of women ordained in the International Foursquare Gospel has held steady at about 40 percent for several decades. The percentages of ordained and licensed women ministers in the Pentecostal Holiness Church (17 percent) and the Church of God (Cleveland, Tennessee; 15 percent) still exceed those of any of the mainline Protestant denominations. But recent surveys indicate that fewer women are serving as pastors in these churches than ever before.[7]

Practical Protocol for Women in Ministry

As I prayed about what to include in this chapter, I felt a practical section for those women in ministry was needed. Some of the information will pertain more to those with traveling ministries as I am most familiar with this kind of ministry. I could practically write a whole book on what I've learned about the many areas of protocol concerning women ministering. Let's consider a few of them...

An important subject we women need to learn about is how we relate to men in the ministry. I have put some practical policies in place as a traveling minister to safeguard myself from gossip or any other attack that may come from my interacting with men in general as well as men in the ministry.

One of my first lines of defense is a personal letter sent from my office before I go any place to speak. I will include a copy of it for you to have in the appendix. In this letter my office states that I am not ever to be picked up by a man alone. At times, I have had to ride with a driver from a major ministry that sent a ministry van to pick up its speakers. I try, however, to make this the exception.

Another personal policy is that I do not ever go out for lunch or dinner alone with a man, other than my husband, unless Mike is there. I made an exception to this once when I had breakfast in an open room and Mike knew about it. I adhere to these policies, at least at this age of my life, even when the man is much younger than I. It keeps both of our reputations clean and above board.

Women, we can actually inappropriately encourage men and not understand that we are doing so. Spending long hours in intimate conversation, as I alluded to in the section on spiritual adultery, can give men the wrong idea. Don't let yourself be put in a compromising situation. For instance, don't sit in a car talking to a married man or talk for long periods of time on the phone. There are times when I give counsel or seek counsel from a pastor when we have an extended conversation but, again, this is the exception, not the rule. I make sure I am also friends with the male pastor's wife.

An area of concern I have is that of women intercessors and how intimately they relate to their male pastors. While it is important to share what God has shown you, do not spend time behind closed doors without your spouse or the other person's spouse being present. Sadly, this close involvement can cause women who are extremely naive to become emotionally entangled in the lives of their pastors and vice versa.

Before I speak at any local church, I ask for a letter of invitation from the senior pastor of that church. I had some problems early in the ministry when an elder or someone else from a church would invite me and the senior pastor was not in complete agreement with a woman ministering. Now, I always ask for a letter of confirmation to keep on file in my office regardless of the kind of meeting I will be going to.

For those who travel in ministry, the subject of finances can be difficult and will require clear communication. As I stated earlier, my secretary sends a letter delineating our requirements for my travel. I have found that sending the letter provides clarity, plus gives a way to make other needs known. I do not personally require a set honorarium when I travel. What I do ask for is enough to cover my travel and lodging expenses as well as a love gift. When I know that the organization for which I am speaking is notoriously low in their offerings, and thus I cannot meet the budgetary needs of our ministry, I will send a letter that states the following:

> Because of the needs of our ministry, we are asking you to believe with us for an amount of $ _____ for the weekend. If you are unable to meet this amount, we will understand, but let's agree together that God will meet our needs according to His riches in glory.

When I first began traveling, I found that the love gifts I received did not even cover my expenses for gas. Eventually I began to resent this, believing that "the laborer is worthy of his [or in my case, her] wages" (1 Tim. 5:18). At first I had real peace about paying travel expenses out of my own pocket. But after a while I found myself resenting it and realized that God's grace for that period of my life had ended.

Today I find that people are generous in giving to our ministry. It's been a long time since I have had to send this kind of letter. But for those who are just beginning in ministry, a letter like this can be quite beneficial.

In this hour, women are preaching and teaching, leading worship, working with the poor, going into prisons and doing many other valuable ministries. The Lord is uniquely calling women to be pioneers in new fields where they never used to walk. It is a privilege and honor to be a pioneer. God calls some women to do what others haven't done to make the way easier for the next generation. I want to be like that. God has given me a heart for young leaders, both men and women. I wish I could spend time individually with the many calls I receive asking for mentoring, but I simply do not have the time. It is often a great frustration to me, because I really do care. This is one of the major reasons I have written this chapter.

If you are called and are frustrated, please be assured that God will make a way for you where there seems to be no way. In all the years I've ministered, I have never done any self-promotion—I let it all come from the Lord. I have never had one door that I cared anything about remain closed. God has opened doors that have astounded me. As I've traveled, I've often been told by the pastor that I was the first woman ever to preach the gospel from that pulpit. These words have rung in my ears from Pakistan to Nepal to many places in Latin America. The fact is, you simply can't keep the Holy Spirit out from a place where He wants to go.

The next and final chapter is quite exciting and eye opening. It's titled "The Cultural Reformation" and deals with the way God views women and their involvement historically in revival and their role in the Church today.

Notes

1. *Christianity Today*, "Ministering Women" (April 8, 1996): 17.
2. George Barna, *Today's Pastors* (Ventura, Calif.: Regal Books, 1993), p. 31.
3. Ibid., p. 31.

4. Ibid., p. 32.
5. Ibid., p. 32.
6. "Female Ministers Gaining Acceptance," *Denver Post* (Sunday, September 27, 1997).
7. Vinson Synan, "Women in Ministry," *Ministries Today* magazine (Jan./Feb. 1993): 50.

The Cultural Reformation

Blessed be He who did not make me a Gentile;
Blessed be He who did not make me a woman;
Blessed be He who did not make me an uneducated man
(or a slave).
—Tosefta[1]

A hundred women are no better than two men.
—B. Berakhot (Talmud)

"A woman is a pitcher full of filth with its mouth full of
blood, yet all run after her."
(Babylonian Talmud Shabbath 152A)

When a boy comes into the world, peace comes into
the world;
when a girl comes, nothing comes.
(Babylonian Talmud)

These sayings depict a world in which women were often marginalized and despised. In the midst of this twisted thinking

came One who would bring cultural reformation—the Savior, Jesus Christ. No wonder the women loved Him. The women were "last at the Cross and the first at the tomb." For the female gender, there never has been nor ever will be one who smashed barriers and set the captives free like He did.

As I've studied Jesus' love for the lowly, the oppressed and downtrodden, I have been amazed with increasing awareness at how He shows Himself to be so personally relational and yet such a cultural reformer. To experience the full impact of this One who tore down the walls of partition, let's take a look at the world into which He was born.

Greco-Roman Attitudes

The following brief sampling of practices characterized Greco-Roman male attitudes concerning women. The following examples come from the time period leading up to the time of Christ:

Infanticide and Abuse

Girl infants were exposed and left to die much more frequently than boys. Girls, after all, were an expensive and unremunerative investment, not only because of the cost of supporting them as children, but also because of the expense of providing them with dowries (Posidippus—who lived between the third and second centuries B.C.).[2]

At one time in Rome, husbands greeted their wives with a kiss. This was not a sign of affection, but rather a test to see if their wives had been drinking wine. Drinking wine was thought to make a woman "loose" and sexually uninhibited. If women smelled of wine, their husbands had a legal right to kill them.

Women usually were married at age 12 to much older men and were expected to bear a child every two years.

Note Seneca's perspective on women: "Women and ignorance are the two greatest calamities in the world."[3]

"Zeus designed this as the greatest of all evils: women. Even if in some way they seem to be a help, to their husbands especially, they are a source of evil."[4]

"Mistresses we keep for the sake of pleasure, concubines for the daily care of our person, but wives to bear us legitimate children and to be faithful guardians of our households" (Pseudo-Demosthenes).[5]

The Jewish Perspective

Divorce

A woman's security in her husband's family was limited by her husband's legal right to divorce her if she caused an "impediment" to the marriage. A man could divorce his wife without her consent for reasons ranging from her unchastity to burning a meal to finding a fairer woman.[6]

Most rabbis repeatedly stressed the inferiority of women in their teachings. Rabbi Yochanan, we are told, quoted the Mishna (the most ancient and important part of the Talmud) as teaching that a man could do as he pleased with his wife: "It is like a piece of meat brought from the shambles, which one may eat, salt, roast, partially or wholly cooked." A woman once complained before Rav (a great rabbi) of bad treatment from her husband. He replied, "What is the difference between thee and a fish, which one may eat either broiled or cooked?"[7]

The wife's household duties included grinding flour, baking bread, washing clothes, breast-feeding the children for 18 to 24 months, making the beds, working with wool and washing her husband's face, hands and feet.[8] Although many of these tasks are not abnormal in themselves (I made our bed this morning!), there are still places in the world where these simple household tasks are taken to extremes. For example, when Mike and I were in Nepal last year, we were told of a practice by some tribal people in which the women wash their husband's feet each night and then drink the dirty water to show respect. And that isn't all!... When the men travel, they wash their feet and bring the dirty water home in a jar so their wives can drink it!

Another example of Talmudic prejudice against women can be found in what is known as "The Ten Curses Against Eve," the commentary on Genesis 3:16.

The Ten Curses Against Eve

1. Greatly multiply refers to catamenia, etc.;
2. Thy sorrow in rearing children;
3. Thy conception;
4. In sorrow thou shalt bring forth children;
5. Thy desire shall be unto they husband (followed by language too coarse for reproduction, leaving no doubt of the rabbinical interpretation of "desire");
6. 'He shall rule over thee' (more and fouler language);
7. She is wrapped up like a mourner; i.e,
8. Dares not appear in public with her head uncovered;
9. Is restricted to one husband, while he may have many wives;
10. And is confined to the house as to a prison.[9]

To be fair, not all rabbis were woman haters. Some, such as Rabbi Jacobs, said, "One who has no wife remains without good, and without a helper, and without joy, and without blessings, and without atonement."[10] However, honoring statements such as this one by Rabbi Jacobs were few and far between.

The more I have studied ancient cultures, the greater admiration I feel for what Jesus did to set precedents for treating women and children with respect. Until I completed this study, I overlooked many seemingly simple little words and actions recorded in the Gospels that I now understand were huge statements in the culture of Jesus' day. Jesus brought an enormous reformation not only for women and children, but also the whole family. These actions and teachings were built upon later in Scripture by the New Testament writers.

The Good News Perspective

From the very beginning of the New Testament, women are given a place of unprecedented equity and prominence. This new place is first illustrated in chapter 1 of Matthew's Gospel where Matthew traces the lineage of Christ. Matthew mentions not only the men's names, but also three significant women ancestors in the Messiah's geneology: Tamar, Rahab and Ruth.

The next powerful cultural statement is evidenced when the angel Gabriel first appeared not to Joseph, or Mary's father, or any other male, but to a little woman probably about 14 years old (see Luke 1:26-38). (Today we would probably label her a teenager and not a woman at all.) And what the angel said was even more amazing... *You have found favor with God.*

No wonder Mary sang, "He has regarded the lowly state of His maidservant; for behold, henceforth all generations will call me blessed!" (Luke 1:48).

It is also interesting to study the way the Holy Spirit inspired the New Testament writers to include male and female pairings through the Scriptures. This is beautifully presented in the story of Jesus' presentation at the Temple as a child. Two powerful leaders, Simeon and Anna, were drawn by the Spirit to witness to the fact that Jesus was the "consolation of Israel" (Luke 2:25). Anna prophesied about Him to all those who were looking for redemption of Jerusalem (see Luke 2:38). The recognition of Jesus as Messiah was announced that day in beautiful gender equity—a foretaste of the day when the Holy Spirit would come upon both handmaidens and servants (see Joel 2:28,29).

Luke's birth account of Jesus lists other pairings of men and women: Zachariah and Elizabeth, Joseph and Mary, and Simeon and Anna.

More male-female pairings come to the forefront in the parables of Jesus. For instance, Luke 18:1-8 tells the story of the woman who refuses to stop crying out to an unjust male judge for vindication. The setting of the story is a male-oriented society where females rarely received the same kind of justice as

men. The woman's cries were heard because of her persistence.
Jesus finishes the parable with the statement: "Shall not God
avenge His own elect, who cry day and night to Him?"
Witherington says:

> Jesus' choice of a woman in need of help as an example for
> His disciples perhaps indicated Jesus' sympathy and concern
> for this particular group of people in a male-oriented soci-
> ety, and also because the aspect of this woman's behavior
> that Jesus focuses on (her perseverance or persistence) is a
> characteristic that in a patriarchal society was often seen as
> a negative attribute in a woman (Prov. 19:13).[11]

Women in the Ministry of Jesus

The second chapter of John starts with a fascinating exchange
between Jesus and His mother. Mary tells Jesus there is a problem. They have run out of wine. Evidentially, she believes He can
remedy the situation. He replies, "Woman, what does your concern have to do with Me? My hour has not yet come" (John 2:4).
To us the address "Woman" may seem rather disrespectful. But
there is no harshness of disrespect here at all, as can be seen in John
19:26, Matthew 15:28, Luke 13:12, John 4:21 and 8:10. Yet Jesus does
seem to be distancing Himself from her as His mother by calling
her "Woman." The phrase "My hour is not yet come" may refer to
the time when she will know Him in an entirely different way—as
Savior—rather than simply as a mother knows her son.

If Jesus was ever-so-slightly distancing Himself from Mary as
His mother, His address really makes His response to Mary much
stronger. He changes the water to wine as a result of a "woman"
seeking His help. This would have been quite unusual in His time.
Not only did He literally change water into new wine, but He was
also transforming the "old wine" prejudice against women into
that of a "new wine" perspective in which there is "neither male
nor female." According to Jesus both women and men equally
approach the throne of God in times of need.

(A parenthetical comment on this passage: One of the gods worshiped during Jesus' time was Bacchus, the god of wine. Jesus' first miracle of turning water to wine very well could have been a direct act of spiritual warfare against Bacchus, the god of disorder and revelry. Jesus came to bring the wine of the Spirit which sets all things into right order.)

The next major blow to cultural prejudice against women was with Jesus' conversation with a Samaritan woman (see John 4:4-26). Scripture records this story as the most extensive personal conversation Jesus ever had with anyone. If Jewish men reviled anyone more than an unclean woman, a foreign woman or an immoral woman, it would have been a Samaritan woman—the very kind of woman with whom Jesus spoke at length. Jesus honored her with much more than a lengthy conversation; He singled her out to receive some of the weightiest theological instruction of His ministry and to be the recipient of His first claim to be the Messiah.[12]

The story of the woman at the well speaks powerfully both to gender prejudice and racial prejudice. Jesus chose to reveal Himself to a woman who was considered little better than a dog. Even His disciples were, no doubt, astonished at His behavior. Jesus came to reconcile both the genders and the races.

The Samaritan woman became the first evangelist! She preached the message to the whole city, men and women. Surely Jesus could have gone into the city and found a Samaritan man, but no, He chose a woman from the lowest class of society and gave her value as one worthy to spread the good news.

(A final parenthetical comment on this passage: Respected rabbis were expected to keep their distance from sinners, but Jesus spoke directly to sinners about matters of the Kingdom. This was very unusual for rabbis in His day.)

Another clear example that Jesus despised double standards of conduct and punishment for men and women is found in the story of the woman caught in adultery:

> The Scribes and Pharisees brought to Him a woman caught in adultery. And when they had set her in the midst, they

said to Him, "Teacher, this woman was caught in adultery, in the very act. Now Moses, in the law, commanded us that such should be stoned. But what do You say?" (John 8:3-5).

I can only imagine the thoughts that ran through Jesus' mind. One immediate thought would have been that the Scribes and Pharisees had only quoted part of the law on adultery. Leviticus 20:10 says that both the adulterer and the adulteress shall surely be put to death. The woman alone had been "caught in the act"— the guilty man was getting off scot-free.

Many other double standards had evolved in the society since the law had been given. Of course, the eternally present Son of God and lawgiver knew. His next statement ripped the covers off the hidden places of their hearts: "He who is without sin among you, let him throw a stone at her first" (John 8:7).

What was Jesus saying? Whichever of you who has never indulged in sexual fantasy, throw the first stone. Whichever of you who has never had a problem with lust, throw the first stone. We know the woman's accusers must have had some kind of struggle because the Bible makes it clear that His statement smote their consciences (see v. 9).

This was absolutely incredible! Jesus saw the sin of a woman and the sin of a man as being equal. He leveled the genders and held men to the same moral responsibility for their actions as He did women.

Another strong statement from Jesus about the value and equality of women is the story of the healing of the woman with the issue of blood (see Matt. 9:20-22; Mark 5:25-34; Luke 8:43-48). What is often overlooked is that a woman could not enter into the Temple precincts during her menstrual cycle. She would have been considered unclean and could only have been made "clean" again through rather elaborate ritual washing. However, when Jesus noted the woman with the menstrual flow was healed, He immediately brought her into His presence. The statement Jesus was making: *There is never a time when you cannot approach Me. You can never be too "defiled" or "unclean" that I will not take you in.*

Jesus and the Children

Unlike the terribly wicked practice of exposing children to the elements at birth to die (infanticide), Jesus went out of His way to proclaim their worth. A cultural background of the terrible practice of infanticide brings a whole different slant to the story of the disciples sending the children away and the Lord becoming indignant over what His followers had done. One of the most beautiful passages in Scripture establishes a strong place for the little ones in His kingdom: "Let the little children come to Me, and do not forbid them; for of such is the kingdom of God." (Mark 10:14).

Jesus and His Healing Ministry

Jesus broke from the rabbis and their oppressive rules concerning women. When He healed the crippled woman on the Sabbath in the synagogue, Jesus both *touched* and *spoke* to her (see Luke 13:10-17), both actions avoided by over-scrupulous rabbis. But that wasn't all....Then the biggest slap on the face to the Pharisees came when Jesus called her "daughter of Abraham." No woman was ever called a daughter of Abraham. Only men were to be called sons of Abraham.

Jesus also healed Peter's mother-in-law of a fever on the Sabbath, right after he healed the man with the unclean spirit in the synagogue (see Mark 1:23-31). Again, He broke precedent by taking her hand. No rabbi would take a woman's hand until sundown on the Sabbath.

Women as Disciples

It is widely known that Jesus included women with His traveling team. This must have seemed absolutely scandalous.

Now it came to pass, afterward, that He went through every city and village, preaching and bringing the glad tidings of the kingdom of God. And the twelve were with Him, and certain women who had been healed of evil spirits and infirmities—Mary, called Magdalene, out of whom had come seven demons, and Joanna the wife of Chuza, Herod's steward, and Susanna, and many others who provided for Him from their substance (Luke 8:1-3).

It has often been claimed that Jesus chose 12 male disciples to set a precedent for men only in ministry. However, we must remember that Jesus came to the Jews, a very patriarchal people. Jewish believers would become His bridge team to the world. To impose a first-century Jewish culture grid on all future Christians would not only too narrowly define those who could be disciples, but also set artificial limits on Jesus' worldwide mission to the Gentiles. Jesus started with 12 men, but by Luke 8 we see that His ministry team had greatly expanded. In fact, it doesn't take much of a stretch to believe that by Luke 10, some of the Seventy-ministry team were also women. And we are explicitly told in Acts 1:13,14 that women were included in the company of 120 awaiting Pentecost in the Upper Room.

Other women besides those in the Luke 8 traveling team were also among His disciples. Remember the story of Mary and Martha? Martha was worried about the meal and Mary wanted to sit at the feet of Jesus and learn from Him. According to Witherington, "the use of the phrase 'to sit at the feet of' is significant because evidence shows this is a technical formula meaning 'to be a disciple of.'"[13]

Evidentially, it was unknown in those days for a rabbi to come into the home of a woman and specifically teach her. Jesus' behavior of being in the home of two women alone would also have been questioned by other rabbis.

Witherington goes on to say: "As in the case of Jesus' relation to His mother Mary, we again see a reorganizing of traditional priorities in light of Kingdom requirements. Martha's service is not denigrated, but it does not come first. One must reorientate one's lifestyle according to what Jesus says is the 'good portion.'"[14]

Paul, Women and the Family

Paul followed Jesus' lead in revolutionizing the thinking of his day concerning the family. He grounded his instructions regarding honoring mother and father (see Eph. 6:2) in the fifth commandment (see Exod. 20:12). But as we know from His theology, He did not slavishly follow rabbinic tradition.

In Roman times, households were governed by a common understanding of "household ethics." This common understanding was the basis for Roman tax and legal codes. The tax and legal codes made it clear that the man was the undisputed ruler of the house. Similarly, the Mishnah or Jewish tradition also put women in a subordinate and subservient position, as I stated in the opening of this chapter.

In the book of Ephesians, Paul gives us the "household ethics" or rules of order for the Christian home. What he wrote under the inspiration of the Holy Spirit rocked the foundations of society with the transforming power of the gospel. Paul writes of the

The power of the Cross cuts through the walls of division and brings dignity to men, women and children....God loves all of His children the same— no matter what their age, gender or race.

wife's submission in the context of mutual submission under Christ (see Eph. 5:21,22). The wife and husband are fully included in the Body of Christ (see vv. 23,24). The husband is instructed to love his wife in order that she may respect him (see v. 33). Her respect for him is to be the fruit of his love for her.[15]

In writing these words, Paul completely redefines the marital relationship. Paul's theology engages the very fabric of society, challenging all established cultural protocols, reshaping human value systems and transforming interpersonal relationships.[16]

The power of the Cross cuts through the walls of division and brings dignity to men, women and children. There is no preferential treatment here. God loves all of His children the same—no matter what their age, gender or race. The good news of Jesus Christ wrought a cultural reformation that continues to reshape our understandings today.

Attitudes of Early Church Leaders Toward Women

I was amazed to find that some of the Early Church fathers had a very negative attitude toward women. The following quotes give some examples:

"Having become disobedient, she was made the cause of death, both to herself and to the entire human race" (Irenaeus, Bishop of Lyons A.D. 177).[17]

"Do you not know that you are an Eve? God's verdict on the sex still holds good, and the sex's guilt must still hold also. YOU ARE THE DEVIL'S GATEWAY, you are the avenue to the forbidden tree" (Tertullian of Carthage, a few years later).[18]

What's sad about Tertullian's statement is that it isn't even biblical! For instance, 1 Corinthians 15:22 says that "In Adam all die," and that, "Adam was not deceived" (1 Tim. 2:14).

Even reformers such as Martin Luther had a bias against women. He once said, "No gown worse becomes a woman than to be wise."[19]

Bible Translation
Bushnell believes that the translators of the English Bible were significantly influenced by Babylonian Talmudic thinking. The following is how: The Babylon Talmud existed as oral instructions for

many centuries but was reduced to writing and published at Babylon about A.D. 800.[20]

In the 1530s, an Italian Dominican monk named Pagnino translated the Hebrew Bible relying on rabbinic interpretation of certain key passages regarding women. The *Biographie Universelle* quotes the following criticism of his work, in the language of Richard Simon: "Pagnino has too much neglected the ancient versions of Scripture to attach himself to the teachings of the rabbis."[21]

Bushnell then shows that later translations of the Bible into English such as Coverdale's and Tyndale's depended upon Pagnino's various renderings.

An excellent quotation sums up one of my life's philosophies as I have tried to study this subject: "Interpret your Bible by what the Bible says, and not by what men say that it says."[22] All of us, including myself, have some biases. The hard thing is to put them aside and try to hear what the Lord is saying in His Word.

The Impact of Jesus' Reformation in Modern Times

As I've studied the impact of Jesus' cultural reformation, it has been both fascinating, and, I must admit, sad. First I would become exhilarated in studying the history of revivals when the Holy Spirit was trying to bring "new wine" thinking into the Church, then I would become discouraged when I saw how cultural influences inhibited what the Spirit was doing.

Around the turn of the last century, a substantial move of God occurred regarding the role of women in the Church. Great reformers were hearing the Holy Spirit say that it is time for the women to come forth.

Leaders such as A. B. Simpson (who founded the Christian Missionary Alliance church) gave women a prominent place in church ministry, and encouraged women's participation and leadership in virtually every phase of early CMA life. In celebrating its golden anniversary, the CMA proudly recalled that "especially in the early days of Alliance, there was a host of Spirit-filled women who labored as evangelists and Bible teachers with great effectiveness. Simpson included women on the executive board committee, employed them as Bible professors and supported female evangelists and branch officers (the early CMA equivalent to a local minister). Half of all CMA vice presidents in 1887 were women.[23]

The Evangelical Free Church provided for women preachers in its original constitution. Charles Finney allowed women to speak in his Presbyterian church to mixed audiences. Dr. A. J. Gordon published his major treatise on women in 1894. Gordon Bible College prepared women to answer any call of the Spirit. Gordon pastored the Clarendon Street Baptist Church in Boston the last 24 years of his life. A woman graduate of Gordon Bible College later went on, after being ordained in 1914, to serve as an assistant pastor of the Stoughton Congregational Church. William Bell Riley pastored Minneapolis's First Baptist Church, one of the largest in the Northern Baptist Convention, for 45 years. Like Gordon, he advocated women preaching, pastoring and doing evangelistic work.[24]

I have noted in studying many denominations that when they were still simply "moves of God," and the Holy Spirit was pouring out His power, no one seemed to mind that women were preaching. Later, when they became routinized, institutionalized and set in governmental structure, the women were voted out. (I wonder somehow if the Holy Spirit was too!)

A study of the Moody Bible Institute shows that under Dwight L. Moody, women openly served as pastors, evangelists, pulpit supply preachers, Bible teachers and even in the ordained ministry. The school's official publication, *Moody Monthly*, listed Lottie Osborn Sheidler as the first woman to graduate from the Pastor's Course in August of 1929. Yet, on August 1, 1979, MBI administration published the following statement about the role of women in public ministry:

Our policy has been and is that we do not endorse or encourage the ordination of women nor do we admit women to our Pastoral Training Major....Although there were women in the Early Church who exercised spiritual gifts, they were not given places of authority in the government of the church.[25]

This policy is quite sad in light of the fact that its founder, D. L. Moody, encouraged Francis Willard to openly and publicly preach temperance, suffrage and the gospel.[26]

The Free Methodists began licensing women as local preachers in 1873, and founder B. T. Roberts wrote on behalf of women's ordination. The Wesleyan Methodist Church, founded in 1842, promoted equality for women and for blacks. Wesleyan minister Luther Lee delivered the sermon "Women's Right to Preach the Gospel" at the 1853 ordination of Congregationalist Antoinette L. Brown, America's first fully ordained woman.[27]

Northern and Southern Baptist churches had different attitudes toward women ministers; however, the culture of the South did reflect a much more restrictive climate to women preaching than that of the North. In the North, women did preach in the Free Will Baptist, Seventh-Day Baptist, Swedish Baptist, German Baptist and German Baptist Brethren churches. When the German Baptist Brethren Church split in 1883, Mary Melinda Sterling became the first ordained Brethren woman in the Brethren Church. In the South, Southern Baptists overwhelmingly restricted females' public roles to singing in the choir and public testimonies. In stark contrast, American Baptist churches in the North ordained dozens of women in the first quarter of the twentieth century.[28]

Some Southern Baptist churches today have ordained women. One of my prayer partners is an ordained woman pastor. Because Southern Baptist churches are autonomous with regard to such decisions, some churches have ordained women even though the practice is not currently encouraged by the denomination.

At the turn of the last century women worked in parachurch agencies such as the Young Women's Christian Association (YWCA). Other denominations such as the Quakers, the Nazarenes and the Salvation Army were pioneers ordaining women in ministry. It is ironic that there was a greater freedom for women in some of these denominations a century ago than we see today. Why is this?

Part of the explanation may be a conservative backlash against changing social values.[29] Separatist Fundamentalists such as John R. Rice wrote books against bobbed hair, bossy wives and women preachers, lumping all three together in one ominous group.

Another factor has been the rise of feminism in its most militant, anti-male state. Any woman who preaches, even if she takes a stance against the errors of extremist feminism, takes a risk of being labeled a "flaming feminist." Actually, the early feminist movement in America for the women's right to vote came from an inspiration of the Holy Spirit to protect the home. I believe that today God is calling many women to be pioneers to pray and speak out against unrighteousness, to protect their homes in much the same way that Frances Willard and other early feminists did.

The Pentecostal movement, which began around the turn of the last century, recognized the anointing of the Holy Spirit upon women's lives. In the predominantly black Azusa Street Mission, charisma (or the anointing) was what counted, not race, gender or class. Those called by the Holy Spirit led the meetings. The movement was led by the prophetic class, rather than the priestly class. Listen to Bartleman, an eyewitness of the revival:

> We had no pope or hierarchy...we had no human program; the Lord Himself was leading. We had no priest class....These things have come in later, with the apostasizing of the movement. We did not honor men for their advantage in means or education, but rather for their God-given "gifts." The Lord was liable to burst through anyone. Some would finally get anointed for the message. All seemed to recognize this and gave way. It might be a child, a woman or a man. It made no difference [30]

This reminds me of my husband Mike's statement during the interview he gave to *Charisma* magazine about why he believes I am called to preach the gospel. He said that it was God who anointed, and who gives the anointings. His answer was based upon an understanding of the function of the prophetic class that Bartleman referred to.

According to an article in *Evangel*, the newspaper of the Azusa Street Revival, published in 1916:

> A marked feature of this "latter day" outpouring is the Apostolate of women. Men have hypocritically objected to women making themselves conspicuous in pulpit work, but thank God, this conspicuousness is of God Himself. They did not push themselves to the front, God pulled them there. They did not take this ministry on themselves, God put it on them.[31]

Sadly, a great struggle ensued throughout the following 29 years during which the roles of women in the Church were added and then subtracted. Women were not alone in this treatment. The color barrier that had once been declared "washed away" by the Azusa Street Revival reemerged. It has been quite clear to me that when the spirit of prejudice has been allowed to rise in the Church, women and minorities have been its focused target.

The shift from the prophetic to the priestly role for ministry took its toll on many women leaders. One of the most outstanding was Aimee Semple McPherson who was an ordained Assembly of God minister for three years. Aimee left the Assemblies to form the International Church of the Foursquare Gospel in 1927, partly because of the lack of consensus concerning women in ministry in the Assemblies. She stated in a lecture in one of her classes, probably in the late 1930s:

> This (the Foursquare Church) is the only church, I am told, that is ordaining women preachers. The Assemblies of God are not ordaining women, to my knowledge....Foursquare-dom is the only work that has given such acknowledgment to women preachers, as well as men. Even the Pentecostal work, in some cases, has said, "No women preachers." But I am

opening the door, and as long as Sister McPherson is alive, she is going to hold the door open and say, "Ladies come!"[32]

Even though the official position of the Assemblies of God today is pro-women in ministry, as I stated earlier, the number of women as senior pastors is still relatively small in comparison with the men. However, Sister McPherson would be proud to know that Foursquare still leads the way for ordained women ministers.

At the turning of the century the Holy Spirit wants to pour out His Spirit just as He did in the last century. The Spirit of God is declaring to the Church that God wants us to be a prophetic class of people who long for a fresh Pentecost. God is longing to pour out His Spirit upon both His sons and daughters.

I have a burning longing in my heart that we not miss it this time and that an outpouring will rain down upon the whole Church, male and female, which will take us to a new place in God, a place we have not yet known, where men and women teamed together will plant their feet on soil held by Satan for centuries to preach the good news that He's Alive.

Psalm 68:11 is a prophetic message for the great army of women who are arising in the land. "The Lord gives the word [of power]; the women who bear and publish [the news] are a great host" (*Amp.*).

According to Dr. Gary Greig, this passage and Isaiah 40:9,10 both refer to God raising up an army of women evangelists in the last days, since both refer to the Lord appearing in glory to bring judgment on the earth and to restore His people in the land of Israel. The verb forms in both passages are in the feminine form, not the usual masculine form, of the verbs in question.

Greig goes on to say the following about Isaiah 40:9,10:

The literal translation with the feminine verb forms in caps is... (9) Onto a high mountain GO UP (feminine singular form of the imperative of the verb "go up") ONE WHO PRO-CLAIMS GOOD NEWS (to) Zion (literally "female evangelist of Zion" using the fem. sing. form of the participle meaning "one who proclaims good news" or "evangelist" or "herald" derived from the verb "to announce good news, proclaim good news, herald good news"). SAY (fem. sing. imperative) to the cities of Judah, "Here is your God!"

See, the Lord Yahweh is coming and His strong arm (a reference from Exodus to God's power working in signs and wonders) rules for Him. See, His reward is with Him and His recompense goes before Him.

What a powerful end-time statement! The incredible thing is that these passages about the Spirit raising up women evangelists has been there all this time, perhaps hidden for this season and hour when God is calling women to come forth and preach and prophesy over cities....Cities, Behold Your God! Verse 10 goes on to tell of God working signs and wonders through this company of women in the end times.

God is speaking to the prophets all around the world that an army of women is coming who will be evangelists to their cities and who will perform mighty signs and wonders.

The gospels end with one of the most powerful and beautiful stories ever told about a woman (see John 20:1,2,11-18): a woman who came to the tomb to do what women did for the dead...anoint them for burial. Mary Magdalene went that day to the place where they had placed her master's body. However, to her surprise, she found that He wasn't there.

Suddenly, someone called her name. It was Jesus. Scripture tells us that Jesus stopped on His way to heaven to comfort Mary and tell her that He was (is) alive. Have you ever wondered why He chose Mary Magdalene? I believe it was because the men could all have gone back to their former respectable professions, but she, a former prostitute, had nothing to go back to. Jesus was the only way out for her.

He must have known this, and in His immense love made a stop, just for her—the woman of least value in all society's eyes—to give her a message...*Go tell them I'm alive!*

I believe that is the message God is telling women today. He's also saying it to men and women together as teams. Maybe you feel inadequate, the last one that Jesus would choose to speak His Words; but you see, He's not like all the others. He doesn't look on the outward form like they do. He only wants you to bow your knee before the King of Glory and give Him all of yourself, and He will fill you with all of Himself. Then you can run to the streets, and your neighbors, and the people in the grocery stores and proclaim with all your heart: *Come meet a man who told me everything I ever did and still loves me....*GO! Go on! Man, woman or child—He's calling all today. Go tell them....He's alive!

Notes

1. Note: This is a form of the *bereka*, the liturgical morning prayer which was recited every day by all devout Jewish males during Paul's time.
2. Quoted by David Joel Hamilton in "I Commend to You Our Sister," (master's thesis, 1981), p. 43.
3. Ibid., p. 81.
4. Ibid., p. 35.
5. Ben Witherington III, *Women and the Genesis of Christianity* (Cambridge, Ma.: The Press Syndicate of the University of Cambridge, 1990), p. 15.
6. Ibid., p. 4.
7. Katherine Bushnell, *God's Word to Women* (Peoria, Ill.: Cosette Joliff and Bernice Menold), paragraph 8.
8. Ben Witherington III, *Women and the Genesis of Christianity*, p. 5.
9. Katherine Bushnell, *God's Word to Women*, paragraph 106.
10. Quoted in Ben Witherington III, *Women and the Genesis of Christianity*, p. 6.
11. Ben Witherington III, *Women and the Genesis of Christianity*, p. 53.
12. Judy L. Brown, *Women Ministers* (Kearney, Nebr.: Morris Publishing, 1996), p. 133.
13. Witherington, Women and the Genesis of Christianity, p. 100.
14. Ibid., p. 102.
15. Quoted by David Joel Hamilton in "I Commend to You Our Sister" (master's thesis, 1981), p. 132.
16. Ibid., p. 134.
17. Katherine Bushnell, *God's Word to Women*, paragraph 88.
18. Ibid., paragraph 88.
19. Ibid., paragraph 619.
20. Ibid., Bushnell, see diagram after paragraph 128.

21. Ibid., paragraph 142.
22. Ibid., paragraph 20.
23. Janette Hassey, *No Time for Silence* (Grand Rapids, Mich.: Academie Books, 1986), p. 16.
24. Ibid., p. 3.
25. Ibid., p. 31.
26. Ibid., p. 33.
27. Ibid., p. 53.
28. Ibid., pp. 61-62.
29. Ibid., p. 137.
30. Charles H. Barfoot and Gerald T. Sheppard, "Review of Religious Research Prophetic Versus Priestly Religion: The Changing Role of Women Clergy in Classical Pentecostal Churches," *Review of Religious Research*, 22, no. 1 (September 1980): 9.
31. Ibid., p. 9.
32. Ibid., p. 15.

Appendices

Appendix A

Clinton—Gender and Leadership

A. J. Gordon's Article on Women in Ministry

Comments: I include the following article in this book for several reasons:

1. A. J. Gordon was a powerful missions-minded Baptist pastor who in the early 1880s and '90s advocated for women in ministry. Some people today erroneously think that anyone who advocates for women in ministry is powerfully influenced by the women's liberation movement, and hence, is disqualified from speaking unbiasedly about the issue.
2. Gordon strongly sees the principle of interpreting confusing passages in light of clear passages and not the other way around. He uses what are in his mind (and mine) normative passages to set the standards.
3. This article shows the difficulty of the passages being interpreted. Godly exegetes have continued to wrestle with these passages. My general observation, therefore, is that to draw a major doctrine out of a passage over which so many learned exegetes differ is not wise.
4. The tone of Gordon's spirit as he examines the issues displays wisdom and grace.
5. He shows how male biases actually influence translation of the Scriptures, which in turn influences views.
6. A. J. Gordon was my historical mentor for two years and has had a powerful impact upon my life. I honor him by remembering him in this way.

The Ministry of Women

By Dr. A. J. Gordon

December 1894
Introduction to Article

The occasion for writing the following article is this: At a recent summer convention a young lady missionary had been appointed to give an account of her work at one of the public sessions. The scruples of certain of the delegates against a woman's addressing a mixed assembly were found to be so strong, however, that the lady was withdrawn from the program, and further public participation in the conference confined to its male constituency.

The conscientious regard thus displayed for Paul's alleged injunction of silence in the church on the part of women, deserves our highest respect. But with a considerable knowledge of the nature and extent of woman's work on the missionary field, the writer has long believed that it is exceedingly important that work, as now carried on, should either be justified from Scripture, or, if that were impossible, that it be so modified as to bring it into harmony with the exact requirements of the Word of God. For while it is true that many Christians believe that women are enjoined from publicly preaching the Gospel, either at home or abroad, it is certainly true that scores of missionary women are at present doing this very thing. They are telling out the good news of salvation to heathen men and women publicly and from house to house, to little groups gathered by the wayside, or to larger groups assembled in the zayats. It is not affirmed that a majority of women missionaries are engaged in this kind of work, but that scores are doing it, and doing it with the approval of the boards under which they are serving. If anyone should raise the technical objection that because of its informal and colloquial character this is not preaching, we are ready to affirm that it comes much nearer the preaching enjoined in the Great Commission than does the reading of a theological disquisition from the pulpit on Sunday morning, or the discussion of some ethical or sociological question before a popular audience on Sunday evening.

But the purpose of this article is not to condemn the ministry of missionary women described above, or to suggest its modification, but rather to justify and vindicate both its propriety and authority by a critical examination of Scripture on the question at issue.

Article Proper
The Ministry of Women

In order to gain a right understanding of this subject, it is necessary for us to be reminded that we are living in the dispensation of the Spirit—a dispensation which differs most radically from that of the law which preceded it. As the day of Pentecost ushered in this new economy, so the prophecy of Joel, which Peter rehearsed on that day, outlined its great characteristic features. Let us briefly consider this prophecy:

In the last days, God says,
"I will pour out my Spirit on all people.
Your sons and daughters will prophesy,
Your young men will see visions,
Your old men will dream dreams.
Even on my servants, both men and women,
I will pour out my spirit in those days,
and they will prophesy.

I will show wonders in the heavens above
And signs on the earth below,
Blood and fire and billows of smoke.
The sun will be turned to darkness

And the moon to blood
Before the coming of the great and glorious day of the
Lord.
And everyone who calls on the name of the Lord will be
saved" (Acts 2:17-21).

It will be observed that four classes are here named as being
brought into equal privileges under the outpoured Spirit:

1. Jew and Gentile: "All flesh" seems to be equivalent to
   "everyone who" or "whosoever," named in the twenty-
   first verse. Paul expounds this phrase to mean both Jew
   and Gentile (Romans 10:12-13): "For there is no difference between the Jew and the Greek...For whosoever
   shall call upon the name of the Lord shall be saved."
2. Male and female: "And your sons and your daughters
   shall prophesy."
3. Old and young: "Your young men shall see visions, and
   your old men shall dream dreams."
4. Bondsmen and bondmaidens: "And on my servants and
   on my handmaidens in those days will I pour forth of
   My Spirit, and they shall prophesy."

Now, evidently these several classes are not mentioned without
a definite intention and significance; for Paul, in referring back to
the great baptism through which the Church of the New Covenant
was ushered in says: "For in one Spirit were we all baptized into one
body, whether Jews or Greeks, whether bond or free" (1 Cor. 12:13).
Here he enumerates two classes named in Joel's prophecy; and in
another passage he mentions three: "For as many of you as were
baptized into Christ did put on Christ; there can be neither Jew nor
Greek; there can be neither bond or free; there can be no male and
female; for ye are all one in Christ Jesus" (Gal. 3:27-28).

We often hear this phrase, "neither male nor female," quoted
as though it were a rhetorical figure; but we insist that the infer-
ence is just, that if the Gentile came into vastly higher privileges

under grace than under the law, so did the woman; for both are spoken of in the same category.

Here, then, we take our starting point for the discussion. This prophecy of Joel, realized at Pentecost, is the Magna Carta of the Christian Church. It gives to woman a status in the Spirit hitherto unknown. And, as in civil legislation, no law can be enacted which conflicts with the constitution, so in Scripture we shall expect to find no text which denies to woman her divinely appointed rights in the New Dispensation.

"Your sons and your daughters shall prophesy." Here is woman's equal warrant with man's for telling out the Gospel of the grace of God. So it seems, at least, for this word "prophesy" in the New Testament "signifies not merely to foretell future events, but to communicate religious truth in general under a Divine inspiration (cite Hackett on "Acts," p. 49) and the spirit of prophecy was henceforth to rest, not upon the favored few, but upon the many, without regard to race, or age, or sex. All that we can gather from the New Testament use of this word leads us to believe that it embraces that faithful witnessing for Christ, the fervent telling out of the Gospel under the impulse of the Holy Spirit which was found in the Early Church, and is found just as truly among the faithful today.

Some, indeed, foreseeing whither such an admission might lead, have insisted on limiting the word "prophesy" to its highest meaning—that of inspired prediction or miraculous revelation—and have been affirmed that the age of miracles having ceased, therefore Joel's prophecy cannot be cited as authority for women's public witnessing for Christ today.

This method of reasoning has been repeatedly resorted to in similar exigencies of interpretation, but it has not proved satisfactory. When William Carey put his finger on the words, "Go ye into all the world and preach the Gospel to every creature," and asked if this command were not still binding on the Church, he was answered by his brethren: "No! The great commission was accompanied by the miraculous gift of tongues; this miracle has ceased in the Church, and therefore we cannot hope to succeed

in such an enterprise unless God shall send another Pentecost."
But Carey maintained that the power of the Spirit could be still
depended on, as in the beginning, for carrying out the Great
Commission; and a century of missions has vindicated the correctness of his judgment. When, within a few years, some
thoughtful Christians have asked whither the promise, "The
prayer of faith shall save the sick," is not still in force, the theologians have replied: "No; this refers to miraculous healing; and
the age of miracles ended with the apostles." And now it is said
that "prophecy" also belongs in the same catalogue of miraculous
gifts which passed away with the apostles. It is certainly incum-
bent upon those who advocate this view to bring forward some
evidence of its correctness from Scripture, which after repeated
challenges, they have failed to do, and must fail to do. Our greatest objection to the theory is that it fails to make due recognition
of the Holy Spirit's perpetual presence in the Church—a presence
which implies the equal perpetuity of His gifts and endowments.

If, now, we turn to the history of the primitive Church, we
find the practice corresponding to the prophecy. In the instance
of Philip's household, we read: "Now this man had four daughters which did prophesy" (Acts 21:9); and in connection with the
Church in Corinth we read: "Every woman praying and prophesying with her head unveiled" (1 Cor. 11:5); which passage we
shall consider further on, only rejoicing as we pass that "praying"
has not yet, like its yolk-fellow, "prophesying," been remanded
exclusively to the apostolic age.

Having touched thus briefly to the positive side of this question, we now proceed to consider the alleged prohibition of
women's participation in the public meetings of the Church,
found in the writings of Paul.

We shall examine, first, the crucial text contained in 1 Tim.
2:8-11:

(8) I desire therefore that men pray in every place, lifting
up holy hands without wrath and doubting. (9) In like
manner that women adorn themselves in modest apparel

with shamefastness and sobriety; not with braided hair and gold or pearls or costly raiment; (10) but (which becometh women professing godliness) through good works. (11) Let a woman learn in quietness with all subjection. (12) But I permit not a woman to teach, not to have dominion over a man, but to be in quietness, etc. (*RV*).

This passage has generally been regarded as perhaps the strongest and most decisive, for the silence of women in the Church. It would be very startling, therefore, were it shown that it really contains an exhortation to the orderly and decorous participation of women in public prayer. Yet such is the conclusion of some of the best exegetes.

By general consent the force of *boulomai*, "I will," is carried over from the eighth verse into the ninth: *"I will that women"* (*vide* Alford). And what is it that the apostle will have women do? The words, *"in like manner,"* furnish a very suggestive hint toward one answer, and a very suggestive hindrance to another and common answer. Is it meant that he would have the men pray in every place, and the women, *"in like manner,"* to be silent? But where would be the similarity of conduct in the two instances? Or does the intended likeness lie between the men's *"lifting up holy hands,"* and the women's adorning themselves in modest apparel? So unlikely is either one of those conclusions from the apostle's language, that, as Alford concedes, "Chrysostom and most commentators supply *proseuchesthai*, 'to pray,' in order to complete the sense. If they are right in so construing the passage—and we believe the *hosautos*, "in like manner," compels them to this course—then the meaning is unquestionable. "I will, therefore, that men pray everywhere, lifting up holy hands, etc. In like manner I will that women pray in modest apparel, etc."

In one of the most incisive and clearly reasoned pieces of exegesis with which we are acquainted, Wiesinger, the eminent commentator, thus interprets the passage, and, as it seems to us, clearly justifies his conclusions. We have not space to transfer his argument to these pages, but we may, in a few words, give a summary of it, mostly in his own language. He says:

1. In the words "in every place" it is chiefly to be observed that it is public prayer and not secret prayer that is spoken of.

2. The *proseuchesthai* "to pray" is to be supplied in verse 9, and to be connected with *"in modest apparel"*; so that this special injunction as to the conduct of women in prayer corresponds to that given to the men in the words *"lifting up holy hands."* This verse, then, from the beginning, refers to prayer, and what is said of the women in verses 9 and 10 is *to be understood as referring primarily to public prayer.*

3. The transition in verse 11 from *gunaikas* to *gune* shows that the apostle now passes on to something new—viz., the relation of the married woman to her husband. She is to be in quietness rather than drawing attention to herself by public appearance; to learn rather than to teach; to be in subjection rather than in authority.

In a word, our commentator finds no evidence from this passage that women were forbidden to pray in the public assemblies of the Church; through reasoning back from the twelfth verse to those before, he considers that they may have been enjoined from public teaching. The latter question we shall consider further on.

The interpretation just given has strong presumption in its favor, from the likeness of the passage to another which we now consider:

Every man praying or prophesying, having his head covered, dishonoreth his head. But every woman praying or prophesying with her head unveiled dishonoreth her head (1 Cor. 11:4,5).

By common consent the reference is here to public worship; and the decorous manner of taking part therein is pointed out first for the man and then for the woman. "Every woman praying or prophesying." Bengel's terse comment: *"Therefore women were not excluded from these duties,"* is natural and reasonable. It is quite incredible, on the contrary, that the apostle should give himself the trouble to prune a custom which he desired to uproot, or that he should spend his breath in condemning a forbidden *method* of doing a forbidden thing. This passage is strikingly like the one just considered, in that the proper order of doing having been prescribed, first for the man, and then for the woman, it is impossible to conclude that the thing to be done is then enjoined only upon the one party, and forbidden to the other. If the "in like manner" has proved such a barrier to commentators against finding an injection for the silence of women in 1 Tim. 3:9, the unlike manner pointed out in this passage is not less difficult to be surmounted by those who hold that women are forbidden to participate in public worship. As the first passage has been shown to give sanction to women's praying in public, this one points not less strongly to her habit of both praying and prophesying in public.

We turn now to the only remaining passage which has been urged as decisive for the silence of women—viz., 1 Cor. 14:34,35:

> Let the women keep silence in the churches: for it is not permitted unto them to speak; but let them be in subjection, as also saith the law. And if they would learn anything, let them ask their own husbands at home: for it is shameful for a woman to speak in the church.

Here, again, the conduct of women in the church should be studied in relation to that of men if we would rightly understand the apostle's teaching. Let us observe, then, that the injection to silence is three times served in this chapter by the use of the same Greek word, *sigao,* twice on men and once on women, and that in every case the silence commanded is conditional, not absolute.

"Let him keep silence in the church" (verse 28), it is said to one speaking with tongues, but on the condition that "there be

no interpreter." *"Let the first keep silence"* (verse 30), it is said of the prophets, *"speaking by two or three;"* but it is on condition that "a revelation be made to another sitting by."

"Let the women keep silence in the church," it is said again, but it is evidently on condition of their interrupting the service with questions, since it is added, "for it is not permitted them to speak,...and if they would learn anything, let them ask their husbands at home." This last clause takes the injunction clearly out of all reference to praying or prophesying, and shows—what the whole chapter indicates—that the apostle is here dealing with the various forms of disorder and confusion in the church; not that he is repressing the decorous exercise of spiritual gifts, either by men or by women. If he were forbidding women to pray or to prophesy in public, as some argue, what could be more irrelevant or meaningless than his direction concerning the case: "If they will learn anything, let them ask their husbands at home"?

In time, we may reasonably insist that this text, as well as the others discussed above, be considered in the light of the entire New Testament teaching—the teaching of prophecy, the teaching of practice, and the teaching of contemporary history—if we would find the true meaning.

Dr. Jacob, in his admirable work, "The Ecclesiastical Polity of the New Testament," considering the question after this broad method, thus candidly and as it seems to us, justly, sums up the whole question: "A due consideration of this ministry of gifts in the earliest days of Christianity—those times of high and sanctified spiritual freedom—both shows and justifies the custom of the public ministration of women at that time in the Church. The very ground and title of this ministry being the acknowledged possession of some gift, and such gifts being bestowed on women as well as men, the former as well as the latter were allowed to use them in Christian assemblies. *This seems to me quite evident from Paul's words in 1 Cor. 11:5, where he strongly condemns the practice of women praying or prophesying with the head unveiled, without expressing the least objection to this* public ministration on their part, but only finding fault with what was considered an unseemly attire for women thus publicly engaged. The injunction contained in the same epistle (1 Cor. 14:34), 'Let your women keep silence,' etc., refers, as the context shows, not to prophesying or praying in the congregations, but to making remarks and asking questions about the words of others."

On the whole, we may conclude, without over-confidence, that there is no Scripture which prohibits women from praying or prophesying in the public assemblies of the Church; that, on the contrary, they seem to be exhorted to the first exercise by the word of the apostle (1 Tim. 2:9); while for prophesying they have the threefold warrant of inspired prediction (Acts 2:17), of primitive practice (Acts 21:9), and of apostolic provision (1 Cor. 11:4).*

As to the question of teaching, a difficulty arises which it is not easy to solve. If the apostle, in his words to Timothy, absolutely forbids a woman to teach and expound spiritual truth, then the remarkable instance of a woman doing this very thing at once occurs to the mind (Acts 18:26), with the entire paragraph to which it belongs, refers to the married woman's domestic relations, and not to her public relations; to her subjection to the teaching of her husband as against her dogmatic lording it over him. This is the view of Canon Garratt, in his excellent observations on the "Ministry of Women." Admit, however, that the prohibition is against public teaching; what may it mean? To teach and to govern are the special functions of the presbyter. The teacher and the pastor, named in the gifts to the Church (Eph. 4:11), Alford considers to be the same; and the pastor is generally regarded as identical with the bishop. Now is no instance in the New Testament of a woman being set over a church as bishop and teacher. The lack of such example would lead us to refrain from ordaining a woman as pastor of a Christian congregation. But if the Lord has fixed this limitation, we believe it to be grounded, not on her less favored position in the privileges of grace, but in the impediments to such service existing in nature itself.

It may be said against the conclusion which we have reached concerning the position of women, that the plain reading of the New Testament makes a different impression on the mind. That may be so on two grounds; first, on that of traditional bias; and second, on that of unfair translation. Concerning the latter point, it would seem as though the translators of our common version wrought, at every point where this question occurs, under the shadow of Paul's imperative, "Let your women keep silence in the churches."

Let us take two illustrations from names found in that constellation of Christian women mentioned in Rom. 16:

"I commend unto you Phoebe our sister, which is a servant of the church which is at Cenchrae." So, according to the *King James Version*, writes Paul. But the same word, *diakonos*, here translated "servant," is rendered "minister" when applied to Paul and Apollos (1 Cor. 3:5), and "deacon" when used of other male officers of the Church (1 Tim. 3:10, 12, 13). Why discriminate against Phoebe simply because she is a woman? The word "servant" is correct for the general unofficial use of the term, as in Matt. 22:11; but if Phoebe were really a functionary of the Church, as we have a right to conclude, let her have the honor to which she is entitled. If "Phoebe, a minister of the church at Cenchrea" sounds too bold, let the word be transliterated, and read, "Phoebe, a deacon"—a deacon, too, without the insipid termination "ess," of which there is no more need than that we should say "teacheress" or "doctress." This emendation "deaconess" has timidly crept into the margin of the *Revised Version*, thus adding prejudice to slight by the association which this name has with High Church sisterhoods and orders. It is wonderful how much there is in a name! "Phoebe, a servant," might suggest to an ordinary reader nothing more than the modern church drudge, who prepares sandwiches and coffee for an ecclesiastical sociable. To Canon Garratt, with his genial and enlightened view of woman's position in apostolic times, "Phoebe, a deacon," suggests a useful co-laborer of Paul, "traveling about on missionary and other labors of love."

Again, we read in the same chapter of Romans, *"Greet Priscilla and Aquila, my helpers in Christ Jesus."* Note the order here; the woman's name put first, as elsewhere (Acts 18:18; 2 Tim. 4:19). But when we turn to that very suggestive passage in Acts 28:26 we find the order reversed, and the man's name put first: "Whom, when Aquila and Priscilla had heard, they took him and expounded unto him the way of the Lord more perfectly." Yet this is conceded to be wrong, according to the best manuscripts. Evidently to some transcriber or critic the startling questions presented itself: "did not Paul say 'I suffer not a woman to teach, nor to usurp authority over the man'? but here a woman is actually taking the lead as theological teacher to Apollos, an eminent minister of the Gospel, and so far setting up her authority as to tell him that he is not thoroughly qualified for his work! This will never do; if the woman cannot be silent, she must at least be thrust into the background." And so the order is changed, and the man's name has stood first for generations of readers. The *Revised Version* has rectified the error, and the woman's name now leads.

But how natural is this story, and how perfectly accordant with subsequent Christian history! We can readily imagine that, after listening to this Alexandrian orator Priscilla would say to her husband: "Yes, he is eloquent and mighty in the Scriptures; but do you not see that he lacks the secret of power?" And so they took him and instructed him concerning the baptism of the Holy Ghost, with the result that he who before had been mighty in the Scriptures, now "mightily convinced the Jews." How often has this scene been reproduced; as, e.g., in the instance of Catherine of Sienna instructing the corrupt clergy of her day in the things of the spirit till they exclaimed in wonder, "Never man spake like this woman"; of Madame Guyon, who by her teaching made new men of scores of accomplished but unspiritual preachers of her time; of the humble woman of whom the evangelist Moody tells, who, on hearing some of his early sermons, admonished him of his need of the secret of power, and brought him under unspeakable obligation by teaching him of the same. It is evident that the

Holy Spirit made this woman Priscilla a teacher of teachers, and that her theological chair has had many worthy incumbents through the subsequent Christian ages.

To follow still further the list of women workers mentioned in Rom. 16, we read: "Salute Tryphaena and Tryphosa, who labor in the Lord. Salute Persis the beloved, which labored much in the Lord" (verse 12). What was the work *in the Lord* which these so worthily wrought? Put with quotation another: "Help those women which *labored with me in the Gospel*" (Phil. 4:3). Did they "labor in the Gospel" with the one restriction that they should not preach the Gospel? Did they "labor in the Lord" under sacred bonds to give no public witness for the Lord? "Ah! But there is that word of Paul to Timothy, 'Let the women learn in silence,'" says the plaintiff. No! It is not there. Here again we complain of an invidious translation. Right the *Revised Version* gives it: "let a woman learn in quietness (*hesuchia*)," an admonition not at all inconsistent with decorous praying and witnessing in the Christian assembly. When men are admonished, the *King James* translators give the right rendering to the same word: "That with quietness they work and eat their own bread" (1 Thess. 3:12), an injunction which no reader would construe to mean that they should refrain from speaking during their labor and their eating.

As a woman is named among the deacons in this chapter, so it is more than probable that one is mentioned among the apostles. "Salute Andronicus and Junia, my kinsmen, and my fellow-prisoners, who are of note among the apostles" (v. 7). Is Junia a feminine name? So it has been commonly held. But the *en tois apostolois* with which it stands connected, has led some to conclude that it is Junias, the name of a man. This is not impossible. Yet Chrysostom, who, as a Greek Father, ought to be taken as a high authority, makes this frank and unequivocal comment on the passage: "*How great is the devotion of this woman, that she should be counted worthy of the name of an apostle!*"

These are illustrations which might be considerably enlarged, of the shadow which Paul's supposed law of silence for women has cast upon the work of the early translators—a shadow which was even thrown back into the Old Testament, so that we read in the Common Version: "The Lord gave the word; great was the company of those that published" it (Ps. 68:11); while the *Revised* correctly gives it: "The Lord giveth the word; the women that publish the tidings are a great host."

Whether we are right or wrong in our general conclusions, there are some very interesting lessons suggested by this subject:

Especially, the value of experience as an interpreter of Scripture. The final exegesis is not always to be found in the lexicon and grammar. The Spirit is in the Word; and the Spirit is also in the Church, the body of regenerate and sanctified believers. To follow the voice of the Church apart from that of the written Word has never proved safe; but, on the other hand, it may be that we need to be admonished not to ignore the teaching of the deepest spiritual life of the Church in forming our conclusions concerning the meaning of Scripture. It cannot be denied that in every great spiritual awakening in the history of Protestantism the impulse for Christian women to pray and witness for Christ in the public assembly has been found irrepressible. It was so in the beginnings of the Society of Friends. It was so in the great evangelical revival associated with the names of Wesley and Whitfield. It has been so in that powerful *renaissance* of primitive Methodism known as the Salvation Army. It has been increasingly so in this era of modern missions and modern evangelism in which we are living. Observing this fact, and observing also the great blessing which has attended the ministry of consecrated women in heralding the Gospel, many thoughtful men have been led to examine the Word of God anew, to learn if it be really so that the Scriptures silence the testimony which the spirit so signally blesses. To many it has been both a relief and a surprise to discover how little authority there is in the Word for repressing the witness of women in the public assembly, or for forbidding her to herald the Gospel to the unsaved. If this be so, it may be well for the plaintiffs in this case to beware lest, in silencing the voice of consecrated women, they may be resisting the Holy Ghost. The conjunction of these two admonitions of the apostle is significant: "Quench not the spirit. Despise not prophesying" (1 Thess. 5:19).

The famous Edward Irving speaks thus pointedly on this subject: "Who am I that I should despise the gift of God, because it is in a woman, whom the Holy Ghost despiseth not?...That women have with men an equal distribution of spiritual gifts is not only manifest from the fact (Acts 2; 18:26; 21:9; 1 Cor. 11:3, etc.), but from the very words of the prophecy of Joel itself, which may well rebuke those vain thoughtless people who make light of the Lord's work, because it appeareth among women. I wish men would themselves be subject to the Word of God, before they lord it so over women's equal rights in the great outpouring of the Spirit" (Works, v. 555).

As is demanded, we have preferred to forego all appeals to reason and sentiment in settling the question, and to rest it solely on a literal interpretation of Scripture. Yet we cannot refrain from questioning whether the spiritual intuition of the Church has not been far in advance of its exegesis in dealing with this subject. We will not refer to the usage prevailing in many of our most spiritual and evangelical churches, but will cite some conspicuous public instances.

Annie Taylor's missionary tour into Tibet has been the subject of worldwide comment. And now she is returning to that vast and perilous field with a considerable company of missionary recruits both men and women, herself the leader of the expedition. In this enterprise of carrying the Gospel into the regions beyond, and preaching Christ to all classes, she is as full a missionary as was Paul, or Columba, or Boniface. Yet in all the comments of the religious press, we have never once heard the questions raised as to whether, in thus acting, she were not stepping out of woman's sphere as defined in Scripture.

When before the Exeter Hall Missionary Conference in 1888, Secretary Murdock described the work of Mrs. Ingalls, of Burmah, declaring that, though not assuming ecclesiastical functions, yet by force of character on the one hand, and by the exigencies of the field on the other, she had come to be a virtual bishop over nearly a score of churches, training the native ministry in theology and homiletics, guiding the churches in the selection of pastors, and superintending the discipline of the congregations, the story evoked only applause, without a murmur of dissent from the distinguished body of missionary leaders who hear it.

When at that same conference, the representative of the Karen Mission having failed, it was asked whether there were any missionary present who could speak for that remarkable work, the reply was, "Only one, and she is a woman." She was unhesitatingly accepted as the speaker; and though at first demurring, she finally consented, and had the honor of addressing perhaps the most august array of missionary leaders which has convened in this century. The clear and distinct tones in which Mrs. Armstrong told her story did not suggest "silence;" but the modesty and reserve of her bearing completely answered to the Scripture requirement of "quietness." And though she had among her auditors missionary secretaries, Episcopal bishops, Oxford professors, and Edinburgh theologians, not the slightest indication of objection to her service was anywhere visible

We vividly remember, in the early days of woman's work in the foreign field, how that brilliant missionary to China, Miss Adel Fielde, was recalled by her board because of the repeated complaints of the senior missionaries that in her work she was transcending her sphere as a woman. "It is reported that you have taken upon you to preach," was the charge read by the chairman; "Is it so?" She replied by describing the vastness and destitution of her field—village after village, hamlet after hamlet, yet unreached by the gospel—and then how, with a native woman, she had gone into the surrounding country, gathered groups of men, women, and children—whoever would come—and told of the story of the Cross to them. "If this is preaching, I plead guilty to the charge," she said. "And have you ever been ordained to preach?" asked her examiner. "No," she replied, with great dignity and emphasis—*"no; but I believe I have been foreordained."* O woman! You have answered discreetly; and if any shall ask for your foreordination credentials, put your finger on the words of the prophet: "Your sons and your daughters shall prophesy," and the whole Church will vote to send you back unhampered to your work, as happily the Board did in this instance.

How slow are we to understand what is written! Simon Peter, who on the Day of Pentecost had rehearsed the great prophecy of the new dispensation, and announced that its fulfillment had begun, was yet so olden of tradition that it took a special vision of the sheet descending from heaven to convince him that in the body of Christ "there can be neither Jew nor Gentile." And it has required another vision of a multitude of missionary women, let down by the Holy Spirit among the heathen, and publishing the Gospel to every tribe and kindred and people, to convince us that in that same body "there can be no male nor female." It is evident, however, that this extraordinary spectacle of ministering women has brought doubts to some conservative men as to "whereunto this thing may grow." Yet as believers in the sure word of prophecy, all has happened exactly according to the foreordained pattern, from the opening chapter of the new dispensation, when in the upper room "these all continued with one accord in prayer and supplication *with the women*, and Mary the mother of Jesus, and with his brethren," to the closing chapter, now fulfilling, when "the women that publish the tidings are a great host."

The new economy is not as the old; and the defendants in this case need not appeal to the examples of Miriam, and Deborah and Huldah, and Anna the prophetess. These were exceptional instances under the old dispensation; but she that is least in the kingdom of heaven is greater than they. And let the theologians who have recently written so dogmatically upon this subject to consider whether it may not be possible that in this matter they are still under the law and not under grace; and whether, in sight of the promised land of worldwide evangelization, they may not hear the voice of God saying: *"Moses, my servant, is dead*; now, therefore, arise and go over this Jordan."

*The following note, which we transcribed from *Meyer's Commentary*, seems to be a fair and well-balanced resume of the case: This passage (1 Tim. 2:8-11) does not distinctly forbid *proseuchesthai* (to pray) to women; it only distinctly forbids *didaskein* (to teach) on their part. There is the same apparent contradiction between 1 Cor. 154:34, 35 and 1 Cor. 11:5, 13. While in the former passage *lalein* (to speak) is forbidden to women, in the latter *proseuchesthai* (to pray) and even *propheteuein* (to prophesy) are presupposed as things done by women, and the apostle does not forbid it. The solution is that Paul wishes everything in the Church to be done decently and in order, while, on the other hand, he holds by the principle, "Quench not the spirit."

Appendix B

Dear ,

It won't be long before it is time for Cindy Jacobs to come to your area to minister. I'm delighted that she has accepted your invitation! It would be appreciated if you could take the time to read this letter thoroughly.

   The purpose of this letter is to inform you of the policies that Generals of Intercession have regarding Cindy's speaking engagements, including information on travel and hotel accommodations, honorariums, and any special requests that may pertain to your scheduled event.

Meeting Location
Please send us the address and phone number for the location of the conference meeting(s). We will be keeping this information in our office records in case of emergency and we need to contact Cindy immediately. If there is a contact person at this location that we should ask for, please include that person's name and position if applicable.

Transportation Arrangements
I will be sending you Cindy's itinerary shortly, as arrangements have been made. Please make arrangements for her to be transported to and from the airport and the meeting(s). The policy of G.I. is for Cindy to be picked up by a woman or a man escorted by a woman, in order to avoid any questionable appearance. On international trips Cindy will be traveling with a companion; please be prepared to lodge this person as well as cover the travel cost for their ticket. As a policy, our office purchases the

airline ticket(s), then submits the cost for reimbursement. The reimbursement must be sent within two weeks from the date that you receive the invoice. Please write the check to Generals of Intercession. Thank you for complying with our policies on these points.

Hotel Accommodations

We do require that Cindy's hotel expenses (other than personal) be covered. Since you are familiar with the geographical area where Cindy is speaking, please make hotel accommodations accordingly for her. It is necessary for the accommodations to provide a quiet and pleasant atmosphere for Cindy (and any additional traveling companions). When these arrangements have been made please contact our office. We need to have the hotel name, address, phone/fax number, and confirmation number in our records.

Honorarium

Generals of Intercession does not require a set honorarium for Cindy to speak because we believe in your generosity as givers, however we do request that you take an honorarium/love offering. When sending an honorarium or reimbursement check, please make it payable to Generals of Intercession. G.I. is a nonprofit, tax exempt corporation, therefore please don't issue a 1099 at the end of the year. Cindy's salary is set by a board, and she doesn't take personal funds. If a check is inadvertently made payable to "Cindy Jacobs," we will not be able to process it and it will have to be returned to you. Thank you for your kind understanding in this matter.

Materials

Many times our office sends materials for resale (books, tapes & videos) to the meeting place where Cindy is scheduled to speak. In overseas meetings this is optional. Please let us know what is needed to be done as far as customs and shipping so we can decide what should be done. If we decide to send materials please be prepared for the following: For the purpose of sending materials, please let us know how many people are expected to attend. It would be appreciated if you would have a person assigned to handle receipt of the materials, as well as facilitating the sale and account of funds collected. An inventory/instruction packet will be sent with the materials to assist in keeping account. Please provide us with this person's name and the address to send the materials to.

If you have any questions, please do not hesitate to contact me at (719) 535-0977 ext. 11 or fax (719) 535-0884.

Many Blessings,

Polly J. Simchen
Executive Secretary

Recommended Reading

Aglow. *Women of Prayer*. Lynwood, Wash.: Aglow Publications, 1993.

Barna, George. *Today's Pastors*. Ventura, Calif.: Regal Books, 1993.

Brown, Judy L. *Women Ministers*. Kearney, Neb.: Morris Publishing, 1996.

Bushnell, Katherine. *God's Word to Women*. Bible studies taught in the early 1920s by Bushnell, a medical doctor. (Currently self-published. Copies may be obtained from Bernice Menold, 10303 N. Spring Lane, Peoria, IL 61615, or Cosette Joliff, 408 Clybourn, Peoria, IL 61614).

Cannistraci, David. *The Gift of Apostle*. Ventura, Calif.: Regal Books, 1996.

Dake, Finis Jennings. *Dake's Annotated Reference Bible*. Lawrenceville, Ga.: Dake Bible Sales, 1963.

Davis, Jim and Donna Johnson. *Redefining the Role of Women in the Church*. Quoted from manuscript self-published in 1997 by Christian International, 177 McKenny Road, Santa Rosa Beach, FL 32459.

Dawson, John. *Healing America's Wounds*. Ventura, Calif.: Regal Books, 1994.

Dawson, Joy. *Intimate Friendship with God*. Grand Rapids, Mich.: Chosen Books, 1986.

Dengler, Sandy. *Susanna Wesley*. Chicago, Ill.: Moody Press, 1987.

Evans, Mary J. *Woman in the Bible*. Downers Grove, Ill.: InterVarsity Press, 1983.

Graham, Billy. *Just As I Am*. San Francisco, Calif.: Harper, Billy Graham Association, 1997.

Groothuis, Rebecca Merrill. *Good News for Modern Women*. Baker Book House, Grand Rapids, Mich., 1997.

Haggard, Ted. *Primary Purpose*. Lake Mary, Fla.: Creation House, 1995.

Hamilton, David Joel. "I Commend to You Our Sister." Master's thesis from University of the Nations: Kona, Hawaii, 1996.

Hamon, Bill. *Apostles and Prophets*. Shippensburg, Pa.: Destiny Image, 1997.

Hansen, Jane with Marie Powers. *Fashioned for Intimacy*. Ventura, Calif.: Regal Books, 1997.

Hassey, Janet. *No Time for Silence*. Grand Rapids, Mich.: Academic Books, 1986.

Haubert, Katherine M. *Women as Leaders*. Marc, a division of World Vision International, Monrovia, Calif.: 1993.

Kroeger, Richard and Catherine Clark. *I Suffer Not a Woman*. Grand Rapids, Mich.: Baker Books, 1992.

LaHaye, Beverly. *The Desires of a Woman's Heart*. Wheaton, Ill.: Tyndale House Publishers, 1993.

Littauer, Florence. *Wake Up, Women!* Dallas, Texas: Word Publishing, 1994.

Lindsay, Freda. *My Diary Secrets*. Dallas, Texas: Christ for the Nations Publishing, 1984.

Lutz, Lorry. *Women as Risk-Takers for God*. Carlisle, Cumbria, U.K.: World Evangelical Publications, 1997.

Malcolm, Kari Torjesen. *Women at the Crossroads*. Downers Grove, Ill.: InterVarsity Press, 1982.

Maxwell, L. E. with Ruth C. Dearing. *Women in Ministry*. Camp Hill, Pa.: Christian Publishers, 1987.

Mears, Henrietta. *Dream Big*. Ventura, Calif.: Regal Books, 1990.

Pickett, Fuchsia. *The Prophetic Romance*. Orlando, Fla.: Creation House, 1996.

Piper, John and Wayne Grudem. *Recovering Biblical Manhood and Womanhood*. Crossways Books: Wheaton, Ill., 1991.

Sherrer, Quin and Ruthanne Garlock. *A Woman's Guide to Breaking Bondages*. Ann Arbor, Mich.: Vine Books-Servant Publications, 1994.

———. *A Woman's Guide to Spiritual Warfare*. Ann Arbor, Mich.: Vine Books-Servant Publications, 1991.

———. *How To Forgive Your Children*. Lynwood, Wash.: Aglow Publications, 1989.

Silvoso, Ed. *That None Should Perish*. Ventura, Calif.: Regal Books, 1994.

ten Boom, Corrie. *The Hiding Place*. Grand Rapids, Mich.: Fleming H. Revell, 1971.

The Women's Study Bible. United States: Thomas Nelson, Inc., 1995.

Trombley, Charles. *Who Said Women Can't Teach*. South Plainsfield, N.J.: Bridge Publications, 1985.

Tucker, Ruth. *Guardians of the Great Commission*. Grand Rapids, Mich.: Zondervan Publishing House, 1988.

Tucker, Ruth and Walter Liefeld. *Daughters of the Church*. Grand Rapids, Mich.: Zondervan Publications, 1987.

Varner, Kelley. *The Three Prejudices*. Shippensburg, Pa.: Destiny Images, 1997.

Wagner, C. Peter. *Blazing the Way*. Ventura, Calif.: Regal Books, 1995.

———. *Your Spiritual Gifts*. Ventura, Calif.: Regal Books, 1979.

Witherington, Ben III. *Women and the Genesis of Christianity*. Cambridge, Mass.: The Press Syndicate of the University of Cambridge, 1990.

Wright, H. Norman. *What Men Want*. Ventura, Calif.: Regal Books, 1996.

Subject Index

S

Sacks, Cheryl 217
Sacks, Hal 169, 217
Saint Francis of Assisi 158
Salvation Army 130, 192
Scott, Rev. Lynn 260
Scripture, interpreting 228, 229, 230, 239
secret sins 47, 48
Severus, Emperor Septimius 113
Shaw, Dave 36
Shaw, Sister Gwen 35, 36, 37
Sheets, Ceci 74
Sheets, Pastor Dutch 74, 136, 216, 251, 253
Sheidler, Lotti Osborn 278
Shepherding movement 212, 213
Sherrer, Quin 58, 60, 62, 252
Silvoso, Ed 55, 57, 74, 102
Silvoso, Evelyn 74
Simon, Richard 277
Simpson, A. B. 277
Sisk, Mary Lance 81
Sisterhood of the Common Life 131
Smalley, Gary 148, 159, 160
Smith, Amanda 132, 133
sons 207
soul ties 164, 165
Springs Harvest Fellowship 191
Sterling, Mary Melinda 279
strongholds, generational 103
strongholds of fear 102
strongholds of intimidation 103
srongholds of the mind 102, 103
strongholds of tradition 103, 104
submission 211, 213, 214, 219
submission, mutual 213, 214
succorer 182
Surviving the Prodigal Years 62, 246
Swidler, Leonard 185
Synan, Vinson 260

T

teachers 194
team ministry 186
ten Boom, Betsie 58, 59
ten Boom, Corrie 58, 59
ten curses against Eve 268
Tertullian of Carthage 276
teshuqah 210
Thayer's Lexicon 185
The Amazing History of the Bible 218
The Desires of a Woman's Heart 95
The Dwelling Place 202
The Early Days of Christianity 242
the Fall 208, 209
The Gift of Apostle 184
The Homilies of Saint John Chrysostom 186
The International Inductive Study Bible 196
The Sanctuary 258
The Voice of God 28, 92, 103, 193
The Wife Beater's Bible 218
The Woman's Study Bible 72
Together in Ministery International 140
tortullian 117
traditionalists 207, 210, 238, 239, 241
Trent, John 148
Trombley, Charles 182, 187, 188

U

Unconditional Surrender 36

V

Van Arsdall, Dan 258
Van Arsdall, LanNora 258
Vaucouleurs, France 119
Vision de Futuro 186

Scripture Index

Renew Your Mind Daily

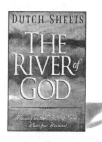

Beyond the Veil
Alice Smith

Experience the power of intimate intercession—and learn how your prayers can bring healing to others.

Paperback
ISBN 08307.20707 • $12.99

Step into the Water
Peg Rankin

Immerse yourself in the presence of God and emerge refreshed by the Holy Spirit. Peg Rankin leads you step-by-step into the flow of the river of God, where life, vitality and purpose are found.

Paperback
ISBN 08307.21452 • $12.99

The Rising Revival
C. Peter Wagner and Pablo Deiros, Editors

Massive revival has been sweeping through Argentina. Discover how it all began in this collection of firsthand accounts by leaders God has used to bring revival to Argentina.

Hardcover
ISBN 08307.21398 • $17.99

The River of God
Dutch Sheets

Dutch Sheets, author of the best-selling *Intercessory Prayer*, describes what we must do to prepare for revival with Biblical teaching in the light of the Holy Spirit's power.

Hardcover
ISBN 08307.20731 • $17.99

Once in a Lifetime
David Shibley

Cindy Jacobs says, "This book is truly God's word for the hour of world missions. If you have a heart for the lost in the nations of the earth, this book is for you!"

Paperback
ISBN 18524.02202 • $14.99

Don't Talk to Me Now, Lord...I'm Trying to Pray!
Steve Sampson

Steve Sampson exhorts and challenges his readers with practical concepts and guidelines for hearing the voice of the Lord and following the Holy Spirit daily.

Paperback
ISBN 18524.00943 • $10.99

The Disciple's Handbook for the Spirit-Filled Life
Dr. Bob Gordon

We must understand why we believe what we believe. From one of the world's foremost charismatic theologians comes a strong foundation for Spirit-filled believers.

Paperback
ISBN 18524.00927 • $14.99

Our Daily Walk
Jack Hayford

Pastor Jack Hayford emphasizes the daily discipline of being alone with Jesus at a personal, intimate level in this challenging, practical and thought-provoking book.

Paperback
ISBN 18524.01923 • $9.99

Renew
FROM GOSPEL LIGHT

Shape Your Destiny

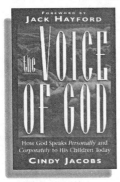

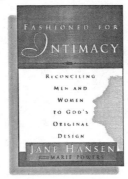

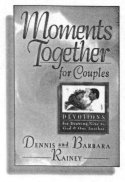

The Voice of God
Cindy Jacobs

In this exciting, biblical examination of the gift of prophecy, you'll get a clear picture of what prophecy is and how it works—in the lives of individuals and churches.

Video • UPC 607135.001195 • $39.99
Paperback • ISBN 08307.17730 • $10.99

Fashioned for Intimacy
Jane Hansen with Marie Powers

From Aglow's President, this book shows how God's original design for men and women points the way toward restoration, intimacy and wholeness in our relationships with one another and with the Father.

Hardcover • ISBN 08307.20669 • $17.99

Moments Together for Couples
Dennis and Barbara Rainey

It's hard for today's couples to find time together, not to mention time with God. This best-selling 365-day devotional makes it easier for husbands and wives to connect on a spiritual level every day.

Hardcover • ISBN 08307.17544 • $16.99

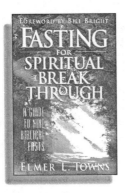

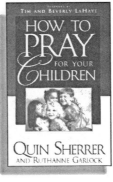

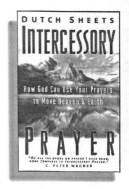

Fasting for Spiritual Breakthrough
Elmer L. Towns

Dr. Elmer Towns presents nine biblical fasts—each designed for a specific physical and spiritual outcome—that will strengthen the faith of your congregation and draw them closer to God.

Paperback • ISBN 08307.18397 • $11.99

How to Pray for Your Children
Quin Sherrer with Ruthanne Garlock

What are your hopes for your children? Whatever your concerns are, whatever their condition is at this moment, this book will inform, instruct and inspire you to press on in praying for your children and their future.

Paperback • ISBN 08307.22017 • $11.99

Intercessory Prayer
Dutch Sheets

This book will inspire you to new levels of prayer, giving you the courage to pray for the "impossible" and the persistence to see your prayers through to completion.

Paperback • ISBN 08307.19008 • $10.99

Renew
FROM GOSPEL LIGHT

Look for these and other Regal and Renew books
at your local Christian bookstore.

Regal
FROM GOSPEL LIGHT